D1594346

REMEMBRANCE OF GRANDEUR

The anglo-protestant elite
of Montreal
1900-1950

To Florence with affection, Margaret

Margaret W. Westley

REMEMBRANCE
OF
GRANDEUR

The anglo-protestant elite
of Montreal
1900-1950

Libre Expression

Données de catalogage avant publication (Canada)

Westley, Margaret W.

Remembrance of Grandeur: Montreal's Anglo-Protestant Elite, 1990-1950

Includes bibliographical references.

ISBN 2-89111-439-6

1. Canadians, English speaking — Quebec (Province) — Montréal — History — 20th century. 2. Protestants — Quebec (Province) — Montréal — History — 20th century. 3. Elite (Social sciences) — Quebec (Province) — Montréal — 20th century. I. Title.

FC2947.E6W48 1990   971.4'28   C90-096475-8

F1054.5.M89B7 1990

Cover photo and interior photos: Notman Photographic Archives, except for pp. 67 top, 71 (By permission of Miss Edgar's and Miss Cramp's School); p. 66 (By permission of Selwyn House School); p. 161 bottom (By permission of the St. Andrew Society); p. 172 (McGill University Archives); p. 190 (Canadian Pacific Archives); p. 273 (Bibliothèque nationale du Québec); p. 278 (*La Presse*).

Graphic Design: France Lafond

Typesetting: Imprimerie Gagné

Legal Deposit third quarter 1990

© Éditions Libre Expression

2016, St-Hubert St.

Montréal, H2L 3Z5

ISBN 2-89111-439-6

In memory of my parents.

Contents

Introduction

I arrived in Montreal in 1951, a complete stranger. My husband was to be a professor at McGill University. I was soon aware that the area of the city around McGill, even the university itself, had once been the geographical centre of an elegant way of life that no longer existed. My husband's office was in Duggan House, one of the private mansions along Pine Avenue which had been acquired by McGill University through gift or purchase. We often ate our lunch in the beautiful gardens surrounding that house. As the years went by and I came to know some of the people who had participated in that vanished way of life, my curiosity increased. I wanted to know what that life had been and why it was no more.

This book is the result of that curiosity. In it, I propose to take the reader on the voyage of discovery which I made of a city, of the people who made it a great commercial and financial centre of a new country, of how they lived and why their descendants no longer live that way.

The city is Montreal which, with its natural advantages at the confluence of the Ottawa and St. Lawrence rivers at a time when waterways were the principal means of transportation and communication, became for nearly a hundred years the commercial capital of Canada.

The people who had the imagination and the drive to make it so were few. By varying estimates fifty to 150 Montrealers (most of them Scots) owned, in the 1890s, one to two thirds of the wealth of the nation. Sir Hugh Allan, Peter McGill, and the Molsons had been building their empires since before Confederation. George Stephens, Richard Angus, and Donald A. Smith, who were members of the syndicate that knitted Canada together by building the Canadian Pacific Railway, were in 1893 the richest men in Canada. At the next level of affluence below them were people who were also economic and social decision-makers. These were well-to-do and able to keep up a modest version of the upper-class lifestyle. Perhaps because the number of the very rich was so small, people in the next social echelon were included as acceptable, if not quite equal, social and business associates and even as marriage prospects. The distinctions were unstable, in any case, because there was much movement up and down between the two social strata. These people built a neighbourhood of mansions set in spacious grounds on the slopes of Mount Royal and there they lived a fairytale existence, an elegant way of life which was worthy of Montreal's preeminent position and their own. The district became known as the "Square Mile."

What was that way of life? The descendants of these entrepreneurs, most of them still living in Montreal, have described in their own words their experiences and observations, from birth to old age, in 191 interviews with 150 individuals. One hundred and ten of these were people who had lived in the Square Mile as children and were the children or grandchildren of the men who had built it. I sought out the people with the longest memories and was passed along from one friend or relative to another, until I had talked with representatives of most of the prominent families whose names appear in Chapter Two. The interviews lasted from two to four hours each. During most of them I asked the informant to tell me about his life: what he or she remembered as being interesting and important. These individual lives, different as they were in some respects, presented a clear pattern of common attitudes and activities. This pattern is what interested me. Thus the anonymity desired by most informants, which I have respected, served also my purpose of emphasizing their common experience. There were more women than men still living whose memories spanned the period to which this book is limited—1900 to 1950. This turned out to be a bonus, I feel, because the woman's point of view has been neglected, on the whole, in accounts of the period. In addition, I interviewed ministers, politicians, medical people, social service workers, artists, musicians, professors, servants, and teachers who had encountered these people in various capacities.

The last and hardest question to answer is why this elegant lifestyle ceased to exist, but perhaps when we see how things were, we will discover why they are no longer that way.

I owe it to the reader to define some of the terms I will use in this book. I use the terms "elite" or "upper class" when

Braehead was the home of Matthew Hamilton Gault until it was sold to G.H. Duggan in 1911. It was later bought by McGill University and was known on campus as "Duggan House". It was the inspiration for this book.

speaking of this composite group. Strictly defined, they were not a true upper class, a term usually reserved for a landed aristocracy, whose wealth and position are inherited. The Montreal barons were "haute bourgeois" or upper middle class, in spite of the fact that a few of them earned titles which could be passed on. Most did not, and their power and prestige were based entirely on money and achievement, rather than on land or inherited position. They were, however, an elite, by which I mean a group of people who possess the greatest amount of wealth and power in a particular arena (government, economy, religion, etc.) and are able to make decisions that affect the whole society. They were also the highest socio-economic class in Canada. This is primarily their story. Middle and working class English-speaking Montrealers are discussed only in relation to this elite. They have their own equally interesting histories, but this study must have limits, and I make the assumption that as leaders of Montreal's Anglo-Protestant institutions the activities of the elite group determined to a large extent the shape and the fate of the whole community, at least in the early years of the century.

Another expression that may need explanation is "French Canadian," which I use throughout this book. During the period with which I am concerned, the word "Quebecois" meant an inhabitant of Quebec City. Since this book is written from the point of view of people who lived between 1900 and 1950, I have kept to their terminology.

In addition to the interviews, four kinds of written material were used in preparing this book: published books and articles; archival material; privately printed memoirs, diaries, and letters; and unpublished diaries, letters, and papers made available to me by various individuals. Written and attributable material is listed at the back of the book in the endnotes for each chapter. Quotations from all anonymous material, whether interviews or diaries, are marked with the symbol ◊. This material is stored on tapes and written notes in my possession.

I am indebted to many people. First and foremost are the people who gave me the opportunity to understand their lives. I am also grateful to the Canada Council for the Explorations Grant which helped me to plan the work, and to the Quebec Government's Fonds FCAC which provided half-time leave from my teaching duties to research the subject. In addition, my thanks go to members of the Dawson College administration who encouraged the idea and smoothed the way to its realization.

Finally, there are individuals without whom, probably, this book would never have been finished: Maysie MacSporran, Dominique Clift, Sheila Arnopolous, Feenie Ziner, Morna Consedine, Carole Levert, Lionel Kent, Frances Bird, and my husband stand out in this respect for their consistent support and valuable suggestions.

PART I

GROWING UP

(1900-1920)

CHAPTER 1

Grandparents, Parents, and Community

Not long after the British conquest of New France in 1760, a race of hard-driving, ambitious men began building a city on the banks of the St. Lawrence river on their way to building a new country in a vast northern wilderness. They were part of that great exodus of squires' and tradesmen's sons who left Great Britain during the Georgian and Victorian periods to colonize and bring civilization as they saw it to India, Kenya, South Africa, Rhodesia, Australia and New Zealand, Hong Kong and Singapore, or, in our particular case, to Canada. These men, unlike earlier emigrants from Britain, were not fleeing religious persecution or political oppression. They were seeking fame and fortune, their own and the Empire's. Sailing up the wide St. Lawrence from the Atlantic to the Lachine Rapids, they found a mission and military post at the confluence of the St. Lawrence and the Ottawa rivers. The Ottawa flowed down from the north and west while the St. Lawrence, past the Rapids, offered access to the Great Lakes. Together they were routes into the heart of the continent. These entrepreneurs quickly saw the potential for a lucrative trade in raw materials needed by the Mother Country and manufactured goods needed by the colony, with themselves as the middlemen. They took over the fur trade and built factories and ships to import what could be sold in Canada and to export what would fetch a good price back home.

Immediately, they ran into money problems. There was not enough sterling or any other single currency in circulation to be

14

accepted as legal tender. Every kind of coin—Spanish, French, American, Portugese or English—circulated and exchange rates had to be negotiated. Trading and long-distance transport required capital. So, in 1817, some Scots organized the Bank of Montreal. The bank printed its own notes, which were soon accepted as the common currency. It also provided the capital needed for commercial transactions. The bank was well managed. Its early directors, for example, Peter McGill, George Moffat, John Redpath, and their successors, became wealthy, not only because their bank prospered, but also because they themselves were importing and exporting, building and speculating. The Bank of Montreal had, by 1900, assets and a volume of transaction as important as any bank in the New York money market. These assets were twice those of its nearest Canadian competitor, the Bank of Commerce.

As the population grew and spread westward, it became clear to these entrepreneurs that Canada was richly endowed as well as vast, and might become a major British colony able to hold its own against its neighbour, the burgeoning United States. In fact, they thought, if they didn't develop Canada's resources, the Americans would.

What was needed to accomplish the first and avoid the second was a railway. A railway would connect the far-flung parts of Canada, bringing settlers to claim the land and transporting wheat, minerals, timber and furs to markets in the east and thence by ship to Britain. A Montreal syndicate of businessmen, George Stephen, Donald A. Smith, R.B. Angus, and Duncan McIntyre persuaded their friends in the government of Canada to support and award them the contract for building the Canadian Pacific Railway all the way to the west coast. Correspondence between George Stephen and Prime Minister Sir John A. Macdonald revealed them to have been close personal friends.

The hopes pinned on the railway were reinforced by a system of national tariffs intended to protect new industries from American competition. East-west transport and communications, wheat and other natural resource development, plus tariffs, would make Canada an independent, economically viable Dominion. This notion, adopted by the Macdonald government in 1879 after years of controversy, was called the National Policy; its effects were to be of considerable benefit to the interests of the Montreal merchants and financiers, who in turn were very active supporters and promoters of the Tory party. They used personal and business

James Ross, engineer for the building of the CPR, whose financial backing made possible the construction of the Montreal Museum of Fine Arts building, with his son, J.K.L. Ross (standing), on the grounds of their mansion.

pressure to secure votes, some even urging their workers to vote Tory. They offered their services for local and national office and so could and did wield influence over and beyond financial contributions to the party. The member of Parliament from Montreal West during the Macdonald years was always a member of the English business elite. In the early years, this was Donald A.Smith, and later, Matthew H. Gault. Gault's brother, A.F. Gault, the textile magnate, along with David Morrice and others, treated the government as their own branch office, instructing Macdonald through personal letters about what tariffs were needed and who was deserving of political favours. In those days, having a "conflict of interest" was considered an asset. It meant that a man had valuable inside knowledge that would help to get things done.

Building the CPR was an arduous task, requiring a roadbed through the solid rock of the Laurentian Shield and through Rocky Mountain passes in a cruel climate; but it was finished in less time than had been expected. Soon the railway was bringing immigrants by the thousands into the West and carrying what they produced to the port of Montreal for trans-shipment. The country prospered and the men who had done all this became rich men for their time and place. By 1900 the power and wealth of Canada were in the hands of a few men. About fifty men, mostly English and Scottish Protestants in Montreal, either owned or controlled more than one-third of the railways, banks, factories, mines and other properties and resources which constituted Canada's economic wealth at the time.

This group included the directors and managers of the Bank of Montreal and the members of the Montreal syndicate who had built the CPR. It also included William Van Horne and James Ross, who as engineers responsible for most of the construction, had also become rich through investment opportunities the CPR generated. Three of them received titles: George Stephen became Lord Mount Stephen ; Donald A. Smith became Lord Strathcona and Mount Royal; William Van Horne was knighted. It is perhaps enough to say of Mount Stephen and his cousin Strathcona that they were dominant figures, personally and financially, in both the Canadian Pacific Railway and the Bank of Montreal, and took ceaseless advantage of the opportunities these positions offered them. Smith was accounted along with McIntyre, Van Horne, and R.B Angus, among the five richest men in Canada in 1893. Twenty years earlier, George Stephen and Sir Hugh Allan had headed this list.

The Allans were equally important in contributing to Montreal's development as the commercial and financial capital of Canada. Sir Hugh founded the Montreal Ocean Shipping Company, which built and sailed ships of the Allan Line. He also founded the Merchants' Bank of Canada, and took his younger brother Andrew into partnership in both projects—again that magical combination of transport and banking which led to control of other industries. For example, the Allans, with George Stephen, controlled the Montreal Rolling Mills (iron and steel). The Molsons owned Molson Brewing Company; but early in their history they had become involved in banking, shipbuilding and shipping; indeed, for two hundred years they had interests in almost every aspect of Montreal business life.

At the turn of the century, the CPR syndicate members were still active and living in the Square Mile. In the Allan family, Andrew Alexander, son of Andrew, and Sir H. Montagu Allan, son of Sir Hugh, had taken charge of the family businesses, inheriting some directorships of other firms, and obtaining new ones. Herbert Molson was the new head of the Molson empire, his father, John Thomas, having recently been incapacitated by illness. Fred Molson, a cousin, was his partner in the brewery, in various real estate projects, and in banking.

These men were surrounded by others who, if not quite so wealthy, possessed the same entrepreneurial drive: James Ross, the general contractor for the CPR, specialized in buying horse-drawn street railways and converting them to electricity—in Montreal, Toronto, Winnipeg, and St. John, N.B. He was one of the promoters of Lake of the Woods Milling Company, he was a director of the Bank of Montreal, the Canada Sugar Refining Company, the Royal Trust, and Dominion Bridge; was managing director of Dominion Iron and Steel and vice-president of Dominion Coal. Sir George Drummond founded the Canada Sugar Refining Company, was vice-president of the Bank of Montreal, a director of the CPR, Ogilvie Milling Company, and other firms. In fact, it would be hopeless to try to list all the directorships these tycoons held.

Charles Hosmer, president of Canadian Cottons and director of the Bank of Montreal and of Sun Life Assurance Company, held thirty-two directorships in all. Sir E.C. Clouston, general manager of the Bank of Montreal, later vice-president of the Bank and considered the financial pundit of the time, was another in this category. Charles Meredith was president of the Montreal

*The Donald A. Smith (Lord Strathcona) house
contained an art gallery as well as the conservatory
seen at right.*

*In 1908, Robert Meighen and his wife, who was
Lord Mount Stephen's sister, gave this garden party
on the tranquil, almost rural grounds of the Mount
Stephen house on Drummond Street.*

"Rosemount", *Mr. W.W. Ogilvie's house, 1894.*

The H.J.Hague house around 1900, showing the spaciousness and the verdure of the Square Mile at the time.

Stock Exchange in 1902 and founder of the investment firm of C. Meredith and Company. His brother, Sir Vincent Meredith, was shortly to become president and chairman of the board of the Bank of Montreal and a director of Dominion Textile, Royal Trust, Mexican Light and Power, and other firms. Thomas Shaughnessy, later Lord Shaughnessy, was president of the CPR, afterwards chairman of the CPR board, and was a director of the Bank of Montreal, the Royal Trust, several insurance companies, and three American railways. Robert Mackay founded a wholesale dry goods firm and was a director of the Bank of Montreal, CPR, Bell Telephone, Sun Life, and many others. By 1900 his son, Hugh, was taking his place. The Gault brothers held controlling interests in Sun Life, Gault Realties, and Dominion Cotton Mills, and A.F. Gault was a director of the Bank of Montreal. M.H. Gault was president of the Sun Life Assurance Company. A.W. Ogilvie founded the Ogilvie Milling Company. and built flour mills across Canada, thus capitalizing on the emphasis on wheat growing and transport which were part of the National Policy. He was a stock promoter of many enterprises, notably Sun Life, of which he was a director. Herbert Holt, not yet knighted, was president of the Montreal Light, Heat and Power Company in 1901. By 1908 he was president of the Royal Bank of Canada, and eventually of five other companies, vice-president of three, and a director of thirteen others including CPR, Montreal Cotton, Ogilvie Flour Mills, and Sun Life.

Sir William C. Macdonald founded the Macdonald Tobacco Company. Although a director of the Bank of Montreal, he most cherished his position as chancellor of McGill University. William McMaster's name is synonymous with the iron and steel industry. He was vice-president of the Dominion Steel Corporation, of the Dominion Iron and Steel Company, and Dominion Coal, and was instrumental in the merger of these and other companies to form the Steel Company of Canada (Stelco). Robert Meighen was a business associate of Lord Mount Stephen and married the latter's sister. With his brother Frank, he founded the Lake of the Woods Milling Company, one of the largest flour milling operations in Canada. The Greenshields family founded the wholesale dry goods firm of Greenshields, Ltd. E.B. Greenshields was a director of the Bank of Montreal, the Royal Trust, Standard Life and the Grand Trunk Railway. His brother, R.A.E.Greenshields, was a judge. David Morrice founded the wholesale dry goods firm, David Morrice, Sons and Company.

He was president of Canadian Cottons, and of Penman's and a director of the Bank of Montreal and Dominion Textiles. Robert Reford founded the firm of Robert Reford Company, Steamship Agents. Alexander T. Paterson founded Alex Paterson and Company, a brokerage firm, and was a director of the Bank of Montreal. Russell Cowans founded McDougall and Cowans, stockbrokers, and was a governor of the Montreal Stock Exchange. Hartland MacDougall founded, with R.E. MacDougall, the brokerage firm of MacDougall and MacDougall. The five sons of Philip S. Ross, founder of P.S. Ross and Sons, one of Canada's earliest accounting firms, played regular hockey matches against the five sons of Jonathon Hodgson, founder of the J. and C. Hodgson Iron and Tube Works, which merged with Montreal Rolling Mills and later formed part of Stelco. Jonathon and two of his sons organized the banking and stock brokerage firm of C.J. Hodgson and Co. The Rosses had wide interests, including real estate and trust company directorships.

Younger men were on their way to the top: the Dawes brothers (Norman, Kenneth and Sidney) of the brewing family; Max Aitken, later Lord Beaverbrook; Hugh Graham, later Lord Atholstan; Paul and Charles Sise; the Nesbitts; J.W.McConnell, and in the 1920s others still, as we shall see.

There were other high status families in the Square Mile who were not so wealthy, but were respected because they were very old families, or because they had a reputation for distinguished service, or had a particular professional or personal distinction. The Fishers and the Marlers, for example, like the Molsons, were descended from some of the earliest British settlers. Duncan Fisher came to Canada shortly after the Conquest. R.C. Fisher, the head of the family around 1900, built the first apartment building in Montreal on Sherbrooke Street. One of his sons, the Hon. Sidney Fisher, was to be minister of agriculture in the Dominion government. Philip Fisher, the son who carried on the real estate business, married Margaret Southam, whose family would rise to control the largest newspaper chain in Canada. For generations, the Fisher family was outstanding in its organization of, and work in, social services in Montreal. The Marlers are descended from Leonard Marler, who was discharged from the British Army after the Conquest and settled in Quebec. Leonard married the daughter of the first Anglican minister sent out to Quebec. The family was represented at the turn of the century by William de M. Marler, professor of law at McGill University,

Sir Vincent Meredith's house at the corner of Pine Avenue and Peel Street, 1906.

Sir George Drummond's house with a view of Sherbrooke Street in the winter, about 1895.

whose son Herbert was to be Canadian minister to Japan, and to be knighted.

McGill professors, such as Sir William Dawson, its first principal; his son-in-law, B.J. Harrington, professor of chemistry; Stephen Leacock, the economist and writer; R.P. Howard, dean of the medical faculty; the doctors Andrew Macphail, Francis Shepherd, Duncan and Charles McEachran; Percy Nobbs, the architect; and others—all were accorded high status, because of their accomplishments but also because of the great respect in which education was then held by Scots. Ministers, too, were much esteemed: a notable example was the Rev. James Barclay, through whose efforts the Trafalgar Institute for Girls was able to open its doors. Evidence of the social standing of successful professionals may be seen in the fact that Lord Strathcona's only daughter married R.P. Howard, while Charles McEachran married a daughter of Sir Hugh Allan.

Finally, there were many other prominent and well-to-do men whose careers and connections between 1890 and 1906 cannot be listed here for lack of space, but their family names make up the social roll: Auld; Baby, Ballantyne, Beique, Bishop, Burland; Campbell, Cantlie, Carsley, Cassils, Caverhill, Clarke, Cramp, Cross, Cushing; Dandurand, Davis, Day, Dow, Duggan, Dunlop, Durnford; Ewart; Fairbanks, Forbes, Forget, Frothingham; Geddes, Greene, Grier; Hague, Hall, Harte, Hayes, Hingston, Holden, Holland, Hope, Hutchison; Jamieson, Joseph, Judah; Kenley; Labatt, Linton, Low, Lyman; Mathewson, McCord, McIntyre, McKenzie, McKim, McLennan, Miller; Paton, Porteous, Pratt; Redpath, Reid, Robertson, Rodier; Savage, Scott, several Smiths, Smithers, Snowdon, Starke, Stephens, Stevenson, Stewart, Stikeman, Stirling, Sutherland; Wallis, Wanklyn; Yuile. A few of these were of French descent; even fewer were Jewish. Otherwise, it was an elite composed entirely of British Protestants, mostly Scottish. Descendants of many of these families provided the personal accounts on which this book is based.

This sample (which does not pretend to be exhaustive) of the wealthiest and the not-quite-so-wealthy members of the English-speaking elite of Montreal at the turn of the century identifies many of the families whose enterprises had made Montreal the financial and commercial capital of Canada. It is easy to see how closely interlocked that business community was. If one looks over the directorships they held, it is obvious that the heads of these families all sat on each others' boards. This interlocking was familial as much as commercial: nearly everyone was related to everyone else, by marriage or by blood.

Without becoming too enmeshed in geneological tables, let us follow one such thread of relationship. Charles Meredith married a daughter of R.B. Angus, while Sir Vincent Meredith married the youngest daughter of Andrew Allan, and Russell Cowans married another. Alexander Paterson married Isabelle McKenzie, whose mother was also a daughter of Andrew Allan, and Sidney Dawes married their daughter, Elspeth. A daughter of Sir Hugh Allan (he had thirteen children) married Dr. C. McEachran and their son married a granddaughter of P.S. Ross. Robert Meighen married one of George Stephen's sisters and R.W. Reford married *their* daughter. Hartland MacDougall married the Refords' daughter Edith, and his son, H.C. MacDougall, married Dorothy Molson, Herbert's daughter. Another sister of George Stephen married J.A. Cantlie. Their granddaughter married a grandson of R.B. Angus and another Angus grandson married Caro Molson. Earlier, J.S. Allan, a son of Andrew Allan, married Adelaide Gault, daughter of the first Matthew Hamilton Gault, and *their* daughter was the wife of Sir Herbert Marler. To complete the circle, Thomas Molson, Herbert Molson's son, married Celia Cantlie, and Kenneth Molson married Isabel Meredith. Thus the Anguses, Allans, Merediths, McKenzies, Patersons, Dawes, Cowans, Stephens, Refords, Meighens, Cantlies, MacDougalls, McEachrans, Rosses, Marlers, Gaults, and Molsons are all "connected." The chain does not stop there and several others could be described; but this will suffice to make the point.

These families built their houses on the slopes of Mount Royal overlooking the lower town and the St. Lawrence River beyond, in what came to be known as the Square Mile. It is not clear when this term began to be used. People do not recall hearing it before World War I, but it was in common usage by the 1930s. Calling the district the "Golden" Square Mile is recent, used only by people who never lived there, according to one resident. This neighbourhood of wealth has tended to move west and north, but in the early 1900s it began near Bleury on the east, extended to Guy street on the west and rose from Dorchester Avenue on the southern edge of the Mount Royal escarpment to Pine Avenue on the north.

They engaged English or American architects to design great houses reminiscent of the grandeur of European manor houses or castles. Occasionally they chose a more contemporary style, the "High Victorian," marked by eclecticism, decoration for its own sake, and by picturesqueness which might be incorporated with, or superimposed on, any of the other traditional styles. It produced the unrestrained lavishness known as "Victorian gingerbread." Examples of High Victorian homes are the H.V. Meredith house with its Romanesque arcades combined with fairytale towers rising to witch's hat peaks, or the James Baxter house (now owned by Corby's), combining different coloured stones, a mansard roof, and Corinthian columns. Sir Hugh Allan built an Italian Renaissance villa which he called "Ravenscrag," near the top of the mountain. After 1900, the taste for exuberant decoration waned. Buildings such as the Mortimer Davis house and the Hosmer and J.K.L. Ross houses had fewer turrets, crenallations, statues, gargoyles, and gingerbread trim, but they were still faithful copies of past styles—monumental, imposing, and derived from the architectural imagery of Europe.

There were stables and often gatehouses and conservatories on the grounds. The grounds of one estate flowed into the next, so that the whole area was a huge park. At the same time it was an area small and compact enough so that everyone who lived there knew everybody else. Even now, people in their eighties can recall the names of all who lived on their block. Like inhabitants of a small town, everyone was intensely concerned with the activities of his friends and neighbours and barely conscious of the existence of thousands of other citizens of Montreal living south, east, and west of the Square Mile.

In public buildings, also, the Victorian Montrealer liked traditional styles evoking the past. The Mount Royal Club, built in 1904, is neo-classic. The Montreal Stock Exchange building (now the Centaur Theatre) is in appearance a Greek temple with its Corinthian portico, as is the Museum of Fine Arts with its Doric columns. The Bank of Montreal on Place d'Armes is Roman in inspiration, while Notre Dame Basilica, across the square from the bank is neo-Gothic. St. James Cathedral (now called Mary Queen of the World) is a small copy of St. Peter's in Rome. The Church of St. Andrew and St. Paul (Presbyterian) and St. George's (Anglican) are neo-Gothic.

The interiors of their houses were lavish. Walnut or oak panelling and woodwork (particularly in dining rooms and libraries), marble fireplaces, and ornate plaster cornices were common. Some, like Ravenscrag or the homes of Sir George Drummond

26

The lavish interiors of Square Mile mansions
at the turn of the century
are illustrated by the staircase …

... and the salon of George Stephen's house ...

... James Ross's art gallery ...

... the Baumgarten's ballroom ...

... the grand salon of Ravenscrag.

and Sir William Van Horne, Lords Mount Stephen, Strathcona, and Atholstan, were as large and elegant as an English manor house and contained collections of paintings and objets d'art. It was the period when the Empire circled the globe and the British were everywhere at home, since they took their customs with them. The Orient had been opened for trade by the European powers and Japanese and Chinese art burst on the European consciousness, first as an inspiration, then as a fashion. Thus Chinese vases, Indian brass trays or carved ivories from Siam were displayed in the drawing rooms of Britain. In Montreal, they were likely to be copies imported from Britain or made by Owen McGarvey or William Coysh, who specialized in copying "art" and antique furniture.

The walls of Montreal mansions were often covered in fabric—some with tapestry, some with velvet or silk with gold threads. Furniture and panelling were heavy and dark. An easel with a painting on it might be set in a corner of the drawing room. A grand piano draped with a brightly embroidered shawl was often a centerpiece of the room. Dark ancestral and scenic paintings in heavy gilt frames hung, rather profusely, on the walls.

In fact, profusion and even confusion reigned. Antimacassars, crotchet doilies and petit point cushions decorated chairs, commodes and the numerous small tables. Rugs were Persian or Indian. Everything was patterned—walls, furniture, rugs, as well as accessories, and all in different, not necessarily harmonious, patterns. It made the eyes dance. A well-known interior decorator of the time recalls being asked by the lady of such a house, "What do I need to put into this room?" Looking at a drawing room of the sort just described, he replied, "Nothing. What you need is to remove about one-third of the things you already have in it." ◇

Besides mansions, the Montreal businessmen built Protestant churches—all kinds of churches: Church of Scotland, Scottish Secession, American Presbyterian, Methodist, Baptist, Congregational, Unitarian, Church of England. There were other people building Roman Catholic or Orthodox churches and synagogues. There were so many of them altogether that Mark Twain is said to have observed that Montreal was a city where a boy would find it impossible to throw a stone without breaking a church window.

Businessmen built the industries and business institutions on which they and the city depended: the bustling waterfront's shipyards and docks; the Canadian Pacific freight yards nearby, where grain and timber were off-loaded; iron and steel foundries and the Angus Shops, in Rosemount, which manufactured and repaired rolling stock for the CPR. Around the industrial plants of Point St. Charles, Verdun, St. Henri, Rosemount, and Maisonneuve, the slums appeared. Often the owners of these sorry buildings were the same men who built factories, churches and mansions. Some housing in these areas was adequate, but among housing officials Montreal slums before World War I were regarded as among the worst in the world. In some respects, the British civilization these businessmen brought to Canada was all too like the urban conditions described by Dickens, but there were differences: Montreal was colder, more heterogeneous in population and—most people would agree—more beautiful.

Tall elms and maples lined the unpaved streets. Sidewalks were made of wooden planks. Roofs were made of tin or zinc, as a fire retardant, with dazzling effect. The reflected sunlight at different times of day or in different seasons, or the glimmering moonlight on these roofs and spires, was magical or blinding, depending on one's capacity to tolerate glare. By 1900, oxidation had subdued them somewhat.

Some people remember especially the sights and sounds of winter in Montreal in the early part of this century. Snowbanks were as high as second-storey windows, reducing the streets to narrow lanes. Sidewalks were at the bottom of canyons, higher than a man's head, made by snow shovelled from lawns on one side and thrown up from the street on the other. Most of all they recall the sleigh bells, for it was illegal not to have bells on any conveyance. Without them, an approaching horse and sleigh could not be heard in the muffling snow—snow which was white and clean all winter long, they say. All over the city, as they fell asleep, children listened to the silvery jingle of those bells and awakened to them on winter mornings.

Other people recall, not the glittering splendour of roofs and spires, but the mud and dust underfoot. In spring when the snow melted, the mud was deep and ubiquitous. "The roads are frightful," one lady wrote in her memoirs, "lakes and pools and slush—rivers of filth everywhere, with patches of boardwalks and flag stones all being heaved up; with heavy accumulation of snow and ice, a perfect disgrace to the city!" In the summer, this knee-deep mud turned to dust so thick as to burn the throat, nose and eyes.

31

Miss Linton preparing to join the afternoon parade of carriages.

Waltzing on skates at the Montreal Amateur Athletic Association rink.

Tandem drives on Mount Royal were regular events in the late nineteenth and early twentieth century.

The pattern of life which the men and women who lived in the great houses of the Square Mile had evolved was modelled, as strictly as local conditions allowed, on patterns remembered from "home." In Canada, these memories were refreshed by frequent trips back to England and Scotland, by constant business contacts, by teachers and servants recruited in the British Isles. The granting of peerages for services to the Empire also cemented ties to the Mother Country. It is alleged that some of these honours were purchased. Whether or not this is true, it underscores the point that to be accepted, on whatever terms, into British aristocracy was the highest social ambition. The aristocratic model in the minds of English-Scottish Montrealers was not only a product of their own upbringing in Britain, or that of their British-reared parents. The British Empire was acknowledged in that age as the greatest power on earth. The British social standards, values, manners, accents; British parliamentary democracy; British economic wealth and military might—all were as widely admired, hated, and imitated by people around the world as are those of the United States today. The heritage of the British Montrealer was that of a hard-working, thrifty, practical, independent, enterprising people. He took these Protestant values for granted, like his own breathing, and never lost his identification with the British Isles and the Empire. Even in the 1980s, a lady in her eighties said firmly, "We still feel that way." ◇

The women of prominent families were neither trained nor expected to do anything useful, except to organize the household servants. Having a large number of servants, they had a great deal of time on their hands. Lady Drummond, Lady Hingston, Mrs. Herbert Molson, and many others used this time to organize and run more than a hundred and fifty church, social, and charitable organizations. Others devoted it to the social whirl, which became the centre of their lives.

For those women whose lives were largely concerned with the social round, the rules of etiquette came to define most of their activities. Ladies had an "at home" day, an afternoon when, around tea time, they would receive any guests who might care to call. If one was entertained at dinner or a dance, it was obligatory to call on the hostess during the following week, and to leave a card if she was not at home, a practice that persisted into the 1920s. "You hoped the lady was not at home when you came to call." ◇ Young men who might have employment during the weekdays were expected to pay their thank-you calls on Sunday afternoons.

It was necessary to have clothes for every occasion, and ladies changed several times a day. Dress was more responsive than interior decoration to European styles. Many Montreal ladies went to Paris to have their clothes designed, or if that was a bit expensive, they had Parisian designs copied by couturiers in Montreal. Women's dresses still reached the floor. They were made of silks, taffetas, wool, satins, or cotton, with inset hand-made lace, appliqué, embossed velvet, tiny beads or embroidery-covered buttons down the arms or bodice; but they were none-theless simpler in design, more flowing, and more comfortable. The bustle was gone. The long skirt might be narrow or longer in back than in front, resulting in a small train. The corsets and stays that bound the waist to eighteen inches were on their way out by the early 1900s. When we consider the fussiness of these dresses and how much care they required, it is easy to see why there were lady's maids to lay out, clean, and mend them, as well as help with the lady's dressing. And then the number of them per day! A lady had morning dresses, afternoon dresses, tea gowns, reception dresses, dinner gowns, and ball gowns. As the day progressed, the dresses became more elegantly decorated, made of more expensive materials, and were more revealing. Only the dinner and ball gowns might be low cut or without sleeves. All the others would have long sleeves, at least to the elbow, even in summer, and high necklines.

These dresses reflected the day's routine. The morning dress was worn for the lady's business: planning, with the cook, butler, and groom, the household activities for the day—the meals, entertainment, and special tasks; telephoning the guests or shops, or actually going shopping in person; and doing charity work. The lady then changed for lunch which might be taken at a club, at someone's home, or (after 1912) at the Ritz-Carlton hotel. If she planned to eat at home, there would usually be invited guests. The afternoon dress was suitable until tea time when, if tea was to be a family affair, an informal tea gown might be worn; but if she were "receiving" she would wear a reception gown. Then a change for dinner, which was very often a social occasion either at home or elsewhere. Dinner parties several times a week were the norm. Balls or dances at home or at various clubs beginning about ten in the evening were frequent and for them, of course, the ball gown was worn.

Aside from social affairs and travel to Europe (the latter being at least an annual pilgrimage, by luxury liner for a stay of a month or more), the principal entertainments for upper class ladies and gentlemen centered around sports. The Winter Club and the Victoria Rink not only provided skating, but also put on fancy dress balls and masquerades. People sledded or toboganned down Côte des Neiges Hill and Mountain Street, and children hitched rides back up the hills on delivery sleighs. Members of the Winter Driving Club, in a procession of sleighs, had outings which started from the McGill gates, wound through country roads to Lachine or Longue Pointe, where a dinner and "hop" (informal dancing to victrola or piano) had been arranged. The drive home in the crisp, moonlit night was one of the great pleasures of the trip. There were curling clubs and snowshoe clubs for the winter; golf, tennis and sailing clubs for the summer. Some people built private rinks and courts, and tied up small yachts at their own docks along the lakeshore. In the fall, there was fox hunting at the Montreal Hunt, then on Côte Ste. Catherine Road. Although many people stayed in the city on the summer weekends, it was already fashionable to own or rent a summer home, or to stay at one of the large resort hotels for several weeks in the summer.

The man who controlled the family fortune was, in relation to the other members of the family, a very powerful figure. He made all important decisions for all of them. His prerogative was the result of his having total financial responsibility, not only for his immediate family, but (if necessary) for nephews, nieces and cousins. He was a rather remote figure to his children, but his word was law—as it was in general to his wife, as well.

His authority was accepted also in the community and in the business of which he was owner-manager. Although there were hundreds of small and medium-sized enterprises in Montreal, owned and managed by people of French, European, or British backgrounds, the biggest manufacturing and financial firms were owned by Anglo-Protestants. They preferred British workers. Their companies were recruiting skilled workers in Britain during the period 1900 to 1913, when one of the largest waves of immigration from the U.K. occurred. These workers, better trained than most local workers because they had served two-to-three year apprenticeships in the U.K., "dug themselves into the various grades of supervision" and soon over half the foremen in the iron and steel companies were British. They were also found in the most highly paid skilled jobs. (It is important, however, to note that 20 per cent of the British immigrants were employed in unskilled labour in 1901 and that even skilled workers received wages too low to support a family.) In the largest financial institutions by 1921, 53 per cent of the male employees doing clerical or supervisory work were of British origin. Wealthy families, too, recruited their domestic servants of the highest status: butlers, cooks, nannies, and governesses in the U.K. Public and private financial aid to come to Canada was offered.

Not only did the British Protestant elite members prefer to hire British workers; in general they preferred to shop at stores owned and operated by fellow Scots or Englishmen: Birks', Ogilvy's, Morgan's, Joyce's, Carsley's, Murphy's, W. Scott and Sons, and Goodwin's. They also preferred to patronize doctors, lawyers, accountants, and other professionals of their own linguistic and religious background. Being British, however, they were class-conscious and such preferences did not lead to equality of status. A distinction was made between people in wholesale and those in retail trade, the former being acceptable in High Society, the latter not. In Montreal, where nearly everybody was in trade of some kind, this distinction was crucial. "I think it was a question of whether you met them over the counter," one lady explained. "It is awkward to receive in your drawing room as an equal a man who took orders and was anxious to serve you the day before." ◊ By the same token, doctors, lawyers and other professionals, who were in a position to give advice—even orders—to people in society, were accorded a higher status than retailers.

Men of wealth within the Protestant community took charge of, and paid for, those institutions needed by the English-speaking Protestants. This they were required to do by the fact that in Quebec religion was the organizing principle of community life. All public schools were either Catholic or Protestant. Hospitals and social services were Catholic, Protestant, or Jewish. Historically and legally, the Catholic Church provided these services for its adherents. Non-Catholic groups were responsible for establishing and operating their own services. Religion was therefore not only a set of personal beliefs and rituals, but a source of personal and community identity, and a support for essential services.

Contacts among the various class levels of the geographically separated Anglo-Protestant neighborhoods occurred in the Protestant institutional structure: at the workplace, and in churches, schools, hospitals, and charitable organizations, where prominent men held leadership positions, and other men and women worked, served, or received aid, according to their abilities, status, and needs. Members of the middle class were high-level employees of the school system, of industrial or financial firms, were professionals or owned their own small or medium-sized businesses. Lower class English were more likely to be recipients than organizers of aid or services. In all institutions, the directors would be drawn from the upper class so that the major institutions of the Anglo-Protestant community were run according to the principles and views of this class. Furthermore, because they were the leaders, employers, and financial supporters of that community, the experiences and activities of its elite members determined, to a large extent, the fate of the whole group.

Montreal citizens of British origin lived in self-segregated neighborhoods in the central, western and southwestern areas of the city. Living among their own kind in near self-sufficiency, Anglo-Protestants of Montreal were able to maintain themselves as one of the "two solitudes" described by Hugh MacLennan, in spite of occasional friendships, even marriages, with French-Canadian Catholics. In the early days, when British soldiers were mustered out in Quebec and British women were scarce, there were many intermarriages. By the beginning of this century, however, such marriages were strongly disapproved on the grounds of religion, not national origin. Protestants of all social levels report being warned as children, at home and from the pulpit, against marriage with Catholics. A French-Canadian Catholic concurs: "We were told as children that Protestants were the devil himself. We were told not to have anything to do with them, let alone marry one'!" ◊ Nevertheless, there had developed a practical, if informal, solution to the not-uncommon mixed marriages of Quebec: it was understood that the sons would follow their father's religion; the daughters, that of their mothers.

Into this community, with such grandparents and parents, living such lives, a generation of children was born with the promising new century, one that the new prime minister, Sir Wilfred Laurier, predicted would be "Canada's century." Those with whom we are concerned were the children of the elite who might have expected to lead in, and profit from, the exciting times ahead.

CHAPTER 2

Getting the Right Start

The Anglo-Montrealer's idea of how to rear his children drew heavily from British examples, either remembered, or known through frequent trips back "home" or drawn from literature. The prominent families chose as their models the top-drawer families "on the other side," families that had provided leaders for the Empire and the world for a century. English Montrealers, hoping to rear their sons to compete, excel, and lead in Canada, and intending their daughters to marry such men, assumed that leaders were produced by the child-rearing methods of the British upper class. Indeed, several European royal households, notably those of the Czar and the Hapsburgs, retained British nannies, on the same assumption.

In a series of studies of childhood from a Canadian perspective, Brian Taylor suggests that the view of the child taken by the Utilitarian movement in late eighteenth century England is useful in understanding later trends in education and child-rearing in Canada. Jeremy Bentham, the Utilitarian philosopher, spoke for the interests of the rising middle class, of which our group of Montrealers were descendants. Bentham believed that a properly educated child would be industrious, sober ("all things in moderation"), and thrifty. He would accept his place or position in the social order, would possess good personal habits (cleanliness, orderliness, honesty, reliability, punctuality) and be respectful of authority and private property.

About the same time, there arose the idea that the child was different from the adult, and that education was an important part of his personal development. This represented an important departure from the view, which had been dominant since the

39

Middle Ages, of the child as simply a small, slightly inadequate adult. These perspectives produced in Britain and Western Europe a new conception of the nature of the child and of the responsibility of parents and society to rear him in the way he should go. "Henceforth it was recognized that the child was not ready for life, and that he had to be subjected to a special treatment, a sort of quarantine, before he was allowed to join the adults."

The confinement of children to the nursery and later to boarding school exemplified this "quarantine." The attitude of English parents of the early part of the century was well summed up by Geoffrey Gorer in his study of English national character: "The formation of a good English character depends on imposing suitable discipline as long as possible: the child's character will be spoiled if the discipline is insufficient or not applied soon enough." Prominent Montreal families took for granted both the quarantine in the nursery and the presence of a nanny or nurse to discipline the child until civility was achieved. In adopting this pattern, parents were providing an aristocratic, not a middle-class, infancy. Trained or not, nannies, especially British ones, were part of an upper-class rearing and they were expected by their employers to turn out little ladies and gentlemen. This was also what the nanny thought she should do. Consequently, we should expect some aristocratic virtues to be added to the Utilitarian ones taught to children in the wealthy households of Montreal businessmen. And so they were, as we shall see.

The British nanny appeared in the mid-Victorian period, and largely disappeared after World War II, although the Norland Nursery Training College in England still turns out nannies. Relatively few Montreal families had a genuine British-trained nanny—although everyone who did not is now slightly apologetic. Several people began interviews by saying, "I had a real British nanny," and then remembered that the nanny might in fact have been Canadian without any training at all. In any case, there were very few Norland or other British-trained nannies in the Montreal area, although there were many English or Scottish girls who took the role without the training and learned on the job. If a nanny had grown up in Britain, trained or not, she might pass for the genuine article since she was likely to understand the values and behaviour expected of the ruling class. As several women said, "British nannies were the best disciplinarians."

Some people went to England or Scotland for nannies and then trained them on the job. Many more hired an Anglo-Protestant Canadian, usually the daughter of a blue-collar worker or a farmer, who lived in the household perhaps for life, almost but not quite a member of the family. If the family was not sufficiently affluent for a permanent, live-in nanny, the mother cared for her children herself, with help from a nursemaid who might or might not live in, and who might very well also do other work around the house—maid's work or cooking. People who employed "a pair of hands," ◊ as one lady called this last category of mother's help, might employ French Canadian girls; but in this case they were "very carefully supervised," as a doctor's wife stated, "because in those days they all spoke *joual,* which wasn't acceptable." ◊ Not only for ease of communication, but as an example for the children, having an English-speaking nurse of at least some education was considered important, particularly if she stayed very long. The principal source of English-speaking immigration before World War I was Britain, where education, even at the lower levels, was considered good. Finally, since religion was of greater importance in those days, Protestants were preferred.

The lower a family's position on the social and economic scale, the more the mother did of the physical work involved in child care and the "spiritual" work involved in character building. Because of this direct association between nanny and social position, *not* having a nanny if you could afford one was frowned upon. Not being able to afford one was a clear announcement of falling on hard times—or worse, of never having been of the right social standing in the first place. One woman who could afford a nanny but wanted to learn to care for her baby herself reports that her family made quite a fuss when she decided to hire only "a pair of hands." ◊

Nannies have almost disappeared in Montreal, but for the generation under consideration, their existence made possible a particular kind of childhood, one that no longer exists. The nature of this childhood helps explain some important elements in the upper class Anglo-Protestant culture of the early twentieth century in Montreal.

There were kind nannies and cruel ones; nannies who by singing and reading to their charges passed on the lore and the heritage of British culture; others who never read; some nannies who denied meals and administered medicine as punishment; others who never did. But they were almost universally snobs, dictating to children who was an acceptable playmate and who was not.

Children and Nannies:
Baby Gordon and nurse (1902)...

Baby Angus and nurse (1897).

Around 1900 in Montreal, baby-nurses began to be trained at the Montreal Foundling and Baby Hospital on Argyle street in central Montreal. The training of an "Argyle nurse" was different from that of the British nanny. She was not expected to stay very long—still less to take complete responsibility for the children. The mother remained in charge. One woman explained that "if the parents wanted the children to be present for tea or to meet guests, it was the *nanny* who would decide whether the children should come and how long they might stay. Argyle nurses never had that kind of control." ◇

The nanny, nurse, and nursemaid were all primarily care-takers of very young children from birth to school age; some, of course, stayed on after the child went away to school if there were other younger children. The general assumption was that a child did not need the services of a nanny or nurse after he or she was about twelve years old. It she got on well with the family, an ordinary untrained nurse might, like the nanny, stay all her life or be passed on to friends, other branches of the family, or kept to take care of the grandchildren.

When a child was about six years old, a governess might be hired. If all the children were past that age she might replace the nanny. On the other hand, she might come in at specified hours, usually in the afternoon when school was over. In the early years of this century, the elementary classes of private schools were in session only in the morning. Children came home at the lunch hour. Afterwards, the nursery became a schoolroom. The governess might come to the house to give lessons, most commonly in French, but sometimes in other subjects as well. Learning French was taken seriously, although it seemed to have had little to do with improved communication with the French-speaking inhabitants of Quebec. The few French Canadians these children encountered, whether working class or upper class, spoke English. With a few exceptions, informants said that they rarely, if ever, spoke French, not even with good friends whose first language it was. The importance of learning French was that it was traditionnally the second language of the British upper class. A lady or gentleman was expected to know it.

A governess who replaced a nurse for the older children would have other responsibilities besides their formal education. She would be responsible for their physical care as well, taking them for walks, supervising their play, having certain meals with them, and keeping their clothes in order. Some girls (but never boys) were educated entirely by governesses.

Governesses were usually "gentlewomen," daughters of middle class fathers and themselves well-educated and cultivated people. Theirs was the highest status of all among the family's employees. They usually took their meals—their dinner, at least—with the parents, something no servant did. They did no housework or cooking. They only supervised and taught the children. At the same time, since a governess was regarded as having an independent profession exercising the role of a teacher, not a substitute mother, she was unlikely to be as emotionally close to her charges as the nurse, and rarely became a "member of the family." Governesses usually stayed about six years, until the child was about twelve years old, at which time the child was sent to boarding school or to a local, probably private, high school where activities and classes filled most of the day.

A child born in 1900 would have been born at home, the birth assisted by a doctor and his nurse. The nurse stayed about twenty-four hours after the birth to care for mother and infant. The baby would be breast-fed. Cow's milk was not always safe; formulas were still in the experimental stage; and Montreal had no tradition of wet-nursing. One woman remembers, "My mother had four children and never quite enough milk to feed them. She told me she had to listen to us scream for hours at a time." ◇ Another recalls that a baby brother died because her mother could not nurse him at all as a result of a post-partum illness and Nestlé's Food—the formula then available—did not agree with him, either. So there was not much choice: mothers breast-fed their babies, if at all possible.

The baby slept in the parents' bedroom, or in the mother's room if she had a room of her own, for the first few weeks or months and then was moved to the nursery on the top floor, where he lived with a nanny or governess taking care of him and his other brothers and sisters, until he was about twelve years old. At that age he began to sleep, eat, and generally live among the grown-ups of the family on the floors below.

The plan of the best Montreal houses of the early 1900s was this: the ground floor or semi-basement level was the servants' quarters and included the kitchen, laundry, and an area in which the servants had their meals; the first floor consisted of a drawing room, the dining room, an entrance hall of considerable proportions, often with a sweeping, handcarved staircase, and extra rooms such as a library, a music room, billiard room, or conservatory, as the personal interests or taste of the family dictated. A

The nursery room which by turns is playroom, dining room and, in the afternoons, may become a schoolroom.

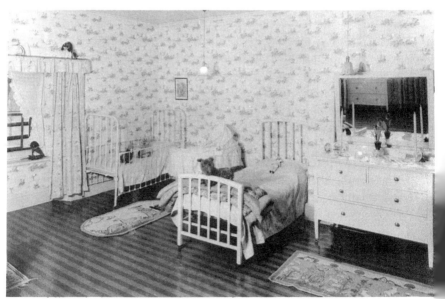

The nursery bedroom

very elegant, large house such as Ravenscrag or the Baumgarten's might also include a ballroom complete with musician's gallery. The great halls for displaying paintings, such as in Lord Strathcona's home, might also be used for dances. On this floor visitors were received, social events occurred, and the family followed hobbies or other recreational pursuits. Adults had their bedrooms, bathrooms and usually an upstairs sitting room or morning room on the second floor. Separate dining rooms for children were not unusual, and were often on the second floor as well. The top floor was the domain of the children and their nurse or nanny. It usually had dormer windows and sloped ceilings. There were bedrooms for the children, one for the nurse, often a room called a day nursery where toys were kept and lessons learned, and a bathroom. There was a dumb waiter by which meals were sent up from the kitchen. There might be a kitchenette or at least a gas burner on which nanny could make tea, but she did no real cooking. If the house had no dumb waiter, the kitchen maid brought meals upstairs on a tray.

Most children were entirely in their nanny's care at some period of their lives. Parents often took holidays or went to Europe on business, leaving the nurse in authority for periods ranging from weeks to years. Also, a great many more serious illnesses had to be dealt with and, lacking antibiotics, illnesses like tuberculosis, typhoid, and scarlet fever, tended to last much longer. Mothers, fathers, or children were often confined, quarantined, or sent away for protracted periods. Finally, for several hours a day nurses were in charge because the social and philanthropic activities of mothers kept them away from home.

This situation easily led to conflict between mother and nanny. Persons who remember such conflicts describe a situation where two strong-willed women were unable or unwilling to divide authority between them clearly.

Mrs. A. remembers that, in spite of the fact that her nurse stayed with the family until she died, " Mother and she used to have awful fights, sometimes, because Nanny was so dominant that she would get Mother quite upset occasionally and Mother would shout loudly at her," ◇ and a lady whose mother left her in charge of a nanny for a very long time reported that "My mother and my nanny never got on very well … when Mother came back from England, my nurse felt I was her child, and I felt she was my real mother." ◇

This uneasy balance of authority in the nursery may still have worked out better from the child's point of view than when

Mothers and children:
Mrs. Paul Size and children, 1910...

Mrs. Herbert Marler and children,
1904...

Lady Allan and children, 1906.

complete authority was given to the nanny, especially if the nanny was too strict, or even cruel. Mrs. C. described a fourth-floor nursery insulated by a panel of glass so that no sound from the nursery could reach the floors below and a system of summoning children with a buzzer (one ring for Johnny, two rings for Mary) when parents wished to speak to one of them. ◇ Another informant, Mrs. E., describes her sister, always a nervous child, being locked for hours in a dark cedar closet for being naughty, and that, the nurse "washed out our mouths with soap when we said a bad word. We were paddled and generally very strictly disciplined. Mother had no idea what went on in the nursery. We never told her about these things." ◇

Still, some parents were uneasy about the treatment their children were receiving. After all, most of them had had nannies when they were children. But when, in one example, a mother became anxious about the screams and yells issuing from the nursery, "My father asked calmly, 'Well, do the children love her?' Mother knew that we did, so that was what mattered." ◇

Some children were not without resources of their own in dealing with disliked nannies. Mr. M. recalls playing on a steep, grassy slope in a park near Pine Avenue, accompanied inevitably by his nanny. He and his sister got behind her and, to her pained surprise, pushed her down the slope. She left the family the next day. Whether she was the same nanny who gave him a bath in turpentine to remove some paint he had got on himself, thereby nearly removing his skin, is not clear. Mrs. G. remembers biting a governess whom she particularly disliked. Some nannies were ineffectual. Mrs. W. says that "our nanny nagged us all the time, but we never paid much attention to her." ◇ Such a case is rather unusual, however. A more common statement was that of Mr. H. who said, "We felt we had to obey our nurse as though she were a parent. We were brought up that way." ◇

Most children of the Montreal elite, however, seem to have been reasonably fond—some, very fond—of their nannies, and in some cases the nurse replaced the mother in the child's affections. "I just adored her and she spoiled me dreadfully. She was not at all the usual disciplinarian nanny and when she left, when I was about twelve, to go to a cousin's (that's what we did in those days; we passed them around the family), I was just useless for months." ◇

Relations between small children and their parents depended largely, of course, on the extent to which the Nurse "took over" their rearing. Mrs. S.,for example, speaking of her own child-hood, says, "We were reared in the worst possible way—confined to the nursery, rarely seeing our parents. They were almost like strangers to us." ◇ Howard Marler has written about family summers spent at a country estate near Drummondville called Grantham Hall:

> As was the usual pattern, Father came out for weekends. One of my earliest childhood memories is the fevered activity on Fridays heralding his arrival. All day the under-gardeners would have been raking the gravel paths and the mile-long driveway.... Then the main gates were shut, not to be opened until his arrival from the station, so that there would be no wheel marks on the gravel. One does not observe one's family, when a child, with any depth of understanding ... but I can now recapture the pleasure that my father must have felt at seeing his beautiful young wife in ankle-length flowered gown and ... his daughter and two small sons in spotless starched dress and suits. I wish that we could have rushed into his arms to greet him, but we just stood there gravely as he mounted the steps, kissed my mother and patted his children on the head. Once the weekly ceremony was over, we children would retire to the nursery in the care of our current nanny.

Not all children were so isolated and remote from their parents. In many households the children were not altogether confined to the nursery and frequently had at least one meal a day with one parent or both parents, but "not *dinner*, when we were very young children, of course." ◇ The pattern seems to have been, in spite of exceptions, that for well-to-do Montreal Anglo-Protestant families, very young children stayed in the nursery most of the time.

Sadly, some mothers who might have enjoyed more active mothering were constrained by social convention and their own acquiescence in the authority of the nanny. Mrs. H., whose chil-dren's nanny had also been her own, remarked wistfully that she liked to be home for nursery tea. "My dear Nanny would serve and I couldn't wait to get home for it because it was so lovely. And I used to love the days when Nanny was off and I could take the baby out in the baby carriage myself." ◇

These, then, were the people responsible for the care of infants in Square Mile nurseries. As every parent knows, given the same nursery, the same nanny and the same parents, chil-dren's reactions can vary widely. In fact, they usually do.

Nursery life was a set of routines for child and nurse, and this was regarded as the best environment for a child. Very young children were lifted from their cribs and changed and dressed in time for breakfast, which would arrive on schedule. If the child was under a year old, he or she would be dressed in "long clothes," the white dresses and petticoats falling a foot or more below the infant's feet. After infancy, little boys might still wear Little Lord Fauntleroy suits of black velvet jackets, short trousers, a wide, black silk sash, and a wide lace collar, especially for dress occasions; their hair still might be allowed to grow long until they were of school age; but both these styles were disappearing to be supplanted by short haircuts and sailor suits. High buttoned shoes for girls were still worn, but sometimes little girls wore strap slippers. Dresses, reaching to mid-calf, were softer and looser than in the Victorian period; but still in vogue were bloomers, numerous petticoats, and long stockings held up by suspenders. Children, like adults, had different types of clothing for different occasions. The sailor suit, for example, was introduced as a play costume. Children were required to wear hats or caps whenever they left the house. On dress occasions, such as tea away from home, white gloves were *de rigueur*.

Breakfast always included, and might consist entirely of, porridge. After breakfast there was "potting": propping or placing the child on the pot and keeping him there until he evacuated his bowels. People were very concerned with "regularity" all through this period, believing it to be essential for health and good disposition. Many children's lives were made miserable by Syrup of Figs, Scott's Emulsion, and in extreme cases castor oil or enemas.

When these functions had been attended to, the nursery made tidy, and the children dressed for the out-of-doors, it was time for the morning walk. Such an outing would be cancelled only if the weather was bitterly cold, the rain pelting, and the child too young to be kept warm by vigorous activity. For any less extreme conditions, the children were bundled up in wool or fur coats, fur caps or hats, ear muffs, hand muffs, boots and leggings; the baby, in bunting bag plus most of the above and a blanket or two. Only in cold weather, of course. The nurse wore a grey or navy-blue uniform over the white one she wore indoors, a coat if necessary, and a hat, always. She took the big English pram which would hold a baby at one end and a toddler at the other, and away they went to the nearest park. When the ground was covered with snow, a pram on runners was used. Nannies and nurses congregated at the neighbourhood park and got to know each other, and these contacts were an important, if not the only, source of social life for them. While the children played and the infants slept, the nurses talked.

As mentioned before, many nannies and nurses were concerned that the playmates their charges encountered there be suitable. Gathorne-Hardy believes that in Britain, the nanny was exceedingly important in reinforcing class distinctions. The same, although probably to a lesser degree, seems to have been true in Montreal. Mrs. B. speaks for several others when she says, ''My nurse always decided who was a suitable playmate and who wasn't. I often wondered how she could tell that some children were what she called 'common,' but however she did it, I wasn't allowed to play with them.'' ◇ We can guess that the nanny based her judgment on her observations as to whether the child had a nurse or was accompanied by his mother and whether the child's clothing suggested a family able to afford the elaborate, varied wardrobe fancied by wealthy families. A child's manners and way of expressing himself would also have been keys to his status. The nanny's charge might not notice these things at first; but children, in general, learn snobbery readily, and nannies helped the process along.

The morning walk over and the play with these carefully selected playmates at an end, nurses and charges returned home for lunch, which was the main meal, also served in the nursery or a children's dining room. When the child is old enough to eat such food, lunch may consist of meat, vegetables and a dessert. People had strong opinions about what children should eat. They believed that a child's diet should be bland, not spicy or fat. Food like sausages or fried dishes were not permitted until a child was about six. As a result, food during childhood is remembered as boring: porridge, bread, butter and jam; rice pudding, junket; a gruel made of milk and bread; ''applesauce interminably''; soft-boiled or coddled eggs occasionally. Plain food in moderate quantities was the rule. Over-indulgence was frowned upon for everyone; certainly, it was not good for children.

Three levels of food were served in most households: one for adults, another for the nursery, and a third for the servants. The quality of the different menus also might vary. One woman maintains that Mrs. Beeton's cookbook (a very popular one at the turn of the century) included a recipe for jam explaining how to use the best fruit for jam, the less perfect fruit for jelly, and finally the pulp left after jelly-making as ''suitable for making a nice jam for the nursery.'' ◇

After dinner and naps, a quiet period, or lessons, depending on the child's age, there might be another walk, weather permitting. Sometimes nurses actually helped older children to learn bicycle riding, tobogganing, or other skills. Then home to tea, served in the nursery around four. Tea really was a light supper, consisting of bread, milk and jam and perhaps a boiled egg. At this point, many children might see one or both parents for the first time since breakfast, or for the first time all day. Sometimes parents came up to join the nursery tea; sometimes children were brought down to the drawing room for an hour or so.

Tea, therefore, was a special event. Nurse bathed the children and dressed them in fresh clothes for the occasion, with the result that by the time they were twelve, dressing for dinner seemed only natural. How exciting, and at the same time how unsettling these visits must have been for the children! The anticipation of seeing adored and god-like figures (an hour or so a day is not enough to produce the kind of stress that causes full-time parents to show their weaknesses) was tempered by the necessity to be on good behaviour, to make Nanny and parents proud. During such visits the adults often read or told stories to the children.

Now it was time to undress and go to bed—by seven o'clock, usually. A light shone reassuringly from under Nanny's door as she mended or ironed the children's clothes for the next day.

Of all the words which Montrealers of this group mention in connection with their early childhood, the most frequent is "disciplined." Most describe their nannies as "strict disciplinarians," and do so with some pride. They feel that it was good for them and that it is precisely what the modern generation has missed. Again, discipline followed the British pattern. English children were punished largely through deprivation of some pleasure, followed by spanking as a second resort. Rewards were rarely used, apparently on the assumption that "the ordinary life of the child is sufficiently rewarding by itself to reinforce good or approved behaviour; though deviations from the proper course call for remedial action, conformity demands relatively little recognition." Montrealers also remember punishment consisting of deprivation, spanking, or scolding, with few if any rewards for good behaviour.

An unrepentant woman, whose son is today an important political figure said, "My son thinks it was awful to have had a nanny. He thinks she was too strict. But I still think the discipline was good for him." ◊ A man who asserts with pride that his parents and his nurse were all strict disciplinarians of "the old British school" said, "I've been spanked, kept indoors, kept from doing things I wanted to do, scolded immensely, but never starved, never threatened. No, it was the right kind of discipline—the same kind I got in school." ◊

This statement suggests the effect on the child of a small, homogeneous community, where the same precepts are taught by the same methods at home, in school, and in the neighbourhood. For example, a grandfather recalls, "It was relatively easy to rear children in those days. Not only because we had a lot of help, but I knew that if I punished my son for doing something wrong, my next-door neighbour would punish his son for the same thing." ◊ Also, the power of adult example and expectation is magnified when a child never encounters contrary ideas. As one man explained, when everyone in one's environment agreed on what were the basic rules of conduct, "most training of children was done by example." ◊

Clearly, elite English Montrealers early in this century believed that certain characteristics were important to instill in children, and that very early. The nursery routine itself demonstrates not only the emphasis placed on order and moderation, represented by the lack of over-stimulation and the unexciting food, but also the emphasis placed on bodily control and cleanliness. The number of routine walks or outings call attention to another point: the belief in regular exercise in fresh air. One woman recalls that even before she was six, she and her nanny walked from Mansfield Street to Westmount Park, about twenty-five city blocks, and back again at least once a day. The value of outdoor exercise was stressed, and became even more emphasized by competitive sports in the boys' private schools, developing lifetime participation in sports as characteristic of the culture, at least for men.

An important feature of the nursery training was the respect for authority represented by the expectation that without question the young child would obey in turn, nanny, parents and, later, teachers. Another was that children learned to respect the property of others, or "things" in general. Unruliness and hyperactivity were not tolerated. "I can recall," a lady says, "that on rainy days my brother and I when very young children would be allowed to play in the drawing room sometimes. That room was full of art objects and valuable furnishings and we played all morning without breaking or disturbing a thing." ◊

The Jonathon Hodgson family, 1904

The P.S. Ross family, 1904.

A reasonable assumption seems to be that differences in the expected roles and behaviour of boys and girls existed even at the nursery stage, since these were so distinct later on. Memories of these are so rare that little can be verified, except those practices which still exist. Boys were taught to be brave, to be protective, to be gallant toward girls, and never to cry. Girls were expected to be gentle, quiet, and non-assertive. Both sexes were expected to be clean and tidy, truthful, well-mannered, and generally considerate of grown-ups.

Toilet training was taken very seriously and begun early, there being some argument as to whether to start at birth or wait a few months. To begin at two years as now recommended would have been totally unacceptable. As we have seen, babies were placed on potties at regular times. If the child performed, the nurse registered great pleasure, and equal displeasure if he did not. None of my informants, I should say, ever reported remembering such an experience when they were children, but they followed the same practice with regard to their own children. This belief in early toilet training held throughout the period with which we are concerned. Masturbation or interest in sex was frowned on; dire threats of insanity and disease followed discovery of a child playing with his or her genitals.

While learning to respect authority, children learned that there were people to whom one ought to defer. At the same time, in daily play in the park, they were discovering that there are people who ought to defer to them. In short, they were learning about social position. Manners were among the most important means of identifying people who "didn't belong" and manners were strongly emphasized in child-rearing. A student of etiquette maintains that courtesy (a general attitude of consideration for others) became etiquette (a set of rules of behaviour) as a means whereby the upper class sought to protect its position against the rising middle class in the early nineteenth century. As an example of how intricate this etiquette could be, *Manners and Tone of Good Society* published in Britain in the mid-nineteenth century contained forty-two pages of instructions on how to use calling cards. Rules about what to wear, how to eat, what to say, and how to say it changed more frequently than etiquette books were published. They were therefore learned at home, and so it was easy to distinguish those who "knew" from those who had to learn. A Montreal woman remembers of schoolmates in a private school, "If they didn't know how to behave, we just ignored them." ◊

Does it seem a lonely, austere childhood? So it was, in many ways; but children of the time enjoyed an enviable fantasy life, perhaps in reaction to this austerity. It was stimulated by the children's books which appeared between 1850 and 1930, many of whose authors had experienced this kind of childhood themselves, and depicted it in their stories. An imaginary world lay just behind the nursery walls. One could reach it through a mirror, or with keys that turned locks in secret doors, or by wishing hard enough. Once on the other side, a child was in Fairyland, Wonderland, Never-Never Land, out of sight of Nurse's watchful eyes. There anything could happen and no one need ever know. There the child who counted for little in the everyday world, whose wishes were rarely if ever consulted, became the central character, righting wrongs and rescuing hapless children or animals, with a little help from a magic guardian.

Parents often found their way back to this world in the company of their children. They read or told stories to them when the children were very young. Later, well-to-do parents often provided a room that could be fitted out as a theatre, especially in country houses. Then, under Mother's guidance, the children and their friends rehearsed and put on plays for family and neighbours—adaptations of some well-known classic, or else something written especially for the occasion by an uncle or friend of the family. Photographs of some of these productions show elaborate costumes and sets. The activity was taken seriously, as well as being great fun; and Montrealers who remember being involved count these amateur theatricals as a memorable part of their childhood.

Without radio, television or cinema, story-telling and reading aloud or to oneself were much more important activities than they are now, and a wealth of great books was available. The books on the nursery shelves were likely to be *Mother Goose*, *A Child's Garden of Verses*, the Beatrix Potter books, and fairy tales by Hans Christian Andersen, the Brothers Grimm, and Andrew Lang.

For older children there were the old classics, really written for adults, such as *Robinson Crusoe*, *Gulliver's Travels*, or *Pilgrim's Progress*. There would also have been more recent books written expressly for children, such as *Treasure Island*, *Alice in Wonderland*, and *Kidnapped*. In this last category, the stories of G.A. Henty and R. Kipling extolled the glories of being British and a soldier. Mrs. Molesworth's and Mrs. DeHorne

A turn-of-the-century doll house.

Vaizey's long-suffering heroines overcame at last. Sir Walter Scott's romances were popular. George MacDonald (*The Princess and the Goblin*) and Mrs. L.T. Meade (*The Girls of St. Wode's*) or Frances Hodgson Burnett (*Little Lord Flauntleroy*) might also have been there. The *Boy's Own Paper*, the *Girl's Own Paper*, and the annuals compiled from these magazines, almost certainly would have had a place.

Anyone who has read these books is aware of certain features they all share. In the first place, nearly all "teach" at least an implied moral lesson. Many were written when literature, especially for children, had to have a moral. The most common lesson in fairy tales is that the honest, loving, gentle, courageous, thrifty and clever person wins in the long run, even (or especially) if he or she is the third son of a king, a poor cobbler, or a stepdaughter. Books and stories for older children were not always so explicitly didactic. Certain values were so taken for granted that even the author seems to have been unaware of promoting them; at other times the character of the author speaks out plainly. An article in the *Girl's Own Annual* of 1903 states: "A real lady must have feminine gentleness of speech, action and manner. Loud talking, brusqueness and a self-asserting or self-conscious manner, do not befit a true gentlewoman." Boys were to be steadfast, loyal, courageous, and if possible clever. A serial in the *Boy's Own Paper* at the turn of the century tells of a luckless lad in a sadistic boarding school who eventually learns to face and not be defeated by his own mistakes and his hard experiences there.

Another common feature of these books and stories is that they are all British. Except for a very few American publications, English-speaking Montreal children before 1914 read books written by British authors about British children, living in Britain. And these characters were the fictional counterparts of the Montreal elite children, with similar big houses on estates or at least set in large gardens. They had nannies and servants, followed nursery routines, and obeyed nursery rules. Even when, as in Charles Kingsley's *Water Babies*, the main character was a poor child, the story is usually aimed at the "well-brought-up" child.

The English of the Victorian and Edwardian periods passionately adored their homeland and were proud of doing so. Kipling, Browning, Tennyson, and indeed almost all British writers since Shakespeare were unabashedly in love with "this scepter'd isle ... this older Eden, demi- paradise/This happy breed of men, this little world/This precious stone set in the silver sea ... This blessed plot, this earth, this realm, this England,'' and this feeling comes through in children's books of the period. This strong sense of nationality bred the certainty that life in England was "how things should be"; that to live anywhere else on earth was to be uprooted. One situation commonly depicted is that of the child whose parents have left him behind in England, while they go to India or to some other colonial posting. Parents took it for granted that the child was better off left in Britain in the care of nannies, elderly aunts, boarding schools, or guardians than to suffer the disadvantages of being "abroad,'' that is, anywhere off the Isles. Canadian children, ingesting this steady literary diet, felt sometimes that everything Canadian was second-rate. They identified themselves to some extent as "British-away-from-home.'' The cement, the symbol of it all, was the Royal Family. A woman in her eighties recalls a childhood visit to London: "I was told that the King and Queen would pass in their carriage along a certain route at a certain time the next day. Well in advance of the time, I was stationed to watch for them and I remember that my knees were shaking as I waited. Members of the Royal Family were like gods to us." ◊

Boys learned through their reading to believe that to be a soldier in the British army and, if necessary, to die for England, were high and heroic ambitions. Kipling and G.A. Henty wrote compelling accounts of historic battles around the world in which British troops triumphed, or, if defeated, went down to honourable deaths in defense of their empire. These stories rarely presented gory details. Wars, especially British wars, seemed thrilling and the true test of a man. Even girls were encouraged to accept this point of view. One of Mrs. DeHorne Vaizey's heroines states that "only a soldier" will do for her husband.

As the child grew older, he read or listened to Dickens and to Anna Sewall's *Black Beauty* and learned, if he did not already know, that there were children and animals who were treated cruelly, who suffered for lack of food and shelter. Not all the world was like his world. His awareness of being privileged was awakened and at the same time his sense of obligation toward the unfortunate, it was to be hoped.

Children are active partners in building their own characters. They choose, in the privacy of their own thoughts, what models they wish to follow, what beliefs they will adopt, what material is worth learning—when they have alternatives. But when the real world and the fantasy world present the same images of truth, the child knows no alternatives. The most compelling models and values would be, then, those common to literature and everyday nursery discipline.

We see that even before school age, young Anglo-Protestant members of the elite born around 1900 had a foundation in good personal habits, respect for authority, self-control, and acceptance of their place in the social order. If we compare this list with the Utilitarian prescription of qualities considered beneficial to the business class in preparing a child to live in an entrepreneurial society, we see that the children born around 1900 were off to a good start. However, it was not enough. The childhood training received by the Montreal businessmen in the early Victorian era was probably much influenced by the Utilitarian views on education, but it was not all they wanted for their children. Having the money and the position to live like nobility, they wanted their children to have the manners and bearing of a ruling class. As we have seen, the model they chose was that of the British aristocracy.

CHAPTER 3

Schooldays

Long ago, a philosopher was asked what were the most necessary things for well-born boys to learn. He answered: "Those things which they will use when they become men." After the nursery age, the children of Montreal's English-Scottish elite were sent to schools intended to prepare them for their future roles and positions. The school experience of the generation of upper-class children born around 1900 is important not only in itself as a phase of life, but also as an illustration of the character and abilities thought desirable in leaders of community and country.

When it was time to think of sending their children to school, parents faced a bewildering set of choices. Education was not compulsory, so parents could decide when—and even whether—to send a child to school at all. It was not unusual for girls to be educated at home by governesses until they were fourteen or fifteen, when they might be sent to boarding school. Boys, however, were always sent to school by age nine at the latest. Their education, in its academic, its character-building, and its social aspects, was considered serious and important. The schools in Montreal around 1906-1908 were of three general types: private "dame schools"; private schools, some with religious affiliation; and the public schools of the Protestant Board of School Commissioners.

"Dame schools" were those held in the homes of teachers, usually women, of widely varying qualifications and abilities. The schools themselves were without any outside regulation or inspection. Some taught boys; some, only girls; others were co-educational in the earliest grades. Some accepted very young children and were an extended kindergarten. A few attempted to provide an entire elementary education; and a few, such as Miss Lyman's, also offered some secondary-level work. Dame schools took the name of the founders and were called "Miss Dunlop's," "Miss Gardner's," "Miss Roberts's," and the like.

Private schools "belonged" to headmasters and headmistresses, who tried to pay expenses from student fees, with occasional loans or other financial support from parents. They picked their own staff. One of the ways in which they made ends meet was by paying substandard wages to the teachers. As a retired recruit said, "In England, we didn't know what the cost of living was here. Salaries sounded much better than they actually were." ◊ Another way of saving money was to have too few teachers. "The hours we worked were cruel. The headmaster dictated what and when we were to teach. I taught everything except chemistry and I think I was spared that only because he was afraid that I might blow up the place. I even taught swimming, and I was such a weak swimmer that if anyone had been drowning someone else would have had to pull him out. I remember once, when I was in charge of cricket, asking for money for two cricket poles and being asked, 'Can't you manage with one?'" ◊ A brisk rate of teacher turnover was the result, though headmasters seemed quite durable.

By 1906, the Protestant Board of School Commissioners was operating fifteen publicly financed elementary schools and three secondary schools, some of which were located conveniently close to residents of the Square Mile. Most renowned was the High School of Montreal.

One of the comments made most frequently by graduates about the High School of Montreal is that there one met and knew people from all walks of life and all backgrounds, something not true of the private schools. The High School consisted of an elementary and a secondary school for boys. Founded in 1843, it came in 1856 under the auspices of McGill College. In 1875 a High School for Girls was added, with an elementary school beginning at the kindergarten level and progressing to the sixth form, or grade eleven. Ever since its foundation, this school had educated the children of the middle and upper class Anglo-Protestant families of Montreal and had produced many famous graduates. Run like a British public school, it often used the same books and courses of study, hired mostly British masters, set the same standards, and dispensed the same discipline as a private school might be expected to do. The High School of Montreal, with its boys' and girls' sections located until 1914 on Peel Street above St. Catherine, had a solid reputation in the community.

However, some changes were occurring. The McGill Normal School was producing trained Canadian teachers. The Report of the Board for 1906 shows that 42 out of 69 new teachers hired for the Protestant system for that year were graduates of McGill Normal School. The British "form" organization was beginning to give way to the American "grade" system. The battle over compulsory Latin and Greek, involving parents as well as staff, had resulted in Greek and Latin becoming optional—a serious blow to the concept of a traditional classical education, although the other option, more science and mathematics, was more in tune with the times. The building on Peel Street intended to house about 350 students was serving more than 700 and was seriously over-crowded. Finally, there being no quota, the majority of students in the academically specialized or pre-university streams were Jewish. Well-to-do Protestant parents, convinced of the virtues of British education, individual attention and a controlled, exclusive environment for their children, began to have doubts about the High School.

Let us summarize the choices before Anglo-Protestant parents for educating their children. For boys there were St. John's School on Ontario and Jeanne Mance Streets, an adjunct of St. John the Evangelist Anglican Church; Wickham House in Westmount, then considered "out of town"; the boys' school of the High School of Montreal; the public primary schools and the various dame schools which took boys. For girls there were Trafalgar Institute, later to become the Trafalgar School for Girls; the Girls' School of the High School of Montreal; the public elementary schools; and the dame schools which accepted girls. This would seem a wide choice, yet according to the historians of Selwyn House School, it was surveying this list in 1908 which led Herbert Holt and his friend Frederick Fairbanks to deplore "the lack of a suitable preparatory school in the neighbourhood to which they might send their sons." Mr. Algernon Lucas arrived from England at this opportune moment and was soon installed by Holt, Fairbanks, Bell, Drummond, Wanklyn and others, as teacher of nine boys in a small flat at St. Catherine and Crescent Streets. Although the remoteness of such schools as St. John's and Wickham House is given as the reason for the establishment of Mr. Lucas's school, it can hardly have been closer than Peel and St. Catherine, where

LUCAS SCHOOL, 1911.
Rear: Mr. Lucas, Mr. St George,
Third row: C. Gault, J. McDougall, A.C. Evans,
J.S.W. Bell, R. Holt, D. Wanklyn, S. Carsley, P.C.
Drummond, D. MacInnes, M. Smith, G. Joseph, W.
Evans, O. Gilpin.

Second row: G. Holt, W.H. Wilson, R. Jacobs, H.
Fairbanks, G. Fairbanks, L. Marler, J. Ross, E.
Hague, P. Ross, A. Barnard, D. Morrice, J.
Pangman, J. McIntosh, C. Black, G.T. Lafleur.

First row: G. Robertson, F. Wilson, J. Barnard, B.
Fairbanks, M.D. Brown, E. Durnford, H. Gordon,
S.D. Cantlie, W.F. Angus, J. Gordon, D.K. Black,
R. Cowans, T.H.P. Molson.

The first location of Miss Edgar's and Miss Cramp's School was on Guy street below Sherbrooke, almost behind the building which housed the Lucas School on Mackay street.

Student cadets on the playing field of Lower Canada College, 1910.

the High School was located. We must conclude that the relevant word is "suitable." The High School had become large, crowded and heterogeneous. A "suitable" school would be one attended by the children of one's friends, offering the advantages of small classes and close supervision by the teacher, and providing a classical curriculum in a controlled environment. It would be less physically restraining than the nursery but enclosed, nonetheless, and consistent in every way with parental values and expectations, reinforced by teachers of similar views and by peers of the same background.

Accordingly, heads of the private schools, usually British-educated themselves in the early days, went to Britain to recruit their staffs. They believed British education was the best available and that standards were more rigorous among British-trained teachers, just as parents had felt about British-trained nannies. A retired headmistress, a Canadian, maintains that the best teachers continued for many years to be those from the British Isles, because there "They needed to know a subject, not educational methods" whereas in Canadian teacher-training, methods were stressed more than knowledge. ◇ In any case, since salaries were generally lower in private schools, Canadian-trained teachers preferred to teach in public schools. Finally, as already mentioned, British teachers could be hired for less money.

Consciously and unconsciously, these teachers taught by precept and example the British traditions and way of life, thus reinforcing the already strong attachment to Britain the children had learned at home. The schools supported the values of the parents in this regard as in most other things. Hugh MacLennan, who taught at Lower Canada College in the early 1940s, describes an atmosphere that must have been even more true of 1910:

> The masters were all Englishmen, and most of them were young. They came from England every fall and worked for a few years before drifting off into other jobs or other schools…. Each master, no matter what his age, took the train for Montreal the day school closed in June and returned to the Old Country for the summer…. The other point on which the staff agreed was the calamitous proximity of Canada to the United States…. They did their best to offset this by teaching the boys British history and geography, and they even tried to teach them British manners as well. This never quite succeeded…. The boys never worried themselves about national problems of any sort; indeed, they did not know they existed. Their home was the English section of Montreal; as a

result of what everyone told them, their country was not Canada but the British Empire.

One of the results of this was that there was little Canadian history taught. In the early days of the century there were few Canadian history texts. One man remembers that his so-called history book was two thirds geography but only one third history. Others remember Canadian history taught as a phase of British history, with no mention of the United States after the Revolutionary War of 1776 had separated the American colonies from the Empire.

As to providing suitable peers, the fact that the new schools were not state-supported automatically required levying higher tuition fees than those charged by public schools; this in turn eliminated the majority of candidates and ensured that the ones who attended the private schools were homogeneous, at least as to financial status. Beyond that, the schools were careful to admit pupils whose family backgrounds predicted that they would "fit into" the school environment. This careful selection of teachers and students produced the controlled environment which had been the founding purpose of private schools. Old Boys at Selwyn House, for example, remember that the staff was "a pretty high-class group, entirely English or Scottish," and that the students were "well-to-do, from a small upper class group of families, all of whom lived in the Square Mile." ◇

There remained, then, only the problem of providing an upper-class education in the British tradition. With regard to the traditions people live by, Joseph Campbell has written that civilizations are built on symbols and myths which, accepted by all members, focus the energies of aspiration, the motivation to live up to a treasured vision. When the mythological canon is no longer cherished, the civilization falls.

The generation of children born about 1900 was one of the last to grow up in the security and certainty of such a mythological canon. The traditions invoked by schools on the British model go back to the earliest days of British history, constantly refreshed by literature from Shakespeare to Walter Scott to G.A. Henty. English and Scottish boys have long dreamed of challenge, of dragons to be slain, of ordeals to be endured through which they could prove themselves valourous and honourable. Certainly since King Arthur became a legend of their culture, British boys have so dreamed. The glamour of this public fantasy was associated with knights, warriors, and soldiers, and may have had something to do with the fact that by 1900 the Empire circled the globe. The dream was kept alive and fresh by the presence of British soldiers in Montreal for so long, adding excitement and colour to life; the patriotism extolled by writers such as Tennyson or Kipling; the elegance of the uniforms of the Black Watch and the other militia in the city who paraded on public occasions, and in which members of the elite were officers. There were cadet corps for boys in the upper forms, which, on occasion, joined the militias in parades or commemorative services. Chivalric traditions were also invoked, one supposes, by the awarding of knighthoods and other titles and insignia of nobility to Canadians in recognition of service to the country or Empire, a practice that continued until the 1930s.

In the Memorial Gymnasium of Lower Canada College a plaque was placed in February 1921 in memory of Old Boys who had died in World War I. Such memorials exist in all the boys' schools. This one has an inscription which begins: "Tranquil you lie, your knightly virtue proved." To a boy, such words might imply that if he fought through all the obstacles and difficulties with which his path was strewn, he might prove himself at last a man among men, in the tradition of King Arthur's knights, the Scottish clan chieftains, or the modern Grenadier Guards. Since everybody he encountered seemed to take this proposition seriously, he saw no reason to doubt it.

It has been said that the idea of Romance is a product of leisure and it is for this reason that the most romantic stories centre around princes, princesses, knights, and ladies. If so, then a girl at one of the private schools must have had many romantic ideas. She was being prepared to marry well and lead a civilized and leisured life as the chatelaine of her lord's castle. While she waited to grow up, she dreamed of ball dresses and silver slippers, of dancing until dawn, and of being carried away by a Prince Charming, a knight in shining armour, or at least an officer in the Grenadier Guards.

The private schools, the preferred choices of most elite families, had slightly different emphases and atmospheres, depending on who founded them, the early conditions of their existence, and, most important, whether they were girls' or boys' schools. The four available in 1909 (about the last year this particular generation of children would have started school) and which still exist today were Lower Canada College (previously St. John's School), Selwyn House, Trafalgar, and Miss Edgar's and Miss

A "crocodile" that is, a line of boarding students on their morning walk from Miss Edgar's and Miss Cramp's School.

Cramp's. Other schools existed before 1914, but many have since closed their doors. These four have simply been chosen to represent the educational experience of the children of Montreal's prominent English and Scottish families at the time.

Because Lower Canada College's founding headmaster, Charles Fosbery, was keen on sports above all else, and because the school possessed excellent playing fields, it became known for its football, hockey, and other competitive games. Mr. Baillie, math and science teacher at L.C.C. for many years, once observed that "if the school has a good football team it has a good year." The College had a secondary school, which Selwyn House did not; and many students went from Selwyn House to L.C.C. for later years of schooling. Having no playing fields, Selwyn House stressed academic standards. "It was clear," said an Old Boy of both schools, "that L.C.C was not as good academically because people who went out there from Selwyn House were at the head of all the classes." ◊ This is not to suggest that the academic side was neglected at L.C.C or that sports were not taken seriously at Selwyn House. Sports were compulsory at Selwyn House because, as Walter Molson pointed out in an assembly address there, they build mental and physical health, develop self-reliance, and foster "sympathy with the underdog, mutual helpfulness, self-discipline, and the benefits of team-work and cooperation." As important as winning was "how they played the game" and boys were to play within the rules not only of the game but of good manners. The "killer instinct" of the sports professional was not extolled. It was the amateur sportsmanship of the gentleman, of the Olympic games, of the Davis Cup which was admired.

The differences between the girls' schools (Trafalgar and Miss Edgar's and Miss Cramp's school) were equally a matter of degree. Sports were not taken seriously at either school. Both placed a strong emphasis on moral training and on "ladylike behaviour, unselfish consideration for others, courtesy and responsibility." ◊ Trafalgar was older, having begun classes in 1887 for girls aged fourteen to eighteen. By the time Miss Edgar's was founded in 1909, Traf was offering elementary classes as well. Miss Grace Fairley of Scotland, its first headmistress, was still in charge. Little is reported by Traf Old Girls about Miss Fairley's academic ideas, but Miss Edgar's are a frequent topic for comment by graduates of her school. She and her friend Miss Cramp were exceptionally well-educated women for the time and had some advanced ideas: for example, that the literature, history, and art of a period and country should be taught as a unit, rather than as separate subjects; and that each girl should progress at her own rate in each subject. Both schools encouraged girls to matriculate at McGill, although few did until after World War I.

The girls' schools had boarders as well as day pupils. They were often taken to concerts, lectures, or church in the city, and there was a daily walk for boarders immediately after breakfast, before classes began. For these outings, the girls lined up in twos, wearing hats and gloves, and walked in lines all the way there and back. It was understood that wherever a girl was she represented the school, and that her behaviour reflected well or badly on its reputation. Loyalty to the school required that she remember "who she was."

Old Boys and Old Girls of all four schools remember the strict discipline. At Miss Edgar's, "You couldn't really miss a day because if you did, you had to go to your box, where the day's lessons and assignments would be waiting for you, and you had to make up whatever you missed. If you were late, you had to go up to the office and say why you were late. Or if you didn't have your black stockings on you were sent home, and then you missed your lessons and had to make them up. It was very strict." ◊ At Selwyn House, "The discipline was strict. I remember a schoolmate and I chasing someone from another school down MacKay Street, two against one, in a fight. We got a strapping from Macaulay about that." ◊

Prefects, sooner or later, were a part of life in all the private schools, as well as in the High School of Montreal. In girls' schools they were sometimes called monitors. The system is important because it was one of the most powerful means of teaching responsibility and the principles of strict discipline considered basic to the training of the nation's future leaders. The prefect was a class representative to the administration, chosen by the headmaster or mistress, or a committee of teachers. In some schools, prefects were always selected from students in the sixth form (the last year), especially in boys' schools where they had disciplinary authority. If the teacher was away from the room the prefect took charge; if the class moved as a group down the halls, to another room or out of the building, he saw that the movement was orderly—that neat lines marched to their destination. If there was any class business, such as an election, which required a chairman, the prefect took charge. Most important, he was responsible, particularly in the boys' schools, for disciplinary action, including any necessary physical punishment. The prefect did not take all the responsibility, of course. The headmaster kept an eye on things. In some schools, masters were allowed to use the strap; in others, only the prefects and the head. In whatever variation, the important point was that conformity to prescribed values was rewarded in a process which taught responsibility. Some of the disciplinary and administrative load of the staff was transferred to the most outstanding and respected students. Equally important, this system, according to a sociological study made by the Maxwells, "co-opts the senior, most mature and articulate boys into the authority hierarchy at a stage when they could cause infinite trouble if excluded."

A man who was a prefect reports that "L.C.C. for a nine year old boy was rough, the discipline very difficult. The prefects were entrusted with a great deal of discipline and we admired them and feared them. They could strap us actually, but on the other hand, they could help us out, too. We had a master who was a rough character and he whacked me across the face a couple of times and left a big welt. The other boys didn't like it and they took it to the prefects, who took it to the headmaster and the instructor was asked to leave. Later I was a prefect myself and what I learned from the whole experience was fairness. I learned that when you have power you ought to take all things into consideration before you act. You ought to be sure the person deserves punishment before you give it." ◊

Wanstall, who succeeded Macauley as headmaster at Selwyn House, was famous—or infamous—for his frequent and enthusiastic use of the cane. If a boy was sent out of the classroom for any misbehaviour by a teacher and was discovered lurking about the halls during class time, Wanstall automatically dragged him into his office for a thrashing, without much discussion or investigation into details. An Old Boy recalls that at his boarding school he was caned constantly, for anything and everything. "After a while it becomes a kind of game. You know you will get it when you have broken some rule, so you just stuff your trousers with newspaper and hope the prefect won't notice the 'THUNK' the cane makes." ◊ However dispensed and by whomever, discipline was rigid and unrelenting.

Physical punishment was rarely, if ever, used on girls. Punishment consisted of having to come in for extra work on

74

Saturday mornings, or of being deprived of some privilege such as recess or an outing. Even in the public schools, a 1906 manual on the use of the strap for purposes of discipline specifically excepted girls. The function of prefects or monitors was supervision and reporting to the staff misdeeds which required disciplinary action.

Somewhere between the ages of fourteen and sixteen many members of the Montreal upper class were sent to boarding school. The ones most frequently attended by boys who did not go to L.C.C. were Bishop's College School in Lennoxville, Ashbury in Ottawa, and Trinity College School in Port Hope, Ontario. Girls were usually sent to King's Hall School in Compton, or to English or American boarding schools. Some of the reasons for sending children away to school seem to have been: first, the belief that it was good for the children to learn to live away from home and with others of their age; second, a last effort to mould the characters of problem children who had somehow managed to resist all previous pressures to conform; third, the wish to prevent early involvement with the opposite sex . In some cases, the point was to relieve parents of some responsibility; and in all cases boarding school attendance contributed a certain prestige. The reason was almost never academic. Most of my informants who had attended boarding school felt that the academic side of such an institution was weaker, or at least no better, than that of the schools they had attended in Montreal. It was a point of pride at Selwyn House that graduates who went on to Ashbury and Bishop's College School took a disproportionate number of the top honours. A teacher who had taught both at Trafalgar and at King's Hall School was appalled at the comparative haphazardness of the English program at the boarding school: ''There really was no syllabus except in the matriculation class and I found that the only way I could get textbooks was to scrounge through the cupboards, which all yielded lashings of Tennyson and Browning, and that was about all. You had to find enough copies of whatever there was for your class and that was what you taught.'' ◊

However, any lack in academic standards in the boarding schools could be and often was made up by the additional tutoring available as a result of the presence of teachers and housemasters living on the premises and on duty round the clock. The McGill junior and senior matriculation exams, which were eventually introduced into all the private schools, also helped to maintain uniform standards; few children who intended to take these exams from the private schools failed. In fact, some schools tried to discourage girls or boys from taking the exams at all if there was a chance they would tarnish the school's reputation by failing them.

There were other advantages. Study was supervised and homework could be corrected immediately, since teachers were always present. Activities such as dramatics or music which require rehearsals could also be more easily and successfully provided because the pupils lived on the premises and their evening hours could be planned by the school. The same was true for cultural activities or trips. Such schools also offered riding, an important accomplishment for some segments of the upper class. Many children had riding lessons on the mountain in Montreal once or twice a week; but this could be intensified in the boarding schools, which had their own riding instructors and stables.

This environment was as nearly hermetically sealed as was humanly possible. Girls or boys were allowed off school premises only at specified times, usually on Wednesday or Saturday afternoons, with early hours strictly set for their return; and in any case they could not leave without being under the care of a teacher or an adult visitor. Boarders were permitted to go home only at Christmas, at Easter, and for the summer holidays. In the boys' schools parents were definitely discouraged from weekend visiting, and they were not exactly encouraged by the girls' schools. Students who did not "fit in"—that is, were too different in their behaviour or attitudes—were asked to leave. Although Jews, Presbyterians, Roman Catholics, and members of other faiths were accepted at B.C.S. and King's Hall, attendance was required at the Church of England prayers every morning.

It was in the boarding schools attended by so many boys from prominent families that boys were molded to the male image of the time and to their expected role in the world. Until the 1930s, and certainly in the earlier years being considered, Bishop's College School and other boarding schools for boys practiced "fagging"—a way of inducting new boys, that here as in Britain, led to such abuses that legislation was enacted against some of its worst features. The published history of B.C.S. describes the system as it worked before Crawford Grier, a new headmaster, changed it in 1931:

> ...fagging was the privilege of "Old Boys," as they were known in the boys' hierarchy of merit: boys with a year's seniority. There

were no published limits to the tasks that might be thrown upon a New Boy.... New Kid concerts, clandestine, sadistic affairs, required each New Boy to perform by song, joke or stunt, and then to run the gauntlet on hands and knees between the legs of paddle-wielding Old Boys.

The commonest use of the system was on-the-spot fagging. An Old Boy merely clapped his hands, and every New Kid within earshot had to come running to see what service was required. Woe betide the boy who tried to beat the game; he could be ''sent in'' to the Prefects for violation of New Boy Rules. In the Prefects' Room a stack of canes, maintained in full supply from the nearby alder and birch shrubbery, provided a ready answer to the problem of what to do with the delinquent....

Senior Old Boys, from the Fifth Form upwards, had specified New Boys assigned to them in the manner of military batmen. Duties included collection of books and materials for all kinds of activities, much cleaning and polishing of boots and brass, running errands, often as far as the village,and an odious shower-fatigue. This entailed the collection and spreading to dry on basement steam-pipes of the fag-master's sweaty sports gear, and presentation of a dry towel and change of clothing as he emerged from the shower.

A man who remembers those days says that this system took so much time that he ''hardly had time to learn anything in the first year.'' ◊ Fagging in this unlimited sense has been modified and now can include only a specified list of services, and boys are not ''assigned '' to a particular older boy. Only prefects, head boys, stewards, and sixth form boys are entitled to this service; but this change was not easy to make because the board of directors and other graduates of earlier days grumbled sourly that what had been good for them must be good for later boys. The possibilities of abuse in any fagging system are obvious. The question is, what use was it?

The youngest boys were learning to obey, to be patient, and to serve their apprenticeship—to *earn* the right to command. The older boys were learning to command, a skill useful in the army, the militia, business, the professions, in short everywhere at that time. In a society where every activity and organization was hierarchical and authoritarian, where some people gave the orders and others followed them, these boys were learning the role of the commander. In boys' private schools before 1914 and for decades after, male aggressiveness and the dominance of the older and stronger over the younger and weaker was institutionalized. Each succeeding generation of boys from these schools developed a conviction that this was the natural order of things. Their conviction not only supported authoritarian structures in every part of the society, but also was immensely important in convincing others to obey their orders and to see them, as they saw themselves, as rightful leaders.

The boys followed a schedule which had them up by 7 a.m., in classes without interruption until mid-afternoon; then, in compulsory games, cadet drill, and supervised homework, when not having meals and changing clothes, until the 9 p.m. compulsory bedtime. This left little, if any, time for reading or other purely recreational or voluntary activity, except on half-holidays, and even that was supervised. Older boys who had some leisure might participate in a school organized choir for chapel or assembly services, a magazine, a debating, or a public-speaking society.

In all the boys' schools, what was admired, what earned trophies, what would get a boy's name into the school history were leadership and excellence in academic subjects, sports, the cadet corps, or debating—areas where he could compete and win. Even when some master or head wished to foster an artistic activity, there often was not enough interest to keep it alive. Art for art's sake was considered a waste of time and, for boys, somewhat suspect. What Old Boys remember most vividly is the discipline they endured. They think, now, that it was good for them. Graduates have the sense of loyalty and closeness to each other that people always have with people with whom they have shared difficult or memorable experiences that tested their mettle. They are proud of their accomplishment, and feel that they have learned and gained much from the experience which others will never know. It helps to explain the "Old School Tie syndrome."

As in day schools, the girl in a boarding school had an easier time of it. Her school may have been strict, but it was not harsh. As a head girl at King's Hall wrote in the school magazine: "Now to my mind, a boy's school would be easy (to manage) because any misdoings and—WHACK! but to run a girls' school successfully—that is another question. The 'brawn' of the Schoolmaster must give way before the originality and inventiveness of the School-marm."

Since physical punishment was not used, it seems that shame rather than fear supplied the motive. For example, at one boarding school a girl's ranking in all subjects, in deportment, and in general attitude was read out every Saturday morning at prayers, followed by appropriate public comments, congratulatory or condemnatory, by the headmistress. Prefects had authority to reprimand girls and report them to the staff but not to chastise them. Manners were stressed even more than in the private day schools, and Old Girls remember statements of teachers and headmistresses which because of repetition and aptness were never forgotten. Graduates of King's Hall School collected some of these rules of etiquette: "A lady will clean the bath after she uses it. Others *must*.... Say 'God be in my head' and think of what you're saying.... Keep your head up and look as though you're proud to be who you are."

As in the day schools, girls were educated to be custodians of art, literature, and music. Even so, they were instructed more as appreciators, or perhaps collectors, than as artists themselves. Perhaps one of the clearest statements of the role of elite women as transmitters of culture was expressed in a letter written by Adelaide Gillard, Lady Principal, and published by the King's Hall School Newsletter:

> ...You are the privileged group. In your short lives, not only have you never known what it means to have to worry about food, clothing, and warmth, not only have you had a large share of the good things in life, but many of you have never had a real wish ungratified.... Do you realize that in return for the good things you have received, you must give something back to the world? ... If girls like you, with your advantages of education and background do not set the standards, to whom can this country look for fixed standards? It is you who should maintain standards of speech, of manners, of integrity, in personal and public life. It is you, the members of the leisure classes, who should encourage a respect for learning and a respect for the best in Art, Literature and Music. If you are satisfied with the third rate and the shoddy— then there will be no best. If you do not put first things first, but let money, material pleasures and superficialities become all-important, you will be betraying all that your school has tried to stand for, and that motto "Noblesse Oblige" "Privilege imposes responsibility" by which you, as members of the privileged classes, are called upon to live, will be merely an empty and meaningless phrase.

It was an inspiring view of the limited role of the elite woman, lifting the emphasis on manners, speech, the social graces, and the arts out of the realm of mere snobbery into that of a sacred trust.

Whether the pupil was a girl or a boy, and whichever one of the schools he or she attended, there would be some experiences common to all. Schools began with a general assembly in which religious observances and Christian teaching played a role. The extent and seriousness of this depended on whether the school had a religious affiliation or not. Selwyn House and Miss Edgar's and Miss Cramp's had none, and so they practiced non-denominational devotions: a prayer, a hymn, a scripture reading, and perhaps a talk on ethical behaviour. L.C.C., Bishop's College School, and King's Hall were founded by, or were connected with, the Church of England, while Trafalgar School was connected with the Presbyterian Church. In these schools religion was emphasized in a specific denominational character. At Trafalgar, for example, ex-graduates recall "We had to learn a Bible verse every day for Devotions, and we were examined on it later." ◊ In general, religion was the foundation for everything taught and took the form most traditional in British culture: either that of the Church of England, or of the Church of Scotland.

After assembly, which might also be the occasion for school announcements, students followed very much the same curriculum at all schools: reading, writing, arithmetic, spelling, geography, French, and history, with Latin, Greek and science in secondary schools. In learning these subjects, the accepted method was to repeat something orally or in writing over and over until it was "drilled into our heads." ◊ In addition to academic subjects, both boys and girls were expected to learn good manners, *noblesse oblige*, and loyalty. Strict discipline accompanied the teaching of all these matters. All of the day schools had a mid-morning recess and closed for the day by one o'clock in the afternoon.

Besides the curriculum, certain values were common to all the schools. Loyalty to the school, and to King and Country (i.e., the Empire) was stressed. School songs and uniforms helped develop attachment to the school, as did competitive sports played against the teams of other private schools. Old Boys' and Old Girls' associations provided financial assistance, and members made frequent visits to the schools with enthusiastic reports of their own experience there, thereby calling forth and reinforcing their own loyalty, while providing an example for children still in school. One of the best proofs of loyalty is the high proportion of alumni who sent their sons and daughters to their old schools. Loyalty also provided the sense of continuity so important preserving traditions. Miss E. and C. often publishes in the *News-letter* photos of girls now attending, whose mothers and grandmothers were Old Girls.

Feelings of loyalty to Britain fostered by schools were not confined to the upper echelons. In the public schools as well, pictures of the King decorated the walls of all classrooms; children prayed for the King and the Empire, sang "God Save the King" and "Rule Britannia"; and read from literature and history series put together in Britain for British children. It reminds us that early in this century a high proportion of the Anglo-Protestants of Montreal, in all walks of life, were in fact first-generation immigrants from Britain.

Honour is a sense of dignity at least partially based on observance of a generally respected code of behaviour. It is an attribute associated particularly with aristocracy since the days of knights and chivalric codes. Breach of the code is shameful. An imputation by others that a breach has occurred threatens one's dignity and standing in the community. Although at the turn of the century honour was no longer a matter to defend with one's life in a duel, it was still a serious thing. Some of the virtues involving honour and being taught then by schools were loyalty, fair play, and honesty. As Miss Edgar said in an assembly speech, "Nothing is more characteristic of the good English public schools than the tradition of truth and honour which obtains in them. This is a national tradition fostered by school spirit."

Fair play—to be a good sport, to lose or win gracefully, to take your medicine when you knew you deserved it—was learned, especially in the boys' schools, through the disciplinary system and on the playing field. It was less emphasized in girls' schools.

Manners were stressed everywhere. Pupils stood at respectful attention when teachers or heads entered the room and always used "Sir" or "Miss." They were expected to stand aside in going through doors and to offer their seats to any older person. One man recalls specifically that on one occasion when, as a schoolboy, he had failed to rise and offer his seat to a lady on the streetcar, his father was waiting for him with a scolding when he got home. The news had arrived before him. ◇ Manners and dress were part of the child's preparation for his social niche. Uniforms bearing a school crest, which all the schools had sooner or later, identified the child who wore it as belonging to a privileged group. So did manners. Schools required even more formal behaviour than could be expected at home.

Fosbery, for example, kept an eagle eye on table manners and all other kinds of deportment. "I asked a question without saying 'Sir' on the first day I appeared at school with my parents. Fosbery checked me immediately and explained that I had to call all masters 'Sir.'" ◊ Another person reports that at Selwyn House and Ashbury: "'Sir' was God. If you didn't say 'Sir' you got a licking. I suppose it was very strict, but that's all right. I don't think they get enough discipline today." ◊

Fosbery was strict not only about manners but also about dress. One of the things he found offensive was a golf cap often worn by the boys until they were in sight of the school, when it would be snatched off and replaced by the required headgear. "One boy caught making the switch was summarily dismissed.... Sometimes a small boy would have his cap snatched off his head so that a large boy could pass muster with the Boss." He inspected every boy in line, every morning, remarking on unpolished shoes, belts instead of the approved braces (suspenders), and other defects of attire. L.C.C. had uniforms even in the early days, (most other schools adopted them only later), and dress remained important. In the girls' schools, emphasis was placed not only on a girl's appearing neat and clean, but also on her wearing hats and gloves. A graduate of Trafalgar remembers Miss Fairley standing at the door to see them off each day, saying in her Scotch burr: "Girrls, Girrls, put on your gloves before you go out. Ya musna go out on the street looking like servant girrls." ◊

Responsibility for the less fortunate was also a value stressed in all private schools. A prerequisite of learning this, however, was that the pupils be class-conscious. Since this was an awareness common to everybody in Montreal at the time, it needed very little reinforcing by teachers. In this connection, it is interesting to note how often the values and attitudes of the English and Scots coincided (if for different reasons), so that they lived comfortably together in Montreal, despite centuries of national rivalry in Britain. English class-consciousness and its attendant exclusivity based on "who you are" was matched on the Scottish side by family pride and loyalty, known as "clannishness." In practice, the two were difficult to distinguish either in manifestation or effect.

Teachers and heads did not intend, necessarily, to foster snobbery; but remarks like Miss Fairley's at the door about servant girls, or discussion of the moral perils of "coming out" which was the subject of one of Miss Edgar's assembly talks say clearly that their girls are of a higher social position than people without gloves or ones who don't "come out." Similarly, in the boys' schools the constant assumption that the pupils will be future leaders conveys the same impression. In any case, this seems to have been what many children learned. Boys who went to Ashbury College from Montreal travelled in a railway car especially assigned to them. One of them remembers now with some chagrin how the black porter on this car shined the shoes of "all of us little brats." ◊ An ex-teacher at Selwyn House remembers that boys he took to cricket or soccer matches against schools outside of Montreal were "irked at the presence of other people on the train. I had to explain that we hadn't hired the whole train—just bought a few seats on it." ◊ Many informants freely confess that by today's more egalitarian standards, they grew up to be snobs. One man was first aware of his attitude when he got to McGill, by which time he "wanted to be known as a member of the top group, socially and every other way. For this reason, it didn't pay to be seen very often with people who weren't top drawer. I really was a snob." ◊

There is another side to this, of course. What appears to be snobbishness may be justified as self-defense, by some people. A lady who was a social leader in the 1920s stated candidly: "There were always people trying to get into what they thought was the inner circle. They might be newly rich or have some other claim, but they were always trying to wangle invitations or trying to get you to accept theirs. Such people are not so much interested in you personally as in being seen with you, you know. It is an intrusion and an attempt to impress by association. Very unpleasant. So we tried to protect ourselves by excluding such people. Which only made them redouble their efforts, I suppose." ◊ A retired headmistress observed that " The worst snobs were not those who had arrived. They could afford to be and often were quite gracious. It was the 'hangers on,' those on the edge of success, who assumed the pretenses that one finds so annoying." ◊

With this sense of social privilege came an awareness which teachers might utilize in teaching that "from those to whom much has been given, much is expected." Not only were there frequent verbal reminders to students of both sexes of their responsibilities to the "less fortunate"; there also were activities organized which taught children the community responsibilities they could expect to assume.

The form and content of responsibility and concern for others were different in the girls' and the boys' schools. Boys were learning to be community leaders. Their responsibility for the less fortunate would be to make decisions on their behalf and to carry out those decisions by financing them. The schools provided a microcosm, a small community wherein this could be practiced. More emphasis was placed on duty and authority than on pity for the less fortunate. Girls were taught direct, personal care and concern for others. At Miss Edgar's, for example, they contributed money each week to the Milk Fund, and decided, with the advice of a visiting social worker, how best to spend it for the poor. They packed hampers for needy families at Christmas; they dressed dolls and gave them to poor children in hospitals. They ran an annual charity bazaar, which provided the girls with experience in organizing and fund-raising. It was made clear to them that they could expect much more of this sort of thing when they grew up. At Trafalgar, there were also weekly collections for a charity fund. In addition, the girls knitted for the Junior Red Cross and sponsored a cot at the Children's Memorial Hospital.

To carry out responsibilities requires that the child learn to postpone his or her own pleasures. As Miss Edgar said in one of her talks to the school: "And of [our traditions] no one is more important for life than that the claims of duty come before those of pleasure."

We have noted that sports or games were compulsory in the boys' schools and not in the girls' schools while music and art were important parts of the school programme for girls and almost non-existent in boys' schools. These differences, plus those in discipline and in the preparation for community service which girls and boys received, remind us that schools were important in supporting the sex roles demanded by a Victorian and Edwardian society. The differences appear in the stated goals of the schools. The stated aim of Trafalgar's founder to teach "lady-like behaviour" is echoed by Miss Edgar's statement that "We want self-control, gentleness and courtesy to be the distinguishing marks of our girls." These goals are distinctly different from those of obedience and self-discipline expressed by a headmaster at L.C.C.: "No one can learn to command until he has first learned to obey ... the conception of self-restraint and of service to the group without thought of oneself should be the basis of all we teach." The headmaster went on to point out that this idea of service was implemented by the election of form and house captains and the appointment of prefects to help in the day-to-day operation of the school and in the maintenance of discipline. A Selwyn House headmaster at a prize-giving ceremony defined a good school spirit as a sign of the successful achievement of the aims of the school which resided ''in taking of just punishment without whining ... in learning that we must obey before we can command ... and above all that privilege is the handmaid of duty and responsibility, and that from those to whom much has been given much also will be required.''

At most schools achievement was promoted by daily or weekly competition among pupils. Selwyn House, as we have seen, published weekly rankings of each boy on every subject, activity, or personal quality. The supreme moment in the school year when the ''energies of aspiration'' were '' evoked and gathered toward a focus,'' came on the annual Prize Day. At the end of the school year, or at some suitable time, the students' achievements were rewarded publicly, with the whole school, parents, governors, and visitors in attendance. The prizes offered an opportunity for the school to make its values crystal clear and reinforce conformity to them. There were prizes for a great variety of accomplishments, in keeping with the goal of private schools to develop each student to his highest potential; almost everyone with any kind of ability might compete for some prize or other.

Miss Edgar's did not have a Prize Day. Miss Edgar and Miss Cramp did not believe in competitive exams, but rather that each girl should develop her own potential as far and as rapidly as she was able, without reference to what others could do. What took the place of Prize Day was the Closing Ceremony. The graduating girls wore white dresses for the latter occasion. The assembly hall, which at the time was the Ritz-Carleton ballroom (Miss Edgar's had no hall big enough), was decorated with masses of flowers. The whole event had the solemnity and simplicity of a religious ceremony. Indeed, there would be scripture readings, prayers, and hymns as well as an uplifting address. Many Old Girls remember it as very moving. The focusing of pupils' aspirations on traditional values and high achievement was provided, but without the competition taught to boys. This would seem sensible in view of the fact that winning a competition in math or history might be actually a handicap in the one race a girl was most likely to enter in the Edwardian era—the matrimonial race.

For the other schools, all the elements came together on Prize Day. It had pageantry and solemnity. Important people marched to the platform, wearing colourful academic robes: a governor-general, the principal of a major university, a world famous scientist or writer, who would give an inspiring address reminding parents, pupils, and teachers of the torch of civilization being passed on here, at this and like schools. The school song, "God Save the King," "O Canada," or "The Maple Leaf Forever," and a hymn would be played or sung, evoking the loyalty everyone felt toward God, country, Empire, and school. There would be prayers, in which God's blessings were requested for the great work being carried on by the group, individually and collectively. And then the prizes. The boys or girls who had struggled so hard all year to learn, to overcome bad habits, to play better at games, to be more polite, and had succeeded better than most would have their names called. As parents, masters, other pupils, and dignitaries watched, they would walk up to the headmaster or headmistress and receive a handshake, congratulatory comments, and the prize. Grown-ups clapped and beamed. Even classmates were impressed: "I found it quite stirring when it didn't last too long. Even if I didn't win anything, I usually made a private resolve to do better next year because I could see it was worth it." ◇

At Selwyn House, as in British schools, it was a tradition that in the course of his address the principal speaker of the day should ask the headmaster to declare a holiday, or at least a half-holiday, at some suitable time. This was always ceremonially granted. Boys waited on the edge of their seats for this moment, wondering, "Will he or won't he, and how long a holiday will he suggest?" ◇ When it came it brought down the house.

Until the secondary years, when school took up most of the day, these children were likely to have additional lessons at home: French, dancing, riding, music, or art. Between such activities and the homework assigned, there was little time for free play. Another event which often occurred and which cut into the children's free time was the tea party organized by parents for their children and the children of friends. Most people report that they hated these affairs. They had to dress up for them, sit quietly through them, minding their manners, with other children whom they might or might not like. "These were our parents' friends' children, not necessarily *our* friends," ◇ as one woman explained. These parties appear to have been another practice in manners, as well as an effort on the part of parents to foster relationships between their children and others of similar backgrounds.

Another part of the instruction of such children at the turn of the century was received in church and Sunday school. At that time, Sunday school was held in the afternoon, and there were two church services each Sunday which children also might attend. At Christ Church Cathedral parents were urged to see that children attended the morning service as well as Sunday school. Our elite children would have attended, most likely, either St. Andrew's or St. Paul's (Church of Scotland, Presbyterian) or Christ Church Cathedral(Anglican), all three being "high" churches and all located near the Square Mile.

The Sabbath school (Presbyterian) or Sunday school (Anglican) movement was just getting under way in the early part of the twentieth century in Montreal. In method and, to some degree, in content, such schools were much like the schools the children attended on weekdays. St. Andrew's Church had weekly assignments and marks, and a prize ceremony in February at the end of the session for "well-prepared lessons, strict punctuality and decorous conduct." As in the private schools, the children in both Anglican and Presbyterian churches collected money for local charities· or foreign missions.

Little Presbyterians were brought up on the Shorter Catechism, made up of 102 questions and the prescribed answers. By this method children were indoctrinated with the chief principles and teachings of their faith: the story of the Fall of Man, the Ten Commandments, Christ's redemption, and the Sacraments. Every Sunday, in addition to a Bible verse to memorize, there was a question and answer from the catechism to be learned and understood. Any child who could repeat from memory the whole Shorter Catechism received a diploma, awarded by the General Assembly of the Presbyterian Church in Canada. In 1914 six children of St. Andrew's received diplomas.

Families were encouraged by the church authorities to subscribe to and follow a *Home Study Quarterly*, which was coordinated with the lessons being learned in Sabbath school and intended to reinforce the child's religious instruction at home. The same general pattern was followed in Christ Church or other Anglican churches at the time. The Anglican catechism had only twenty-five articles, plus the Commandments, Lord's Prayer, and Apostle's Creed, but the Anglican child had also to learn the Order of Service. About 1905 Christ Church instituted, as well, a program of teaching children to chant psalms and canticles. The emphasis on the catechism at both churches presumed submission to authority and discouraged independent religious thinking. Thus Sunday school supported the weekly school experience.

Following school and boarding school, there remained for girls only finishing school. This was usually a year spent in a small, private boarding school in France, England, or Switzerland, the purpose of which was to polish their French; to give them a broader, more sophisticated knowledge of the world; to develop greater appreciation of art, music, and architecture through exposure to the cultural treasures of Europe; and finally, to put the finishing touch on manners and the social graces expected of upper class women. Boys also went abroad for a year, but not necessarily to boarding schools. They might well be in pensions or in flats of their own. After this exposure to the outside world, the young men usually went to McGill or to the Royal Military College in Kingston.

It was a hard schooling, and one not likely to produce spontaneity, self-expression, or creativity. Traditional values, particularly British; discipline, responsibility, obedience to rules, duty, hard work, and strenuous play; the primacy, privacy, and exclusivity of one's family and one's class; God and the *status quo*; all were unquestioned. It is doubtful if many children of the Square Mile ever thought of the blessedness of humility or of persecution for beliefs as applying to themselves. The rebel and the creative genius were not heroes. In the accepted scheme of things, the elite members were educated to see themselves as proud leaders and the custodians of things as they were.

CHAPTER 4

Play and the Holidays

Life was not all discipline and instruction, however, and the attachment of the elite group of Anglo Montrealers to their way of life was due as much to the fun it afforded as to its values.

Children did not leave home for boarding school or spend the entire day at L.C.C. or Trafalgar until they were about twelve. Therefore, before that age, they had some free playtime each day and on Saturdays. The first freedom from supervision was enjoyed during the walk to and from school, which provided their first independent awareness of the city, or at least of the neighbourhood between home and school. Some things they saw and did were the perennial events of childhood: fights between boys from the High School of Montreal and their rivals from Lucas school; tempting candy displays at Bryson's Drug Store. But some of the everyday sights and sounds of that period are gone forever: the early morning horse-drawn delivery wagons of the baker, the butcher, the dairyman; the local farmers clopping along their daily house-to-house rounds or, in winter, jingling their sleigh bells; the clanging and banging of the St. Catherine Street trolley and, in winter, the smell of scorched wool produced by standing too close to the pot-bellied stoves in the cars; the horse-trough in front of the Mount Royal Club; the wooden sidewalks.

Other now-vanished sights were then seen every afternoon. One was the parade of carriages. Just before tea, the ladies of the Square Mile could be seen driving on Sherbrooke Street to call on other ladies who were ''at home'' that day. Sometimes they were driven by a coachman, but often they drove themselves. In either case, they were dressed in jackets, long skirts, and hats of expensive fabrics (or, in winter, furs) all beautifully tailored in the latest fashion. The Allans had a tandem carriage (several horses harnessed one behind the other) and this was considered the most elegant of all. In the pre-war era, the first automobiles began to appear, and to have their own parade on Saturdays, with uniformed chauffeurs at the wheel. If an automobile passed in the street on other days it was a great curiosity. The children, as well as other pedestrians, would stop to stare— that is, if they could see the car through the cloud of dust it raised.

And then there were the hurdy-gurdy men with their monkeys. Unlike the hurrying crowds today, the children and adults who passed would stop a bit, making a circle around the organ-grinder, and listen to popular or operatic tunes and watch the monkey. People did not feel so pressed for time—certainly not children coming home from school.

Once home from school, or on Saturdays, they played on their own block, where they knew all the other children. They were permitted to roam rather freely, "as long as we were within ear-shot of our parents or Nanny." ◊ Since most of the houses above Sherbrooke Street had large grounds and gardens, children had ideal play space and could run back and forth from their own to other children's grounds. In the fall or spring, if there were enough of them, they might play "Mother, May I?" (mostly girls) or "Mossy" (mostly boys), although these were more often played at recess at school because they required a number of players. A game that has now disappeared was "Conkers," again mostly played by boys, and always in the fall. When the horse chestnuts fell, boys selected large, firm ones and dried them until they were hard, having inserted a string through them. The game was to challenge others to try to crack or knock one's chestnut off the string by swinging them at each other until they collided, and one of them was "defeated."

The real fun began with the first snowfall. Everybody remembers sliding down Peel Street, Mountain Street, or Côte des Neiges on their sleds or toboggans and hitching rides back up by attaching the rope to a delivery wagon—a forbidden, and therefore a delicious, pastime. There was so little traffic on the streets that they could coast for blocks. People did not ski then, but there was a lot of skating—at the Coliseum and at the Winter Club. Some families had small skating rinks on their properties where girls might skate and the boys practice hockey or curling. Children dug long tunnels in the snowbanks that bordered the

Children stopping to hear the organ grinder.

Toboganning in the park.

streets. "I don't know why some of them didn't cave in on us, but I don't remember that any ever did." ◊ And of course there were snowball fights, snow fortresses, and snowmen.

As the day waned, the lamplighter would move along Sherbrooke, turning on the gas jets and lighting them with his long pole. The flickering yellow light shone on the snow just as the commercial sleighs of the day were giving way to the sleighs of the evening, bringing fathers home or, later, taking grown-ups to dinner parties, the theatre, or other entertainments. In the moments of relative quiet between, the nannies could be heard calling the children. Reluctantly, the children turned homeward, to nursery tea, probably homework, and then to bed. Tomorrow would be another school day.

The reader may be wondering at the absence of French Canadians in the experience of these children. They were growing up in a city where the majority of the inhabitants were French-speaking yet none have appeared in this account. The fact is that a child of the Anglo-Protestant elite probably knew none, except possibly a maid in the household. Murray Ballantyne, who grew up in the Square Mile, son of an eminent Anglo-Protestant businessman and politician, writes that during his youth he encountered only two French Canadians personally: a maid who remained in service to his family all her life and a pupil at his private school whose parents were not practicing Catholics. There were three prominent French-Canadian families living in the Square Mile. They were "received" by the English families and seemed more at home among them than with people of their own origin, Ballantyne felt. He adds that one could live and die in the Square Mile without ever pronouncing a word of French, nearly without hearing one. Everyone he encountered either was English or spoke the language well. He first became aware of the existence of French Canadians as a people different from his own group during the conscription controversy toward the end of World War I. Ballantyne's memories were confirmed by the people who contributed to this study. Children accept the world as they find it and these children found their world in the Square Mile to be a small town isolated from contact with people who were "different."

There were festive holidays of course, and some of the practices connected with them have changed or disappeared. Christmas meant stirring the puddings for good luck, early in December, and waiting for Santa to fill the stockings on Christmas Eve.

It also meant a Christmas tree decorated with real, lighted candles on Christmas morning—with a bucket of water kept handy in case of fire. Hogmanay was a Scottish celebration of the New Year which involved much visiting on New Year's Day. Dignitaries and all the women held open house while men called and paid their respects. Wine was offered at each house, though the original Scottish custom required that ale and white bread be offered. A man might spend five or six hours at this, even though each visit was expected to be short, because he must stop at the homes of all friends, business associates, and certain dignitaries, especially clerical. There were St. Andrew's, St. George's, St. Patrick's and St. David's days, with parades and balls, although only the parades were of interest to children. But the Queen's birthday did interest them. "May 24th is the Queen's birthday /If we don't get a holiday, we'll run away," said the children's verse. And of course they always did get a holiday. Halloween, then more a matter of tricks than of treats, was a rather strange affair. The Anglicans, like the Catholics, celebrated All Saint's Day following Halloween, but the Presbyterians did not. As Marion Lochhead remarks in her description of Scottish life in the eighteenth century, "In Scotland we banished the saints, but kept the devil and his attendants."

However, the day that really counted, that every child anticipated impatiently through the school year was the beginning of the long summer holiday from late June to early September. For the elite child particularly it was a journey to another world, to a freedom unheard of in the city or in his school. As soon as schools closed for the summer, the great exodus to the summer places began in the Square Mile. One woman has written about anticipating childhood summers at Métis Beach, "One year Dorothy and I, who owned tiny valises, packed them in February, although at that time all we could put into them were pajamas, a bottle of ginger ale and a spare toothbrush." ◊

Among the families who could afford it, it was an accepted fact that a country holiday of several weeks or the whole summer was necessary. Montreal was widely regarded, for good reason, as "unhealthy in the summer." In fact, it was unhealthy all year around. If one considers the uncertain quality of milk, the untreated water, and the open toilets neighbouring on the wells in the poor districts, in all of which the hot weather encouraged even higher bacterial counts than in the winter, this was undoubtedly true. Typhoid and dysentery were common, and the rest and fresh air

Snowbanks on Union Avenue when the streets were cleared by shovelling the snow into piles between the sidewalk and the street.

of the country also might have been expected to cut down on the exposure to tuberculosis—a disease with a high incidence at the time, especially in Montreal.

Every family had a special place it loved, and in spite of inconveniences and hard journeys, the adults seem to have loved these summer holidays as much as the children. "Mother and Daddy's generation must still have had some of the fortitude of the early pioneers, coupled with a deep love of Métis, for there would have been water from a rain barrel or well only, a wood stove, oil lamps and candles. It was not until 1929 that water was piped into this area." ◊

Having a summer place at all was a status symbol. There were summer resorts where middle class people went for their two weeks' holiday, which was the standard length of time allowed by most businesses for employees' vacations. Such families did not usually stay away all summer.

For affluent families, preparing for this trip, the trip itself, and settling in at the summer place were high points of the whole experience. The number of people, and of trunks, boxes, and parcels involved depended not only on the size of the family, but also on its social status. The mother, the children and some servants went out toward the end of June and stayed until the reopening of school, usually the first week in September. Families of sufficient means certainly took a nanny, and might also take a butler, cook, maids, and a gardener from Montreal, with all their gear, as well as the dishes, pots and pans, sheets, table linen, towels, and clothing needed by the family to set up a second household. Families of less lofty status might bring only a nanny and hire local people on a sliding scale from daily to weekly, depending on the family means. Except in the Eastern Townships, which were largely English-speaking, the local summer servants were nearly always French Catholic. Father came on Friday nights or Saturday mornings and returned to Montreal on Sunday nights, except for his annual vacation period, which again might be anything from two weeks to all summer, depending on his occupation.

There were many summer places near or on the island of Montreal, in the Laurentians and even as far away as Nova Scotia or Maine. The patterns of summer living were quite similar everywhere. A summer resort may have been frequented by any number of people who discovered its particular delights of scenery or climate, but it would become fashionable at the point where a prestigious Montreal family adopted it as "their" summer place.

Perhaps the most *socially* important resorts were Cacouna on the south shore of the St. Lawrence, and Murray Bay opposite it on the north shore. Sir Montagu Allan built an imposing summer house at Cacouna, where Lady Allan gave famous parties. Their relatives the Kennedys, Patersons, Daweses, Sutherlands, had beautiful homes in Murray Bay. The Manoir Richelieu there was an elegant hotel which attracted other prominent Montreal families. There life was carried on as nearly as possible like life in the upper social circles of Montreal: the same round of entertaining and being entertained, the same retinues of servants. If the season was dull at Cacouna, according to one informant, Lady Allan fled to Murray Bay. Few, if any, old English Montreal families now frequent Cacouna and Murray Bay always had some famous and wealthy Americans whose presence affected the character of the place: the Tafts from Ohio, the Cabots from Boston, for example.

Let us consider four other examples of summer places: Como on the Ottawa river; the Hermitage Club on Lake Memphramagog; Knowlton on Brome Lake; and Métis Beach, on the lower St. Lawrence.

Although Como was the closest to Montreal, getting there was complicated before 1930. People came from Montreal by train to Ste. Anne de Bellevue, transferred to a boat or ferry to cross the river, and then were met by a horse and buggy for the last part of the journey.

Knowlton was served by the railroad from Montreal. The trip to the Hermitage Club (between Magog and Georgeville) was by train to Magog, after which everything was switched to horse-drawn vehicles or to one of the boats which plied Lake Memphremagog and called at the Hermitage dock. There farmers met the vacationers with horse and buggy or wagon and took them to their cottages.

Métis Beach, being the most distant of the four, was perhaps the most notable for the impressiveness of "getting there." Before 1920 many people came by boat down the St. Lawrence, after that, as a man whose family has been coming to Métis Beach for more than a hundred years recalls: "Everyone went by overnight train from Bonaventure Station in Montreal, arriving early in the morning at the 'old station' about seven or eight miles from Métis Beach. The train was met by the farmers around and about who transported everybody in their black buggies or buckboards to their houses. Everybody brought everything, you know, fifteen trunks for a house like this and this is not a very pretentious house compared to some around here ... and they contained dishes, towels, sheets, pots and pans—the bundle.'' ◊ Everyone interviewed agreed that the ''train trip is what we all remember'': eating chicken sandwiches in pajamas, legs dangling from the top berth; drinking milk from a silver cup; being helped on by Mitchell, a conductor who worked on that train for twenty years, at least, and knew all the Métis-bound families. ◊ And once there, ''What an exciting world it was after the city, with the freshness of the salty air, the sound of cow bells, the scent of the fields just showing the first of the summer buttercups and daisies. On arriving at the house there was a rush to get in 'just to smell it.' The mystical aroma seemed to be a combination of the heat of the iron, wood-burning stoves, and the still fresh woody scent of the walls ... there was also a rush to the shore to stick one's fingers in the sea, then taste, just to be sure it was still salty,'' one lady wrote in her memoirs. ◊

Métis was known, as one man explains, as ''the poor man's Murray Bay.'' When the men at Métis dressed for dinner, they wore blazers and white flannels; but in Murray Bay they dressed more formally. ''My father tells about a group from Murray Bay who came over for a tennis or golf match, I've forgotten which, and for dinner afterwards put on their dinner jackets. They were hoisted into the river by Métis men right after dinner.'' ◊

The population of Métis in the summer increased by about 3,000 people from a few hundred in the winter. Many people spent their holidays there, as in other resorts, not in their own cottages, but in hotels. The most notable hotels in the memories of Métisians were the Seaside, the Boule Rock and the Cascade. A cottager recalls that ''whole families came, with nannies, and the children stayed on the third floor of the Cascade with their nannies and had their own dining room.'' ◊ Not onerous, even if less prestigious than owning your own cottage. The hotel guests were met by buggies or buses from the hotel.

The summer places were located in or near already existing rural or fishing villages offering the facilities needed by the local inhabitants. Although the doubling or tripling of the population of a village for two months of the year must have been a bonanza in monetary terms, it also must have severely taxed village resources at times. The first things needed by the Montreal summer people were, of course, food, drinking water, and services of all kinds.

There were general stores, grocers, butchers, and farmers who delivered whatever food was needed. Some families had their own farms or gardens, especially in the Knowlton, Como and Georgeville areas, where there was good agricultural land. A family which had a gardener expected him to appear at 10:30 each morning (the hour seems to have been the same at places as far apart as the Hermitage and Métis) to inform the cook what was ready for eating. The cook would then compose the menus for the day in consultation with the mistress of the house, and the gardener was expected to bring the produce needed, washed, to the kitchen by 11:30. If the family did not have a garden, as was often the case, food was brought to the house. Farmers would bring fresh produce in wagons. Butchers with horse-drawn unre-frigerated carts, and people bringing milk and fresh-caught fish came to the door daily. "You didn't go grocery shopping. Each of these people who came to the door had a little book with a string on it which they hung inside the customer's kitchen door. When they brought their produce, the cook or whoever was in the kitchen selected what was wanted and this was written in the little book and settled up from time to time." ◊ On the other hand, at the Hermitage Club, George Campbell wrote of the period during and shortly after World War I: "Going to the village [Magog] for supplies was a necessity, and a job, as there were no deliveries. We either had to use our motor boats or hire a horse and carriage."

Drinking water was not a big problem in most of the resorts. The lake, or even the river, could be used for water since they were still unpolluted, and good wells were easily dug if a cottage happened not to be located on the water. But at Métis Beach, where the St. Lawrence is salt and has tides, water was always a problem, and some people had to get water from farmers or some more fortunate cottager.

So much for the problems of obtaining water and food. Services, as we have mentioned, were provided either by servants brought from Montreal or hired from among the locals, whether as temporary servants or as farmer-caretakers. Often whole families worked for the vacationing family.

Mrs. R. W. Reford of Montreal, a niece of Lord Mount Stephen, was considered one of the outstanding hostesses of her era. Her thirty-seven room house and extensive gardens at Grand Métis are now a provincial park and museum. Her summer household constituted one model of an elite style of life. Mrs. Reford's

The Cascade Hotel, Metis Beach.

*Sir Montagu Allan's summer house at Cacouna,
1901.*

British-trained butler served the family both in Montreal and in Grand Métis. His daughter lived in a cottage on the grounds when she was a child, and later worked in the big house herself. She describes a routine which (except for the fishing) is very like the one that was followed in Montreal:

Father came down from Montreal in the middle of June, or earlier, once the children grew up, to get the house ready for Mrs. Reford. For about a week a whole crew of people would be working on it—washing windows, taking down blinds, raking the driveway, cleaning, repairing. Then the Reford family and the rest of the servants came out about a week later. Some servants stayed in the Montreal house, some came down, but there were always a butler, cook, kitchen maid, chauffeur, footman, laundry maid, lady's maid, upstairs and downstairs maids, an odd-jobs boy and in Métis two or three gardeners. Those that stayed in Montreal were replaced by local people in Métis.

Morning tea trays were brought to every adult in the house at 8:00 a.m. sharp. The servants ate their breakfast in the kitchen before that. At 9:00 there was a sit-down breakfast served in the dining room, although Mrs. Reford was not present. She had her breakfast in her room and came down to see the cook at about 10:30, to decide on the day's menus. After that Mrs. Reford went to the gardens where she worked or supervised the work of the gardeners (the gardens cover 175,000 square feet) for the rest of the morning. Meanwhile, the maids cleaned the house, the odd-jobs boy put flowers in every room and changed them every second day, and the laundress washed and ironed all the linen daily). The cook served the servants their dinner at 12:30 and the Refords at 1:30. Coffee and tea were served in the sitting room after lunch.

Dinner was at 7:30 p.m.unless there was fishing in the after-noon, in which case it might be as late as 9:00. Mrs. Reford always came down to dinner in evening dress, and men wore a suit or blazer, flannels, and tie. The table was elaborately decorated with silver candlesticks with shades, and silver serving dishes, vases, etc. On special occasions the butler might compose a landscape of moss, leaves, grass, flowers and figurines running down the centre of the table and at all times each guest would find a small vase of flowers at his place. After dinner, port and cigars were brought for the gentlemen while the ladies retired to the drawing room. Meanwhile, the downstairs maid had pulled the drapes as it got dark and the upstairs maid had turned back the beds. ◇

From 1906 to 1942, the Refords owned a considerable stretch of the Métis River and used it as a private salmon fishing preserve.

Visitors of the highest standing—Princess Alice, the Countess of Roberts, or the Governor General—came for two to four weeks, primarily for the fishing, bringing four or five servants with them. These servants were treated like guests, with their own private rooms. There were guides and professional fishermen who lived on the grounds during the summer. One at the bow and one at the stern of the canoe, they would take the visitors to fish the many salmon pools of the river. People fished in the late afternoons or early in the morning. Mrs. A. recalls the fishing boats drawn up at the river banks between 7:00 and 8:00 a.m. An early tea was provided in the house for the fishing guests.

The work of service was expected to be invisible. A woman whose mother was a cook for one of the great summer houses recalls being told as a child that she was not to be seen around or even outside the big house. A man whose family was employed on a large farm in the Georgeville area owned by a wealthy Montrealer remembers his mother taking him and his brothers and sisters into the woods behind the house when dinner parties were going on, so that they would not disturb the proceedings by being seen or heard.

Vacationers' spiritual needs were not neglected. There might be a Catholic and an Anglican church, but not always a Presbyterian church in a small rural Quebec town. Particularly in the early days of the century religion was considered necessary and the Sabbath taken seriously, so if a church of the proper denomination was not available, one had to be built.

Almost everybody went to church; anyone not in church on Sunday morning took care to make his absence as inconspicuous as possible. A man who spent summers in Como as a boy remembers being cautioned by his mother not to play under the cottage porch on Sunday mornings, for fear of disturbing the Sabbath quiet. In fact, the question of keeping the Sabbath was one of the greatest issues at the summer resorts. The minutes of the Knowlton Boat Club of July 11, 1911 show that since some members had objected to the sale of soft drinks at the Club House on Sundays, a motion was passed that the Boat Club House be closed from midnight Saturday until 6:00 a.m. Monday and that no food or drinks be sold on Sunday. At Métis, it was believed for a long time that Mr. MacNider, who had willed the land to the community for a golf course, had put it in the deed that there must not be any golf played until after noon on Sunday. Then, according to a director of the club, "somebody did some research

102

and found there wasn't anything in the deed about that. So then we had to fall back on the argument that this goes back to the traditions of the place." ◇

Montrealers brought their games with them. The first prominent families in a summer resort built their own tennis courts and sailed their own boats or yachts from their own boat docks or houses. Dr. Shepherd at Como even had his own golf course. By 1920, however, clubs had been formed in all the summer resorts. These tennis/golf/sailing/swimming clubs were at first largely confined to adult activities and a man of seventy recalls: "We weren't allowed to go to the Cascade Club, [Métis] when we were children. We were considered too young." ◇ People who as children or young people were summer residents at Como during the 1920s, recall that they never went to the Royal Oak Club, but were entertained by their nannies when very young, and invented their own games and pleasures when they were older. Ever since World War II, however, these clubs have served the function of occupying the young with tennis, golf, swimming and sailing lessons organized by professionals.

The clubs also provided an exclusive social environment of people "like ourselves." A summer visitor to the Magog-Hermitage Club area and now a member of the club illustrates this with the following story: " I remember a Crown Prosecutor, a French Canadian, who bought a nice property with a big house on it for his family near, but not on, Hermitage property, with the idea that he was going to join the club. Well, they never would let him in, and in the end the guy sold the place and went away very bitter and I'm sure became a strong nationalist. It was many years before the first French Canadian was allowed into the Club." ◇

Exclusivity is evident in the selection procedures for new members. The Hermitage Club requires not only a proposer and a seconder for a new member, which is usual in such clubs, but also the names of four additional members to whom the applicant is known and the approximate length of time they have known him. After these requirements are met, the by-laws state that "The names of the applicants with the names of their respective proposer and seconder shall be sent to each member of the Club and ... shall also be posted for at least one week in the Clubhouse." The directors then choose by majority vote from among those applicants to whom no objection has been raised. It is unlikely that anyone not wanted would slip through this net.

Unlike the other clubs we are discussing, the Hermitage Club (formed in 1917) which owned and still owns about 150 acres of land on Lake Memphremagog and Eaglet Island has sold building lots to its members. A member of the club need not own a house or lot on the club premises, but no one may buy a lot there unless he is already a member of the club. This way, not only the club, but the neighbourhood is harmonious.

What has come to be called male chauvinism was taken for granted. The Knowlton Golf Club, founded in 1920, and with only slightly less scrupulous screening of applicants for membership, was a shareholder's club. Common stock was issued to shareholder members (originally the club founders), "in whose hands the administration of the club rests and who are the only ones eligible for official positions or to vote at meetings ... nor shall the holder if a woman or a junior member have any right to attend or vote at any meeting of the club."

The clubs were, therefore, the proving ground and focal point for the social status hierarchy that existed at all the summer resorts. The intensity of this status-consciousness varied slightly. Status based on wealth is more easily passed on to the next generation than is status derived from a skill or occupation. If Como was slightly less concerned with social standing than Métis Beach, perhaps that was because its most prominent summer resident was an eminent surgeon and dean of medicine at McGill, rather than a member of an old and rich family.

Social distinctions also separated the people who stayed in hotels from the cottagers, and even operated within hotels. A woman who always stayed in a hotel remarked that "There were no social relations between hotel people and cottage people, unless they were friends in Montreal. Transient guests were not welcomed by the hotels, and everyone tried to keep the French out." ◇ One Métis summer visitor remembers that at the Seaside Hotel tables were assigned in terms of one's social standing and history of summer residence. The dining room had tables looking on the street, tables in the middle of the room, and tables with a view of the sea. The first year a hotel guest was assigned a table on the street. If he or she kept coming back to the hotel over the years "you would be moved first to the middle and finally to a seaside table, provided your social status warranted it." ◇

What people did for fun depended, of course, on their ages. Young children throughout this period were largely under the supervision of nannies or their mothers. For children old enough

104

not to need constant surveillance, there was an exhilarating freedom in long hours of invention or imaginary play, especially after the restrictions of the long winter at school and at home. Mrs. McEachran is worth quoting at some length on this:

> The building of sand castles with moats seemed to go on for endless hours. Almost daily we climbed up on the great rocks [on the beach], everyone trying to snatch a chance to reach the highest point, and once there relish the opportunity of screeching, "I'm the King of the Castle, and you're the Dirty Rascal!" There were more exciting pastimes as we grew older, perhaps exciting because we thought they would probably be taboo. If you could snitch some matches, you could light tiny secretive fires in the corners of the rocks. One could also try to light and smoke a cigarette length of dried beach straw.... At times, we would find on the beach a horrible looking rusty can with jagged edges. This we filled with salt water and then boiled mussels in it on a little fire. We thought them delicious, although actually they were very tough. As far as I know this type of *casse-croûte* never seemed to have any ill effects.
>
> In those early days, before the advent of the motor car, picnics were great events, and few and far between. We drove with horses and carriages to the favourite picnic areas—perhaps up the rolling hills of the back country to a river site or to the fields and brook closer by. Several families went together and great preparations were made some days ahead.... [Once there] the men built a fire to hold a cauldron in which probably soup or pork and beans were heated. Whole hams and loaves of bread had been baked at home, and potato salads made.... A great white damask cloth would be spread in the field. The men would have on their tidy shirts and ties, maybe white flannel trousers, panama hats; the ladies, their long, white linen Edwardian frocks, bandannas to protect their hair from the smoke of the fire, perhaps some with hats with wide brims and ribbon bows.

Life really picked up after the age of sixteen. At resorts where there were hotels, such as Knowlton or Métis, there was a very active social life for young people. Cottagers might rent a dance hall or hotel ballroom for an evening, or the hotel might offer dancing; or a club might have a program that included regular dances, as the Hermitage did. Métis seems to have been particularly lively, because it had so many hotels as well as a club and private parties. Some of the hotels had ballrooms and there was a small orchestra of young men from Bishop's College, the Dawson Brothers, who used to play there in the summer for dances. " We danced three or four nights a week in Métis ...

Lake Memphremagog, on the shore of which stands the Hermitage Club.

George Foster's summer house grounds on Brome Lake.

and it *wasn't* in blue jeans. The men wore white flannel trousers, blazers, neckties and dancing shoes; the girls wore evening dresses." ◊

After the first World War, the Scott Act allowed counties in the province of Quebec to decide whether liquor could be sold. Métisians found themselves in a dry county, a difficulty easily surmounted by writing to Rivière du Loup, a hundred miles away. The bottle (or bottles) arrived by mail within a day or two. The liquor was then taken to dances in a hip flask.

At Como, which was not in a dry county during the 1920s, liquor was a different kind of problem. Although minors never drank or had liquor served at their dances, the young bachelors just back from the war, who used to stay at a local boarding house, brought heavy drinking to parties for young adults and "added a lot of gaiety and even wildness to the place." ◊

Meanwhile, the adults, from the "rocking-chair brigade" (elderly ladies on hotel verandas clicking their knitting needles over their yarn and their tongues over the manners and morals of the young) to the young married couples or ladies going to teas or dances, or men playing golf, were having their own fun. A woman who summered on Brome Lake as a child recalls "lots of children and nannies gathered on the beach in the late afternoon while parents went to parties." ◊ A man reminisces that when he was a boy in Métis in the summer, the ladies used to have tea on the gallery of the Cascade Club "in those huge hats they used to wear, with their white gloves and parasols, and eat thin sandwiches served by maids in uniforms." ◊

Bridge was popular; but sports were the main recreation. Older children and teenagers, who were generally just handed a racquet or golf club and told to go out and play, were eager and ready to do what adults spent most of their time doing. Others might prefer fishing, swimming, or sailing. In any case, it was not unusual for whole days to be occupied with one or more sports. Athletic activity, especially for men, was *de rigueur*.

Another important activity, as one can imagine at a time when all schools were segregated as to sex, was flirtation and courtship among the young adults. Here, where parents need not worry about a young person getting involved with someone unsuitable, young people had more opportunity to get to know a member of the opposite sex than was possible at home, during school years. Many engagements are reported to have occurred at the end of summers, and marriages among families frequenting the same summer resort were quite common.

107

The constant coming and going, particularly of the men, but also of families, provided a pleasant ritual, described by a Métisian in memoirs written for her family: "meeting the train or seeing it off were the most exciting times of the week. On Sunday nights, the 'week-ending' fathers and young men returned to town.... I remember one summer when several friends ... and I would go up to the Station on Sunday nights well ahead of train-leaving time. Three young couples had become engaged that summer.... We waited patiently to see their tender or passionate kisses which threw us into the greatest of school girl raptures."

There was never a lack of visitors or relatives spending a good part of the summer at the cottage or farm, but the ample supply of servants made entertaining them more of a pleasure than a chore, and the two months of summer were passed in gaiety and relaxation.

Everyone who has been going to the same summer place since childhood, uses the words "love" or "adore" to describe his feelings about the place. The Quebec countryside is easy to love and the summer resorts are always places that are quiet, rural and include vistas of mountains, hills, water and fields to soothe the soul of anyone whose roots are British and who carries in his mind's eye scenes described by Wordsworth, Keats, Robert Burns, or Walter Scott. The British are nature lovers and brought this sensitivity with them to Canada. They love nature in its unspoiled state, not improved by man. Corners of Quebec are forever reminding visitors of Scotland or the Lake District of England or the cliffs of Cornwall. Of course, there are certain differences. Quebec is wilder, less intimate, with sharper contrasts of colour, light, and climate than Britain. Perhaps the most striking difference is the flora: the predominance of dark spruce, fir, and pine slashed by strokes of white paper birch and electrified in the fall by the intense reds and golds of the sugar maples. Such vividness is not found in the United Kingdom. Como, Knowlton and Georgeville-Magog are gentle and rolling in terrain, and receive the rainfall to be expected in the eastern part of the continent. Métis is another matter. It is like Scotland in climate, with days on end of fog and rain and temperatures dropping to frost level even in the summertime. The water is so cold that several people whose families have been going to Métis for generations freely admitted that rarely does anyone learn to swim there as a child. Children nowadays are sent elsewhere for part of the summer to learn to swim, notably to Camp Ouareau for girls and Camp Nominingue for boys. When my informants were growing up, they swam in a pool called "the tank" at the Boule Rock Hotel. This pool had the dubious distinction of becoming warmer and dirtier as the season went by because the water in it was changed only once a year. It was the gathering spot for young people, in spite of that. Some learned to swim in it, and there is no record of anyone's being poisoned by it.

Perhaps because Canadians admire ruggedness; or because the Scots who chose Métis as their summer place felt a nostalgia for the spare beauty of the Auld Countrie; or because it has to be defended so often before skeptics—whatever the reason, Métis seems to inspire a fierce devotion not found elsewhere. A young woman from Toronto who married a man whose family members were third-generation Métisians assured me that her husband was concerned to know whether she would like Métis before he married her because the annual summer holiday there was such an important part of his life. Alice Baldwin maintained that "Do you like Métis?" is as important as determining the race, religion, social, and financial status of anyone being considered as a potential spouse by a Métisian. In her short history of the place, Mrs. Baldwin has written a glowing litany of Métis in all seasons, reminiscent of Elizabeth Barrett Browning's "How Do I Love Thee?"

> They love her in the early Spring when the first fruit blossoms mass like drifted snow in the sheltered spots of hills and poppies dance in the old world gardens.... They love her in the Autumn when the alders and sumac and soft maple cast crimson colour over the landscape, where the sharp dark accents of the firs and balsam set off the gold-decked white ... birches, when sea and land are bathed in purple light, the curlews wheel and cry, the ducks fly starkly against ... the sunset....
>
> They love her in the summer when the air is light as spun glass, the sunshine spills its liquid golden light over fields of daisies and buttercups, fragrant with pink clover, tasty with little wild strawberries.... They even love her in her perversity, when she may sulk for days withdrawn and hidden ... in trailing veils of mist and fog, changing to a grey land of shadows, still and quiet, her only voice, the monotonous hoarse cry of the fog horn ... with an occasional answering wail from a ship at sea and the intermittent patter of rain.

A reporter for the *Montreal Daily Herald*, on August 9, 1902, waxed eloquent over Brome Lake:

109

Brome Lake, which is five miles long by three miles wide, nestles in the midst of some of the most noted mountain ranges in Eastern Canada, their peaks rising on three sides, as if appointed by nature to be the guardians of one of her fairest gems, its clear, sparkling waters fed by mountain rills and streams that teem with pickerel and bass. These are a paradise for disciples of the rod and furnish unexcelled advantages for boating and bathing, while from a scenic point of view this magnificent expanse of water, with woods, meadows and the lawns of the lovely residences along its shores and a beautiful wooded island presents a panorama that would require the pen of a Scott to do it justice.

In addition to the sights, are the sounds that evoke a place ever after: the distinctive fog horn at Métis with its short wail at ten-second intervals which people coming by boat in the early days could recognize as ''our own fog horn,'' even in a dense fog, and know they had arrived; or the mournful cry of the loon which no one who has heard it in the grey early morning or late evening on Lake Memphremagog and Brome Lake ever forgets. People would say to each other at breakfast, ''Did you hear the loon this morning?''

And so the summer passed. When it was time to go back to Montreal, the mothers and children boarded the same train which had carried the men back every weekend. Mrs. McEachran writes of her sharp impressions as a child when, with her family, she was met at the Grand Trunk Station in the early morning by a horse-drawn cab. She recalls the clip-clop sounds of the milk wagons and the scarlet geraniums in Dominion Square flower beds. ''The streets ... glistened after an early morning bath by the horse-drawn watering carts; and although the sun was out, a warm, moist, misty air seemed to embrace the city. We were home again.''

CHAPTER 5

Years of Trial: World War I

On August 4, 1914, during such quiet summer holidays, the announcement *GREAT BRITAIN GOES TO WAR* flashed across the front page of the *Montreal Star* and telegraph wires hummed with the same message. "I remember that we were at Métis and my uncle, who had just come in on the train to spend the weekend, told us about it. My mother was quiet for a moment, then said, 'Oh, it won't last until Christmas.'" ◊

In Montreal's English communities men and boys old enough to enlist presented themselves. By September 8 of that year, 32,665 Canadians had volunteered and were gathered at Valcartier, a hastily erected camp north of Quebec City. Canada had at the time a population of about eight million and nearly 620,000 men (most of them volunteers, since conscription came only in the last year of the war) were in the Canadian Forces by the war's end. It was as large a proportion as the major combatants contributed, and larger than that of Belgium, Russia, and Greece. Unfortunately, there are no statistics on exactly how many soldiers were from Montreal, or what their ethnic backgrounds were, though it is known that nationally French Canadians constituted 10 to 15 per cent of the forces. If the same proportions held for Montreal, we can say that the Anglo-Protestants made up 70-80 per cent of those who enlisted from the city. Of the 465,984 volunteers from across Canada, 51 per cent were native-born Canadians; the majority of the rest were British-born, reminding us of how large the British-born population of the country was at the time. The first contingents were made up almost entirely of members of this group, who naturally rushed to the defense of their country. However, can anyone who has read the preceding chapters on the rearing of Anglo-Protestant Montrealers doubt that they too, would rise to defend King, Empire, and Country? Recalling the quick response of the Montreal English community to recruiting needs, the Canadian-born son of a prominent family, who was wounded at Passchendaele, explained, "Britain was at war, and we were British." ◇

The majority of the officers in the first contingent in Montreal were Canadian-born and came from the middle and upper classes, primarily the latter, since it was this group which tended to send sons to the Royal Military College, or to private schools with cadet corps, after which the young men served in the militia. This training and experience, together with the qualities of leadership and the connections fostered by their education, meant usually that they were already commissioned officers in the reserves, or acquired commissions quickly in an army where most men had had no training whatsoever.

For many of the boys brought up in the Square Mile this was the great test for which they had been prepared. War was still visualized as glamourous, a high calling, where men in resplendent uniforms on spirited horses charged across fields to meet the enemy, banners flying, bugles blowing, pipes skirling. A veteran of the war said that "I think we were all dying to get into the War ... we were influenced, I think, by people like Henty who wrote about how romantic wars were." ◇

The whole community supported them. The first contingent of troops to leave Montreal was the 13th Battalion of the Royal Highlanders, which had called up militia reserves from the Black Watch and within a month had processed and equipped more than a thousand volunteers. The historian of the battalion, R.C. Fetherstonhaugh, describes their departure:

At approximately 9:15 p.m., Col. Loomis gave the sharp commands which started the unit on its way to the war. At his orders the great doors of the Armoury swung open, the pipers struck up a martial air, company after company passed into the street, and with the Colonel himself leading, the Battalion headed for the station.... Down Bleury St. and west along St. Catherine St. the Battalion made its way, the ranks almost demoralized by a cheering, swaying mob of humanity ... people waved and cheered and cheered and waved without much thought of where the men were going. The men themselves were carried away by the prevailing excitement.... At Peel St. where the unit swung south, the crowd was even denser ... and the skirl of the approaching pipes caused such a wave of enthusiasm that the pushing, jostling, cheering citizens nearly broke up the parade. The police were helpless and the Battalion's ranks were broken repeatedly.

The enthusiasm continued. Even almost a year later, in June 1915, by which time the first battle of Ypres had given Montrealers some idea of the kind of war it was to be, the 42nd Battalion of the Royal Highlanders got the same kind of send-off when it left, even at 4:30 a.m.

People took things into their own hands, which in view of the general lack of preparedness was probably a necessity. J.K.L. Ross, son of James Ross, gave $500,000 to aid the war. Hamilton Gault raised and equipped a regiment, the Princess Patricia's Canadian Light Infantry. Officers bought their own firearms and other accoutrement, and even their own horses, on occasion. "What was needed was bought at once and permission sought afterwards," a process aided by contributions of enough funds "to tide over this difficult time" by the older and wealthier men, as honorary members of the regiments.

Lt. Kenneth Duggan, in a letter to his mother dated February 18, 1915, asks her to buy him a sword and thanks his father for the compass he has received. In another letter in March 1915 he writes that he does not need them to buy him a horse (which had been discussed in other letters) since these are being provided by the cavalry.

Some members of elite families followed the men who went overseas and did war work in England. One man took his eleven-year-old son along as bugler for the company of which he was the captain. A mother followed her husband to England, leaving her daughter in the care of a nanny for nearly four years. Dorothy MacPhail, a young girl at the time, whose mother had died when she was an infant, managed to follow her brother and her father, Andrew MacPhail, as far as England, and saw them on the rare occasions when one or both might be there for rest or on military errands. The wife of a prominent Montreal businessman was caught in Switzerland with her son and two daughters when war broke out. When the father of the family arrived in London to do war work (he was too old for the service), the rest of the family crossed the channel in the dark, bitter cold on a troop ship escorted by five destroyers. Later, the son joined up and went to the front. The mother, when she received a telegram telling her that her son had been wounded and was in a certain hospital in France, crossed the channel again, alone, and made her way to the hospital near the front to see him. Upon returning once

113

more across the channel in the thick of the war, she made arrangements with a London hospital to take her son and had him moved there. She may have been more intrepid than most; but certainly London teemed with prominent Montrealers getting things done in their usual strong-minded way. They established organizations to make life easier for every branch of the service in England and even in France, behind the lines. The Bank of Montreal was a haven, acting as a post office and as a meeting place almost like a club for Canadians in London. Its staff, besides performing their regular banking duties, helped in locating lost or wounded men, and aided people stranded without return passage to Canada.

While the men gathered in Valcartier to await orders to sail for England, or later began to arrive at the front, and later still to engage in bloody battles and the horrors of trench warfare, the women and children back in Montreal threw themselves into whatever war work was needed. School children collected money or made parcels for servicemen. Voluntary societies provided medical supplies and ambulances. One woman remembers as a child seeing the group of women who gathered regularly in their billiard room to roll bandages. The IODE founded and equipped a Red Cross hospital in London. Women drove ambulances, ran canteens and clubs. Twenty-four hundred nurses went overseas, while another five hundred staffed hospitals in Canada. Women kept the economy going. Twenty thousand were employed in making shells and aircraft; thousands worked on farms, replacing the men who had enlisted. Over ten thousand women entered business without previous training.

Thousands of socks, mittens, caps, scarves, and sweaters were knit, not only for family members in Europe, but by groups and organizations for anonymous soldiers who might not have women of their own to knit for them. Cookies were baked, food parcels packed, medical supplies bought or prepared, individually and collectively. Victory gardens were planted and municipal authorities and private individuals contributed plots for the purpose, one of which was the area in front of the Westmount City Hall.

The outpouring of money, work, and supplies from all parts of Canada as well as from Montreal is perhaps best illustrated by the activities of the Canadian Red Cross, through which much of it was channelled. The Red Cross Society issued 56,398 cases of medical supplies to the field; operated a motor ambulance convoy, built recreation huts at general and stationary hospitals, including furniture and musical instruments; opened and operated a rest house for nurses in Boulogne, where in the last eight months of 1918 nearly 7,000 nursing sisters and other women workers had an opportunity to rest. In England in the four years of the war, 248,673 cases of supplies assembled from farms, villages, and cities were sent from Canada.

All the Red Cross personal service activities in England were under the charge of Lady Julia Drummond of Montreal. Someone from Lady Drummond's Information Bureau visited every man who reached hospital in England, offering sympathy and supplying anything he wished, such as razor blades, books, newspapers, food, all of which flooded into England from Canada for this purpose. Every two weeks they sent three ten-pound parcels to every prisoner of war in Germany. The information bureau required the services of 200 workers and 1300 hospital visitors; casualty index cards were kept; in one day as many as 1,076 reports were sent out, in an effort to reassure anxious families.

Then the blows began to fall, the casualty lists to appear, the telegrams to arrive. What was supposed to be a brief and glorious war began slowly to reveal itself as a terrible squandering of human life. In Quebec enlistment of French and Irish Catholics was comparatively small, although there were many soldiers from both groups and they and their families suffered as did the Square Milers. But there is no question that in Montreal the brunt was carried by the Anglo-Protestants of all classes.* There was hardly a family that did not lose at least one member or had someone badly wounded, perhaps crippled for life. As an example, Merrill Denison reports that forty-two members of the Molson family were in the armed forces, of which five were killed and many more wounded. Lady Drummond lost her only son; Sir Montagu and Lady Allan lost two daughters in the sinking of the *Lusitania*, while their only son was killed in France. Sir Neil Ritchie in a Remembrance Day address to Selwyn House School translated statistics into personal experience: "Out of the 1913-14 football team of my school there were only four of us left alive at the end of that war."

*Here I should mention that it was difficult to interview members of elite families who remembered that war about their experiences. They do not consider it good form to talk too much about that or any personal tragedy. Therefore, much of this chapter is based on written records of the time kept by members of the elite group: diaries, letters, and the war histories written by them, those of Canon Scott, Sir Andrew MacPhail, R.C. Fetherstonhaugh, and Col. Beresford Topp.

The manner of that loss of life and limb has been described in graphic detail in the many histories and novels of World War I. The following are a few examples of that experience taken from histories of Montreal battalions:

The Battle of Mount Sorre (June 2, 1916: The morning of June 2nd dawned in peace and stillness under a cloudless sky. The Salient, verdant with the growth of early summer, presented an unusually calm sight. Suddenly at 8 a.m. there was the crash of hundreds of guns of all calibres firing in concert. The whole front of the 8th Brigade and about half of the front of the 7th Brigade held by the Patricias seemed almost in an instant to burst into smoke and flame. "It seemed," said an N.C.O. in a letter afterwards, "as though that part of the line had been transformed into an active volcano so continuous were the flashes of bursting shells." It early became apparent that no troops could long survive in the front line and that supporting units would be called upon.... All ranks of the 42nd "stood to" at once and quietly went about such preparations as were possible for the expected order to advance.

Later, when the 42nd had advanced in support of the Princess Patricia's Light Infantry:

... The trenches were little more than a shapeless mass of debris choked in places with the dead and wounded of the front line troops.... Of the woods all that remained was a grotesque tangle of shattered trunks and branches devoid of any vestige of foliage; undergrowth had disappeared; the earth was churned and plowed into mounds and craters; wire, bath mats, material of corrugated iron, rifles, equipment, tools ... were jumbled together with the bodies of those who had borne the brunt of the first bombardment.... "Everything was shot to pieces," states one report, "and the line is just one shell hole after another with beams sticking up in the air, dugouts completely fallen in and parts of the trench buried." Everywhere among the wreckage were bodies of the Patricias' dead and there were also many wounded who had been hastily attended to and laid out in such shelter as could be found.

The Somme (October 5, 1916). Throughout the next day heavy shelling continued as well as a steady downpour of rain and the plight of the wounded was desperate as there were few places in the trench which were not at least knee-deep in mud and water. Many of them had been lying out in no man's land in the mud for twenty-four hours or more, without attention.

Passchendaele (October 26, 1917). The condition of the ground baffles description. Rain has fallen and overflowed shell holes

Fixing bayonets in the trenches, Sept. 1916.

*No man's land in front of Canadians, Courcelette,
Sept. 1916.*

until acres are a quagmire.Through these swamps to the waist in water, carrying ammunition and equipment and under sheets of machine gun fire, the men have advanced week by week. It is a story of immortal heroism.

These long stretches of bog were impassable except by a few well-defined tracks, which became marks for the enemy's artillery. Col. Topp says: "To leave these tracks was to risk death by drowning, and ... on several occasions both men and pack animals were lost in this way."

Dr. Andrew MacPhail, a noted Montreal physician, served with No. 6 Field Ambulance, and later wrote the official medical history of the war. He describes the problem of medical corps trying to find the wounded in such a terrain. A message arrived before 9:00 p.m. concerning a wounded officer in a dugout about four miles from the medical station. It took the ambulance team until 4:00 a.m. the following morning to locate the injured man. They were back at the advance dressing station by 5:30 a.m.—a full night's work to find one man four miles away, whose approximate whereabouts had been known; but with the disappearance of all landmarks and roads in the pitch darkness, neither maps nor eyes were of any avail.

The airplane, the dirigible, the submarine, the tank, and poisonous gas were new technological developments in warfare. The decisive weapon at sea was the submarine. There were several prominent Montrealers on the unarmed *Lusitania*, which was sunk without warning and without apologies by a German submarine. Horses were still used, and only toward the end of the fighting did the tank become an important means of storming trenches. The Allies did not use dirigibles and the Germans gave them up because they proved to be such easy targets that they were too expensive to use. Gas was used for the first time as a weapon by both sides. Col.Nicholson describes the gas attack on the Canadians at the first battle of Ypres on the afternoon of April 22, 1915:

> The deadly gas enveloped the whole of the 15th Battalion's right company and most of the 8th Battalion's left one, as well as part of each unit's centre company. The damp cloths over their mouths and nostrils, untreated with any chemical (gas masks had not yet become standard issue) helped but little against the chlorine, and with eyes blinded and throats burning men collapsed on the floor of the trench in suffocating agony.

118

Casualty lists were posted in every community, outside government buildings, or post and telegraph offices. Every day, people stood in anxious groups or crowds, all across the nation, looking for names of friends, husbands, sons, brothers, and fathers. In cities like Montreal, the lists appeared in the daily newspaper. The lists were not always accurate and it was often days or weeks, sometimes even longer, before the reported death or missing-in-action could be confirmed. In England the Bank of Montreal, the Red Cross, and the Canadian military did their best to track down individuals when there was doubt. Still, for some it was a heart-breaking suspense while they waited to know for sure what had happened. Comrades-in-arms often sent letters verifying a death and offering consolation. A series of letters to a well-to-do Montreal family, the Duggans, illustrates this agony.

The family had two sons, Herrick and Kenneth, both in the army. When Herrick was killed in 1915, the family received a telegram explaining that he had died from shrapnel wounds in the spleen. The parents asked their other son, also in France, to obtain more particulars. Ken sent a letter explaining that the nurse who was on duty until late in the evening before Herrick's death reported that he was quite conscious and comfortable and that he had been cared for by a distinguished surgeon. "It is some comfort to know that everything possible was done.... His conduct all through was most gallant—we are all proud of him."

Major Kenneth Duggan himself was reported wounded and missing at Passchendaele in October 1917. After months of unsuccessful efforts to confirm the report and to locate their son, the Duggans received from the Canadian Red Cross Society an eye-witness report by Sgt. Horace Brooks as follows:

> I was with Major Duggan on the morning of October 30, 1917 at Passchendaele. We went over the top at 6:10 a.m., our objective being Vine Cottages, which we gained and held. About 20 minutes after leaving our trench, we had advanced about 250 yards when Major Duggan was hit by a shell in both legs. He lay in the open between two shell holes until 8 a.m., when I saw him killed by shrapnel. I myself was wounded and lay within sight of the place where Major Duggan lay.
>
> The stretcher bearer dressed both his wound and mine and whilst dressing the Major's was himself wounded, falling into a shell hole. I did not see him again. I lay in the open all night and next morning I managed to crawl into a trench from where I could distinctly see that Major Duggan was dead.... I know no more as to what became of Major Duggan's body.

Finally, in June, Mrs. Duggan received an additional letter from a Capt. Marten, which verified the account of Sgt. Brooks. The letters do not tell us whether Major Duggan's body was ever found.

Ernest Spiller wrote of his experience with bringing in the bodies of dead comrades:

> ...We take pride in the manner we fix up our dead.... The corpse is taken out at night to the cemetery about four miles behind the line. I am used to these sights—they don't have to prime me with rum before I can handle a man.... I don't worry very much over it now but there were times when I would figure it out that that shapeless mass was some mother's son, somebody's husband.
>
> I have looked through some of the letters in their pockets; letters full of hopes and plans for the future and, above all, someone longing for the time when they shall come home again. I receive similar letters myself and ... sometimes I ... wonder if someone will have the privilege of performing the last sad rites for me as I have done for so many others.... Great good may be the outcome of this war, but, to me, the price is far too heavy.

It was not all like that, of course. The airman was far above the mud and the gas. In fact, the real glamour was in the air. It was only there that men could still feel like knights and warriors in the traditional sense. The battle between two flimsy, unprotected fighter planes was individual and its outcome dependent on the skill, courage, and ingenuity of each man. Canadian pilots excelled. Ten of the twenty-seven "aces" in the RAF were Canadians as were two of the top five aces from both sides: Major W.A. ("Billy") Bishop who shot down 72 planes, and Major Raymond Collishaw with 60 to his credit.

For the men who were taken prisoners of war, the war was a matter of doing menial jobs for their German captors, being constantly harassed, often underfed and waiting, waiting, waiting for release. But without doubt it was the trench warfare, the mud, the gas attacks, the slaughter on the ground which will never be forgotten and which had the greatest impact on the greatest number.

Men laughed and joked in the midst of the death and devastation, as people always must when fear, grief, or horror are too much to be borne in any other way. Men shook the stiff hands of corpses, made jokes about shells and death. A group of soldiers formed The Dumbells, an entertainment company, which put on original shows with complete casts of characters (impersonating females where needed) which were mostly humourous and mostly about the war. They toured the front. Canon Scott recalls that in the midst of a bombardment he remarked to some soldiers that it was a beautiful night and pointed out to them "the extraordinary romance of being actually out in the front line during such a bombardment." The next morning he was wakened by the laughter of men in the adjoining tent, to whom one of the soldiers had recounted the episode. "We were out there with the shells falling round us," he said, "and who should come up but the Canon, and the first thing the old beggar said was, 'Boys, what a lovely night it is.'" Scott heard the men roaring at the idea.

The war strengthened Canada's sense of independent nationhood while at the same time posing a most serious threat to its ability to hold together at all. There were scandals in which officials in Ottawa were accused of taking bribes to place war contracts, often with American firms (while that country was still neutral) and sometimes with Canadian firms. In some cases, shoddy equipment, poor uniforms, and rifles that would not fire properly in combat conditions were shipped to the front. The Minister of Militia, Sir Sam Hughes was involved, personally, in the Ross Rifle scandal. He continued to defend the Ross Rifle even while Canadian soldiers were throwing them away on the battlefield and arming themselves with the Lee-Enfield rifles of the fallen British.

Even more serious was the conscription crisis which was the first event to isolate Quebec politically from the rest of Canada. It also may have been, as Murray Ballantyne reported, the first event to call the attention of our young Anglo-Protestants who remained at home to the existence of French Canadians as an organized community holding ideas and beliefs contrary to those of people they knew.

In 1917, after repeated statements that he did not intend ever to propose conscription, Sir Robert Borden, the Prime Minister, introduced the Military Service Act as the only fair means of raising the additional troops needed at the front in view of declining voluntary enlistments. The December 17 election of that year was fought on that issue. It was widely asserted that this necessity was brought on by the French Canadians themselves, since if they had carried their share of the load by volunteering to enlist there would have been no necessity for conscription. In fact, there were many English Canadians who opposed conscription on grounds of unwarranted infringement of liberty, while others

121

argued that Canada had already done her part. Certain leaders of French Canada whipped up anti-war sentiment by reminding French Canadians of their traditional anti-imperialism, their anti-militarism, their belief that they should fight only to protect Canadian soil, and that they had little debt to either France or Britain. Quebec was vilified in the press of other provinces and abroad. Even staid, conservative papers like the *Toronto Mail and Empire* said that a vote for Laurier was a betrayal of sons at the front and a vote for the Kaiser. The *Toronto Daily News* printed a caption calling Quebec "the Foul Blot on Canada." In revenge, Quebec returned 63 anti-conscriptionists out of her 65 representatives in Ottawa. The rest of Canada, on the whole, elected men committed to conscription. A "Union" government, intended to produce national unity during wartime, was re-elected, in which Quebec had almost no part. The only Quebec representatives willing to serve were P.E. Blondin and Albert Sévigny, whose support in the province was minimal because of their pro-conscription stand. Sir Wilfred Laurier had fought long and bitterly against conscription on the grounds that it would divide the country, perhaps fatally. He was right.

When it became evident that the Military Service Act would be enforced, there were meetings and demonstrations in the streets of Montreal night after night during the months of July and August, 1917. Hotheads proposed armed resistance to the conscription. Late in August a crowd of about seven thousand were urged to clean up their old guns and a collection was taken for the purchase of arms. In some demonstrations, "Long live the revolution!" was heard, and marchers broke windows along the streets. When police tried to break up one such meeting, a man was shot and four policemen were hurt.

Reactions among those who felt identified with the British Empire were mixed. Some felt that "it was all the fault of the federal government which handled the issue with incredible insensitivity. They sent an Orangeman into Quebec to organize recruitment!" ◇ Others were bitter about the inadequate enlistment which made conscription necessary.

Dorothy MacPhail wrote from Montreal to her father, Dr. Andrew MacPhail (then in England) on March 27, 1916. " The hockey match left me in a state of ferment and fury. The arena was packed with men, eligible, too, the most of them, and there's the 148th with only 900 since January." Women and young girls handed out white feathers, signifying cowardice, to young men not in uniform. "My brother had rheumatic fever when he was a child and was rejected for any kind of military service. The time he had during the war was unbelievable. People handed him white feathers and women came up to him on the street and said, 'What are you doing not in uniform?'" ◊ Troops passing through the province of Quebec were pelted with rotten vegetables, ice, and even stones. French Canadians maintained that the troops had brought it on themselves by openly taunting the youth of the towns through which they passed, for not being in khaki.

On the other hand, an Anglo-Protestant Montrealer of a well-known family recalls that the conflict was present within the English community itself. "Truly violent feelings were aroused and there were riots. Most Anglophones, except for the staunchest Liberals, were in favour of conscription.... but it ... left very bitter feelings.... Antagonism was not confined to race—my mother, not normally very political, quarreled with a long-standing Liberal friend [English] in a disagreement which lasted for a surprisingly long time."

In spite of all resistance 121,124 men were taken into the armed forces as a result of the Military Service Act, although only about 40,000 were sent to the front before the war ended. Quebec did not actually rebel, but the experience was not forgotten.

By September 1918 there was a turn in the war. Canon Scott described this in religious terms evoking the Arthurian legend and chivalric codes still present in the cultivated Anglo-Protestant mind:

> (*September 1918*) We felt ... that nearer and nearer the hour of the great victory was approaching. Who amongst us would be spared to see it? How would it be brought about?... to me it seemed that a new and mysterious light that was born of heaven hid behind the sunshine, and cast a glory upon men and even nature. To dine at the rude board table with the young officers of one of the companies of a battalion, perhaps in a bare hut, on the floor of which lay the lads' beds, was something sacred and sacramental. Their apologies for the plainness of the repast were to me extremely pathetic. Was there a table in the whole world at which it was a greater honour to sit? Where could one find a nobler, knightlier body of young men?

Canon Scott's "hour of victory" had in fact already begun in August with the breakthrough at Amiens. For the next "Hundred Days" Canadian troops spearheaded one victory after another. At Cambrai they were the first to enter the city; advancing steadily eastward, the Canadian Corps took Valenciennes and were the first troops to enter Mons, the scene of British defeat early in the war. Their prominence in the battles of those last days was built on their earlier record. They were a decisive factor in the victory at Vimy Ridge, at Courcelette, Hill 70, and at Passchendaele. The Canadians had proved themselves such tough fighters that for the remainder of the war they were brought along to head the assault in one great battle after another. "Whenever the Germans found the Canadian Corps coming into the line they prepared for the worst," Lloyd George said.

At about the same time that Scott was sensing the advent of victory, another eyewitness reported that "when a soldier thinks that his army is better than anybody else's ... his morale must be high. Everybody believed that the Canadian Corps, all by itself and single-handed, was actually flogging the hide off the German Army and winning the war, and you could see it."

But the cost was heavy. During the period between the end of August 1918 and the Armistice, over 30,000 Canadian troops were killed or wounded. A Montreal woman says, "We were proud of them, tremendously proud. Day after day the newspapers would report important victories won by Canadian troops and stories of heroism. Then, a few days later, the same papers would have in bold, black type the names of the casualties. And we would wonder if it really *was* a victory." ◊

The influenza epidemic of the fall of 1918, was still raging when the "false" armistice was announced. Between October 1 and November 8 there were 3,063 deaths in Montreal from the disease. Law courts, theatres, churches, schools were closed. The city was a gloomy and sad place. Then a false cable, a hoax, arrived from New York announcing that the Armistice was signed. The news threw not only Montreal but the whole continent into delirium. An eyewitness recalls:

> In Montreal a bulletin posted on the "Notice" board of the *Star* announcing: "Germany has surrendered. Fighting to cease at 2 p.m. today," started the excitement here. Almost on the instant the city put on gala and carnival apparel, odd dress gear and fancy costumes. The "flu" was forgotten, all civic regulations tossed aside. Exalted crowds gathered indoors and outdoors, in cafés and bars, in the squares and streets; the factories blew their whistles ... impromptu parades, bonfires, the Kaiser beheaded, scenes of girls impetuously kissing in the open invalided soldiers ... sailors holding up the traffic and dancing hornpipes.

When the real armistice celebration occurred on November 11, the wild hilarity had spent itself and what occurred was a three-and-a-half-hour Victory Loan parade. However, to lighten things up, at eleven o'clock Paris time when the armistice was signed, a CPR engine started out from Windsor Station with its whistle blowing as loud as possible. Soon the bells, whistles, horns, and sirens of the entire city took up the clamour, announcing the end of the War.

Of Canadians who had fought in the war, one in ten was dead: sixty thousand in all. The total number of Canadian army casualties of all categories in all theatres was 232,494 out of a total enlistment of 619,636, a rate of 37 per cent. Montreal had her share of these, a cup full and overflowing, especially among Montrealers of British origin. There were seven infantry battalions, not to mention medical, engineering, artillery, cavalry, signal and machine gun companies, which were organized in Montreal and which were largely Anglo-Protestant in composition: the 13th, 42nd, and 73rd Royal Highlanders; the 14th Royal Montreal; the Victoria Rifles; the 60th Victoria Rifles; and the 87th Canadian Grenadier Guards. The 22nd Royal Canadians (a French-Canadian Battalion) was mobilized in St. Jean, P.Q., but included many French Montrealers. Let us examine the losses in two of these units.

The 42nd Battalion of the Royal Highlanders of Canada had 43 officers and 1,043 other ranks when it was formed in June, 1915. Official statistics show that 588 per cent of the original officer strength and 432 per cent of the other ranks were casualties. The 13th Battalion of the RHC, was one of the first Canadian battalions to go overseas, arriving nine months before the 42nd. It included 48 officers, of whom 30 were Montrealers; and 1,209 other ranks, of which 966 were from Montreal. It suffered 185 casualties among its officers, or 3.8 times the original number; and 4,074 among the other ranks, or 3.3 times the original complement. In effect, the battalion was reconstituted more than three times. Non-fatal casualties were not necessarily out of the war, nor did all these wounded represent different soldiers. The historian of the Black Watch (which raised both these battalions) says that what characterized them was great loyalty which caused officers and men to return over and over from hospital to rejoin their units.

If we consider that the 13th recruited a total of 5,810 men of all ranks, of whom 4,259 were casualties, we see that this is a casualty rate twice as high as that of the Canadian Expeditionary Force as a whole—73 per cent compared to 37 per cent. Even if the rate was highest in the 13th, because it was longest at the front, it is obvious that there was a staggering loss to a small community. The vast majority of these men were Montrealers from the Anglo-Protestant community. If we consider that most of the officers came from the 2,000 families of the upper class, we begin to understand why many feel that the decline of that group began with the loss of the best and bravest of a generation. The casualty lists in the histories of the Montreal battalions, on the plaques displayed by the private schools, the High School of Montreal, and McGill University show that almost every prominent family in Montreal lost a son or close relative. An even larger number were crippled, or suffered impaired health for the rest of their lives. Since there was no conscription, it is fair to suppose that those who enlisted were the healthiest, the most adventurous of their generation.

There was another effect. The young woman of marriageable age, in an era when marriage was the expected career for women, no longer had an even chance of achieving that status. The ratio of the sexes in English Montreal had been approximately equal; by 1921 there was an excess of females over males of about 5,500. In Westmount, a census district where 88 per cent of the population was of British origin, there were 2,771 more women than men in a total population of about 17,500. This may have been an important factor in the fight for women's suffrage and education and their entry into the workplace—a movement initiated mostly by Anglo-Protestant women in Quebec prior to 1930.

How did families handle this devastating victory, this war which had begun in valour, heroism, and loyalty to the Empire and ended, with the Kaiser defeated, to be sure, but with so many young men dead? They did not talk about it much. On the outside, families kept up a brave front, during and after the war. One man, whose two uncles were killed, and whose father died in the twenties as a result of war wounds, recalls a pervasive sense of sorrow which never went away—a sense of loss over ''what might have been'' that was never addressed or aired, but always felt. He heard stories of the heroism of his father and uncles, who became important to him as examples—and, of course, had no flaws. He went to Remembrance Day services. ''Danny Boy'' was played often, ''and to this day, that song represents all the sadness of my childhood spent in the shadow of that war." ◇ Another man says: "We didn't talk about it much when I returned from the war. My only brother was killed and several cousins. But the feeling was 'the past is past. Now let's get on with what needs to be done.'" ◇ People at home were sustained, to some extent, by the feeling that they and their men had had no choice; all their principles and beliefs had required that they defend the Empire, and they had quite simply offered their lives for the principles in which they believed. They had learned how to bear the long waiting, to sew, to knit, to wrap parcels endlessly, to write letters that never brought a reply, to read casualty lists without skipping over the names they were hoping not to find, and when the bad news finally came, they accepted it quietly. They had lived with death for a long time. Fortunately, it would be many years before people began to tell them that the sacrifice had been pointless. For the immediate future, the point was to cope.

PART II

COMING OF AGE

(1920-1930)

CHAPTER 6

The Winds of Change

The young members of Montreal's English elite families, those who had been too young to go to war, had heard stories of how life had been before 1914 "which were hard to believe in the midst of war-time austerity." They were eager for life to "return to normal," and in this they were joined by their elder brothers and sisters. But there was disquieting evidence that it might not be so easy to keep things the way they were. The cataclysm of the war could not be ignored: the winds of change that swept the Western world in its wake carried the despairing voices of the old whose past was in ruins; the frightened voices of children with no future; the angry voices of men defrauded, and of soldiers disillusioned; the voices of young girls sighing for lovers, of widows weeping for lost lives; the mocking laughter of the cynical, the shrill gaiety of those abandoned by faith. These anguished voices mixed with the joyous and triumphant voices of those to whom the war brought hope and opportunity: the new creators and the new power-seekers; those who had profited by the war and those who were freed from old dispensations. No longer speaking in unison of a common view of things, the voices were discordant, like saxophones crying and chattering in the dissonant music of jazz and Stravinsky. The effects of these different reactions are important because they led some people on the edge of the Montreal English elite to question the old values. Thus, holes appeared in the invisible social membrane which insulated their class from self-doubt.

Young women of the Square Mile rarely read the newspapers. "We didn't need to," because all the news that was of any importance in their lives could and would be picked up at lunch at the Mount Royal Club or at someone's dinner party that night. They felt that they were at the centre of the world, and anything of real importance happened *there* to people they knew. ◊ This lack of awareness of national, international, or even local, events which did not involve them directly was reinforced by the taboos against discussing controversial issues at social events, or business with wives and family, or of "unsuitable" subjects with the young. "I don't remember conversing with them [parents] about many issues. Even when I was sixteen or so I often did not have meals with them, and besides, they wouldn't talk about things about which they felt strongly before the young. They never talked about sex, birth control, all kinds of things were taboo." ◊

Men read the newspapers more regularly, but often only to have their own views confirmed. Newspapers were quite openly political and partisan. The *Montreal Star* and *The Gazette* were both conservative. The *Star* was owned first by Lord Atholstan, and later by J.W. McConnell. The White family, part of the old family elite, owned *The Gazette*. The *Montreal Standard* was largely concerned with social gatherings, fashion, and household advice. The *Montreal Witness* was taken up with Protestant religious issues. Only the *Montreal Herald* occasionally espoused liberal causes. The press could be counted on not to rock the boat. In fact, it sometimes misled readers if the facts were unpleasant or disturbing, as we shall see.

As a result, certain portentous changes, such as the emergence of the United States as stronger economically than Britain after World War I and its displacement of Britain as Canada's chief trading partner, were not evident to young Montrealers just reaching adulthood. Indeed, the full implications of this shift were not yet evident even to many of their businessmen fathers, whose fortunes had been built on east-west trade when Britain was able to protect their interests against the Americans.

Young people did notice some physical changes in the city connected with technological changes. Increasing automobile traffic was making the downtown area and the Square Mile less attractive for residence. In addition to automobiles, the radio and the airplane were bringing distant places closer and changing perspectives. One man remembers: "My father had one of the first radios on our street. The first time I heard it as a boy, I heard someone speaking in New York and I can still remember my sense of awe. I thought, 'New York must be closer than I thought it was.' I couldn't quite imagine voices travelling through the air for hundreds of miles without wires." ◊

The airplane was still largely regarded as a war machine or a pleasure craft. Young men learned to fly in flying clubs, just as they had learned to drive automobiles for fun in the preceding generation. But air pioneers were beginning to use them to fly men and materials into the north of Canada, to areas almost inaccessible previously.

The automobile, increasingly used for ordinary transportation, was changing not only the way people lived and where they lived; it also was having a noticeable effect on customs and morals. It made it difficult for parents to guard and supervise their daughters in the traditional way. According to one lady, "In the early twenties, the man I eventually married had an automobile, and I wanted to drive up to Kingston with him to an RMC ball. My parents had a fit. You didn't drive any distance with a man in a car in those days. But I was determined to go, and I did." ◊

The new freedom gained by young women was expressed in the new styles: bobbed hair, short skirts, and loose clothing. Divorce, along with smoking and drinking by women, became less scandalous. One man (still active today in a large investment firm founded by his father) explained that before the War, the Church of England, like the Catholic Church, did not grant divorce or remarriage, as a general rule. Infidelity did not necessarily break up a marriage. " Some people had flings or affairs and then came home and all would be forgiven. Sometimes people might go off with someone else's husband or wife, say to Edmonton, and never marry but pass themselves off as such in the new community. The West was far away and Montrealers didn't travel there much. Also, the mass media hardly existed, so that this solution was possible then. But World War I was devastating to morals and beliefs as well as to the general strength of the community." ◊

Another sign of a change in the status of women was that some began to enter university for training in professions other than teaching and nursing. Their initiatives met with strenuous objections. Throughout the 1920s the *McGill Daily* debated whether women had the constitutional ability to endure the rigours of university work. Margaret Gillett, in *We Walked Very Warily*, has documented this struggle in detail, and has confirmed that higher education for women met determined opposition not only in Montreal, but in most parts of the world. McGill was on a par with Oxford and Cambridge in its reluctance to admit women, and more conservative than many universities in the United States or the rest of Canada. Both Oxford and Cambridge had had complete (though separate) education for women with the same professors and curriculum as men, and with all examinations open to them, since the latter part of the nineteenth century; the University of London had accepted them fully since 1878, while in Canada, Mt. Allison, Acadia, Dalhousie, Toronto, and Trinity all preceded McGill by a few years. In the United States, Oberlin, Cornell, and all the mid-western state universities offered co-educational opportunities by the 1860s and 70s.

The battle at McGill had begun in 1871, when some of the grandmothers of the young ladies whose lives we are following, led by Anne Molson and Lucy Simpson, organized the Montreal Ladies' Educational Association, which offered university level courses taught by McGill professors in the Redpath museum (not in McGill classrooms). The courses were financed through tuition fees, and led to an "Associate of Arts" diploma granted by McGill. This organization included, in addition to the two mentioned, Mesdames Andrew Allan, Durnford, Atwater, Greenshields, Lyman, Moffatt, and Redpath. The success of these courses and the existence of such a pressure group among McGill benefactors exerted a softening influence on public and private resistance to university education for women. Throughout the subsequent years, the Montreal Council of Women continued to petition for greater educational opportunities.

In 1884 Lord Strathcona provided the financial support for the first McGill program open to women, in a move that evidently surprised Sir William Dawson into acquiescence by removing all financial barriers. His bequest specified that women were to be educated in separate classes. This program, called "Donalda,"(in honour of Donald A. Smith) admitted women to the Arts and Sciences faculty as "occasional," "partial," or full-time students. They had the same professors and courses as the men, but at different times and in different rooms. Later, in 1898, Lord Strathcona carried his interest in women's education a step further by endowing one million dollars for a women's college, to be affiliated with McGill. It was to be named Royal Victoria College and was to be a residential college, with its own tutors. Actually, only the first two years were taught in the college by tutors, the last two years being taken in mixed or separate classes at McGill, with degrees granted by McGill. The first women to successfully apply for entrance to McGill were from the Girls' High School of Montreal in 1884, shortly after the first Strathcona bequest. Although elite women were involved in this struggle as bene-factors, very few of them actually tried to obtain a higher educa-tion themselves. This is not surprising, given the nature of their relationship to the men on whom their financial security depended.

In spite of this, by the 1920s all the private girls' schools were urging their graduates to apply for university places. Grad-uates of The Study, founded during World War I, believe that this pressure was especially felt there perhaps because Miss Gascogne, the first headmistress, was such a firm believer in higher education for women. In 1922, The Study was the first girls' school to introduce the House system, common in boys' schools, to encourage competition for grades and other activities. It tends to develop in girls the same academic ambitions as boys have. Some upper class girls began to expect to attend university. Not all took degrees, at first; some attended courses as partial or occasional students. This was a compromise which recognized the possibility and importance of being educated without commit-ment to a career, or even any serious intention of competing with men in the classes they attended. Even if they took a degree, elite women were still not expected to work. A student of interior decorating was offered a most interesting and important contract, but refused it because she was planning to marry a war veteran. "To have taken the job would have been a slap in the face of my new husband, and after all they had been through in the war, we were certainly not going to make things difficult for them. My friends felt the same way." ◊ This feeling is echoed in the statement of another lady who was offered a job in an organi-zation where she had worked for three years as a Junior League volunteer. "Since it carried a salary and I could be fired, I couldn't accept it because it would have been an affront to Father. It would look as though I didn't think he could support me." ◊

The distaste felt by many men for the educated woman must have been an equally important factor. Several men now in their seventies or eighties volunteered the information in interviews that the girls who went to McGill in the pre- and post-World War I days were largely the "unattractive" ones. It was not only men who felt this way, either. Some women reported that their moth-ers were "terribly afraid I would turn into a blue stocking" because of some intellectual interest or pursuit. ◊

With such opposition, only the bravest would have insisted on going to university. The result was that during the thirty-five years between 1884 and 1919, a total of 184 women graduated from McGill—about five a year. On the other hand, we know that there was a shortage of young men after the war and many young women were unable to find a husband. In fact, every woman of this elite group whom I interviewed who took a university degree or some kind of professional training during the early 1920s either married later than her peers or not at all.

By 1920 the number of women at McGill had risen to 329. There were still ten times as many men (3,914 in that year) but a change was occurring. Some upper class women had made reputations for themselves as teachers, writers, artists, and nurses without university courses. The idea was certainly abroad that women, even of this group, could not only be educated but have careers as well.

Another significant change was the increasing shift in the balance of ethnic power in Montreal. Montreal's population of 267,730 at the turn of the century included a total of 12,864 of non-British, non-Canadian origins. By 1931 the population had grown to 1,020,018, which included 29,000 people of Central and Eastern European origin and 58,029 Jews. The Italian population had grown to 22,000, and the number of Asiatics had increased from less than a thousand in 1901, to 4,725.

Most of the new inhabitants of Montreal, however, were French Canadians. Quebec farms had long been unable to support all their sons and daughters and whole families had migrated to the western Canada and to the textile towns of New England. Montreal had also received a steady flow of migrants from Quebec farms and the French-Canadian population of the city grew from 230,000 in 1901 to 604,827 in 1931. From being an English city as it was before 1850, Montreal had become a French city. Sixty per cent of the population was French-speaking.

A Westmounter who was "a great walker" used to take the streetcar from Westmount to St. Lawrence Boulevard and then up towards the Back River. There she would cross the bridge at St. Vincent de Paul and walk to Cartierville. On the way, she had a view of that area just east of St. Lawrence to which many of these migrants were moving. "And I saw what was happening. Unfortunately, the government of the city of Montreal was corrupt and had a mayor, Médéric Martin, who sent out a call to the countryside: 'Come in to Montreal and I'll give you jobs, if you

136

vote for me.' So they flocked in from all over the nearby countryside; and the jobs that Médéric had for them were in cleaning streets and that sort of thing, because they weren't prepared for anything else. And they built themselves wooden shacks with tarpaper roofs.'' ◊

In fact, Médéric Martin had been one of the earliest politicians to appreciate and take advantage of the change in the population balance between French-speaking and English-speaking Montrealers. Before his time, mayors of Montreal had alternated between French and English by a gentlemen's agreement of long standing. In 1914, when George Washington Stephens, the English candidate, should have been automatically elected, Martin refused to honour the agreement. He ran a vigorous campaign: his most startling technique was to leap to the platform of political rallies organized and paid for by Stephens's supporters and harangue the crowd on his own behalf. The established rules of courtesy prevented his being ejected without a hearing. By promising to protect the interests of the French Catholic poor against the English Protestant rich he thought he could win—and he did.

One event everyone remembers was the church union issue, although its significance was not appreciated by the young as much as by their parents. The movement to unite the Presbyterian, Congregationalist, and Methodist churches in Canada, and its partial success in 1925, forced a change in one of the most fundamental bases on which the English-Scottish culture rested: the identification of the Scots of Montreal with their native Church of Scotland. The union issue caused much bitterness and division among members of the Protestant community of Montreal, as it did elsewhere in Canada.

Religion has always been important in the history of Canada, as sociologist S.D. Clark has demonstrated. In Montreal and Quebec it was the basis of the social structure. Every institution in the province and the city was either Protestant, Catholic, or Jewish. When Montreal was still a small garrison town in the late eighteenth and early nineteenth centuries there was of necessity considerable cooperation between all religious organizations. The Sulpicians of Notre Dame permitted the Protestants to use their chapel for services, while Presbyterians and Church of England members worshipped together. For some years, there were simply too few Protestants to support more than one church. By the mid-nineteenth century this had changed. The population

137

of Montreal had grown to 100,000, and people of British origin made up a majority of the population. At this point religious beliefs reasserted their alliance to national origin. The Scots worshipped in Presbyterian churches; the English went to the Anglican church; the Northern Irish, to the Methodist church. Even the Americans in Montreal started their own church. Norman Mair, a religious historian, believes that "this was important during the church union debates because people were giving up a national identity in joining. It seemed particularly hard for the Scots who over and over talked about not deserting the old Scots ways."

Many of my informants expressed strong national feeling for the churches to which they belonged. One man, who admitted to having little religious feeling himself, said: "People like us, English in background, naturally belonged to the Church of England." ◊ By the time of the first World War, "everyone had an active church connection" which was part of his ethnic identity.

Another change which complicated the religious issues of the immediate post-war period was the "social gospel," a largely Methodist religious movement originating in the latter part of the nineteenth century and given great impetus by the war. Its followers rejected the traditional order as un-Christian in its materialism and its injustice to the poor and weak. The message was taken up by other denominations as well and some young people of Montreal were much excited by this questioning of the establishment. "People used to go to church, especially in the evening. I remember full congregations with students sitting on the steps for the evening service. Afterwards we would discuss all the main points of the sermon. This was not uncommon. Sermons were very meaty in those days: social issues, peace and war, the world for Christ in our generation, the concept of taking science and medicine, as well as Christianity, to save the poor, the sick and the disadvantaged. Christianity was then considered *the hope* for mankind." ◊

This is not to imply that the Square Milers were particularly spiritual in outlook. Religious fervour on the part of any member of the social elite was regarded with acute embarrassment, far more so than a moral lapse would have been. The community was certainly not unduly concerned about the implications of the social gospel. Studies of the relationship between religion and social class have shown consistently that elites take an instrumental view of religion: that it is important more as an agent of social control than as a source of personal and moral salvation. This study has arrived at similar conclusions. As one gentlemen remarked, " Religion had very little effect on my values, but as an adult I have spent many years involved in the work of Christ Church Cathedral because I think there should be churches and that I should set an example. Whatever influence the churches have must be one for good." ◊

Between the mid-nineteenth century and the pre-war era, Protestant churches competed to secure converts and provide services for widely and thinly scattered settlers in the West of Canada. They soon realized that their competition was both too costly and counter-productive. The idea of church union, already an old and widespread one in Christian circles, was available as a solution. It had first been proposed in 1889 by the Anglicans. Some small denominations, such as the Regular and Free Baptists in the Maritimes, and the four branches of the Presbyterian Church, had formed unions of churches. However, the first step in this direction by quite different denominations occurred in 1902. Presbyterians, Methodists, and Congregationalists formed committees to draw up proposals for union of the three churches. This was completed by 1908 in a Basis for Union, and many Western communities proceeded to set up community churches serving all three denominations. However, when the Presbyterians found that in a national plebiscite nearly one third of their members were opposed to union, they decided to postpone commitment in the hope of securing unanimity. The war years intervened. In 1915 another vote showed that the sentiment in favour of union had declined. The Presbyterian assembly again decided to postpone its decision until the soldiers came home. The Presbyterians were in a difficult situation. Many of their western congregations had already amalgamated, and they risked losing their standing as a national church.

The proposal for union reflected both theological and practical concerns. A sense of guilt over schisms in the church had existed since the Reformation. The dream of Canada as a Protestant part of Christendom, with a United Church of Canada as a step to World Christendom, was also a factor. As well, the financial cost of competition between denominations of not very different beliefs had become evident. Finally, there was the practical consideration of maintaining Protestant power and effectiveness in competition with the Roman Catholic Church in Canada. This last motive was rarely expressed. In Montreal, there was a protest when Principal D.J.Fraser of the Presbyterian College was reported by *The Gazette* to have said that "the organization of a United Protestant Church was being formed in order to fight the Roman Church with its own weapons and on its own ground." The Presbytery's Committee on Church Union immediately sent an official pronouncement to *The Gazette* stating that "Never to our knowledge has any such reason or motive even been remotely hinted at.... in advocacy of the proposal to form 'The United Church of Canada.'" Nonetheless, some Roman Catholics also took this view of it. George Thomas Daly, rector of the Cathedral of Regina, urged support of the Catholic Church Extension Society "to meet this combined strength of Protestantism on the western frontier."

Although there were battles within all the denominations which were party to the union, the most bitter conflict occurred within the Presbyterian Church. The non-concurrents in the Presbyterian church rallied all their forces to prevent it and win votes for a continuing Presbyterian church in a conflict that was both devisive and tumultuous. The enabling legislation in 1925 produced huge controversy in Parliament where the prime minister, Mackenzie King, was the chief spokesman for the non-unionists and Arthur Meighan, leader of the opposition, defended the unionist position. The Church Union Bill provided an opportunity for any congregation, it if so desired, to vote itself out of the union. The Presbyterian Church Association which had spearheaded the opposition to union, now set about to force elections in every church. Controversy between the two Presbyterian factions became exceedingly acrimonious during the last frantic days of voting, not only setting neighbour against neighbour, but even dividing families.

When, in 1921, the general assembly of the Presbyterian Church resolved to accept union, there was great tension in Montreal. "People talked about nothing else for months," recalls a man who was in the thick of it. ◊ The old family Protestants tended not to favour union. It is significant that most of these belonged to the established churches—the Church of England or the Church of Scotland. Their religion was aligned with their British traditions as well as their social position. Unionists were likely to be the more evangelical members, or the advocates of the involvement of the church in social issues, or those concerned with the waste and inefficiency of too many, too small congregations. They thought of themselves first of all as Canadians.

140

The Presbyterians in fact had a very strong inter-church committee of pro-unionists made up of such prominent businessmen as J.W. McConnell, Lorne Webster, Henry and William Birks, W.H. Goodwin, and A.S. Ewing.

The *Daily Witness*, the mouthpiece of Protestantism published by John Dougall and read by most Protestants in Montreal, was full of articles, editorials, and letters to the editor covering the arguments on both sides. Dougall himself in an editorial on June 14, 1922 supported union partly to strengthen religion "in the face of the disdain of young people for it and the availability of foreign cults." Archbishop Thornloe in a speech to the Anglican Synod of Ontario called denominational divisions a "sin" that prevented the work of the church. The Church should speak with one voice for Christ. Businessmen in all churches felt that "union would be more efficient, would save overlapping of missionary and philanthropic activities, permit pooling of financial resources."

In a letter to *The Witness* dated December 26, 1923, the Rev. W.B. MacCallum, an anti-union Presbyterian, wrote of the unionists: "It does not seem to have dawned on such persons at all that the real objection to this scheme is not so much, or even at all, what we are entering into—it is regret and fear of leaving behind what perhaps we now especially need." This statement brings us to the heart of the anti-union sentiment. The Montreal elite, certainly the Old Guard, was in this camp. Murray Ballantyne's family was against union, he says, entirely for emotional reasons. He explains that "the scheme took its impetus from the Methodist side and ... many Presbyterians feared the loss of their distinctive personality. Snobbery also played its part, for the proud Presbyterians of Scotland felt that they formed no mere conventicle, they were a historic national Church in their own right."

A regular *Witness* columnist, whose *nom de plume* was "Scrutator," satirized the anti-unionists' position by pretending to speak for them.

> But why ... does no one of our great leaders with frankness...come out and admit—no, declare—to all and sundry that our real reason for opposing Church union is because we consider we are different from and better than the Methodists? That is the real reason we are taking such strong ground. (March 12, 1924)

The battle in Montreal was particularly acrimonious because it was the home of two of the most vociferous anti-union Presbyterian leaders: the Rev. Mr. Ephraim Scott, and Robert Campbell, who was the senior clerk of the Assembly of the Presbyterian Church. Scott scandalized many by calling on Catholics as well as Protestants to oppose the Church Union bill or "your turn may be next." A storm of protest followed in the pages of the *Witness*. J.N. Beckstead summed up the unionist position in a letter dated January 9, 1924 in response to Scott. "The Church ... has already decided [the question] on the grounds of expediency, right reason, the testimony of Scripture and of history and the age-long prayer of every Christian liturgy for the healing of our unhappy divisions."

When the battle was over, the Presbyterian church had been split in two. In Montreal, of 422 Methodist, Congregational, and Presbyterian churches representing 45,863 members, 391 churches with 38,498 members entered the United Church of Canada. Thirty-one congregations, representing 7,365 members, all Presbyterians, stayed out. Many ministers who backed union found themselves without churches, while some churches who had rejected union were now without ministers. Many of the wealthy, however, stayed with the "continuing" Presbyterian church which was able to reorganize in a surprisingly short time. The day after the last General Assembly of the Presbyterian Church in Toronto, Dr. Ephraim Scott was "elected moderator of a reconstituted assembly and entered the pulpit to denounce church union as 'our country's greatest national crime.'"

Every church in Montreal was divided. Some members of St. Andrew and St. Paul left to join the Erskine and American, a United Church which included the American Presbyterian. Similarly, members of "uniting" congregations broke away and joined "continuing" Presbyterian churches.

For some Presbyterians, the wounds were never entirely healed. One family which was anti-union Presbyterian, but whose church joined the union, attended services for a while at the Church of St. Andrew and St. Paul. Then it returned to its old pew, finally settling down in the United Church. Years later, the son of the family decided to go into the United Church ministry and remembers his father standing by the window saying sadly, "What a pity you couldn't go into the ministry of our own church." ◊

The following story told by a church member illustrates the difficulties of integrating worship among people of widely different traditions in a church that had recently "united."

Mine was a Presbyterian church that joined the Union. The congregation was mostly made up of Presbyterians and was not given to effusive self-expression or religious fervour. The minister was also Presbyterian and, as was usual at the time, he gave great care to preparing thoughtful and well-expressed sermons. The union brought us an ex-Methodist member who customarily, whenever he strongly agreed with a point the minister made would rise from his place and cry ''Praise the Lord!'' Both the minister and the congregation found this disruptive and discomfiting.

The minister went to the ladies' organization of the church and asked them if they could tactfully put a stop to this. The ladies, in carrying out this mission, discovered that the elderly man lived alone and was in straightened circumstances. In fact, he had only two threadbare blankets on his bed. They bought him two handsome, thick wool blankets and in the course of making him a present of them, tactfully made their point that his fervent comments interrupted the sermon and disturbed some of the congregation. He seemed to understand and for several Sundays there were no more outcries. However, a Sunday came when the minister preached a particularly moving and inspiring sermon and in the midst of it, the gentleman leaped to his feet and exclaimed, ''Blankets or no blankets, praise the Lord'!'' ◇

The success of Church union represented the rise of Canadian nationalism and the weakening of old British ties after the war. It also represented the declining importance of sacred values which accompanied the advance of science. Religious doctrines and religious differences were losing their importance in an age of relativism.

It can be argued that religious ideas produced disturbances and doubts in the minds of Anglo-Protestant capitalist leaders, although they might not readily admit it. The social gospel suggested that society ought to be reorganized in the name of justice and Christianity. Although it was the evangelical sects such as the Methodists which were proposing these views (and they could be ignored) these ideas began to creep into the cathedrals of the wealthy. In 1920, the Lambeth Conference *Report of the Anglican Bishops* raised serious questions about the role of Christianity in the industrial world. This encyclical letter pinpointed low wages, inadequate provisions for health and safety, unemployment, and bad housing as evils of the industrial system. As a partial remedy, they advocated ''perfect freedom of organization on the part of workers, with leaders and spokesmen of their own choosing.'' Furthermore, Resolution 76 stated:

> In obedience to Christ's teaching as to covetousness and self-seeking, the Conference calls upon all members of His Church

to be foremost both by personal action and sacrifice in maintaining the superiority of the claims of human life to those of property. To this end it would emphasize the duty which is laid upon all Christians of setting human values above dividends and profits in their conduct of business.

The war had released forces of change that diminished the possibility of a "return to normal." New ideas that began to question the old order supported greater freedom and more opportunities for women, criticized the capitalist on the grounds of Christian ethics, and promoted "Canadianism" and "modernism" over "Empire" and "tradition." Such ideas struck at the basic traditions and beliefs of the Anglo-Protestant elite of the 1920s. Even its religious and ethnic identity was threatened in the Act of Church Union. Some of the exponents of these ideas belonged to the fringe of the ruling group. The old wealthy families in Montreal could surrender, fight them, or ignore them. For the most part, they chose to ignore them, and return to normal—if at all possible.

CHAPTER 7

The Return to Normal

In spite of this evidence of rapid change, young people just coming of age in Montreal's elite English families tried, like their parents, to carry on as they had before the Great War. The period between the world wars can be seen as a constant struggle around new values which the old families consistently opposed. Of considerable importance to the generation born around 1900 and now reaching adulthood were the social patterns which provided the setting for courtship and marriage. The careful exclusivity of clubs, summer places, balls, and teas, plus their own well-trained class consciousness, ensured that young men and women met suitable candidates.

The organizing focus for this—perhaps the most successful reestablishment of pre-war customs—was the return of "coming out." Young girls who had been "finished" at school in Europe or Britain, or by touring the continent, were ready at 17 to 19 (there was no firm rule about age) to be "presented to Society." In the twenties, as before, girls "came out" at the Hunt Club ball; at the Ritz-Carlton, the Windsor, or the Mount Royal Hotels; or at the St. Andrew's Ball, or at a private ball in their own homes. Some girls might even be presented at Court if their fathers' position entitled them to it, or if their mothers had been so honoured. This meant that they would be introduced to the King and Queen in London, or to the Governor General in Ottawa at a "Drawing Room." These were the most prestigious presentations, of course. Girls who were honoured by such an invitation wore for the occasion elaborately decorated, long dresses with a train and the traditional three white Prince of Wales feathers bobbing above their coronets.

People in less affluent circumstances who regarded their daughters as eligible debutantes might give dinners or even teas in their honour, at home. Lower in the social scale were girls who did not come out themselves, but who were nonetheless invited to a taste of the social whirl at the coming-out parties of girls they might have met at school or in church. Not that this was always a pleasant experience. One woman remembers, somewhat bitterly, "I didn't come out myself, my family couldn't afford it, but I was sometimes invited to parties of the girls who did, or would be invited by a boy to such a party. I remember calling my father to come and bring me home once because the other girls there wouldn't even speak to me, and when that happened, sometimes the boys (except the one who had brought you) wouldn't dance with you. It was awful! I didn't want to be left out of the parties, but often they were most painful." ◊

For those who felt socially comfortable, however, the twenties and the round of parties which went on all year for the debutantes are remembered as a carefree time of unalloyed pleasure. None of the coming-out balls were more glamourous or full of tradition than the St. Andrew's Ball.

The St. Andrew's Ball was (and still is) organized by the St. Andrew's Society, a Scottish fraternal organization whose original purpose was to assist new and old Scottish immigrants to Canada, in any way they needed, and to provide friendly contacts among Scots here. The Ball soon became the most glamourous of the debutante season. One had to be invited (after inquiries as to one's suitability) to be one of the debutantes presented. Everyone attending the ball went to private dinners first. The result was they were late arriving and the ball often started late. If the ball didn't start until midnight, it meant dancing until dawn—so much the better!

The central lobby, staircase, and ballroom of the Windsor Hotel were decorated with flags, banners, and tartan hangings of the clans. The guest of honour was either a Scottish nobleman or the Governor General of Canada, especially if he was Scottish and titled. In the hotel's Regal Suite, a reception would be held where a small number of invited guests could meet the patron and his wife and have aperitifs or whisky. The society page reporters of the Montreal English newspapers circulated in this room, noting the material, colour, and the couturier of each lady's dress, and getting the names right. This was one of the most important social events of the year in high society and misspelled names would not be taken lightly. Except that the mess dinner is now served before the ball, and that it no longer takes place in the Windsor Hotel (now closed), the pageantry and splendour of the ceremony remains much the same today as a hundred years ago. It proceeds as follows:

At the appointed time, the Black Watch pipe band appears at the door of the Regal Suite, led by the drum major. The swaying tartan kilts, the red hackle in the black feather bonnets, the military skirl of the pipes evoke ancient masculine rituals and battles and wind-swept Highland moors. The band leads the Patron and the reception guests into the ballroom. Down the wide festooned staircase, at the bottom of which the paying guests have assembled, the Patron and Patroness and his reception guests march, two by two. As they pass into the ballroom, the people who have bought tickets, equally elegantly and formally attired, fall in behind them.

The Patron and his wife, the President of the Ball and his wife, and a few very special guests take their places on the dais at one end of the long ballroom. The hundreds who have bought tickets line the walls, leaving the centre of the ballroom floor clear. After an exchange of ceremonial greetings and thanks between the Patron and the President, the pipes announce the arrival of the debutantes. Each young girl in her long white dress clutches the arm of her father, who is wearing white tie and tails. One by one these couples walk the length of the ballroom and approach the dais. The girl's name is called, and she curtsies deeply to the patron, who acknowledges the introduction with some inaudible words. The young girls, with their thin necks, uncertain smiles and nervous hands look like offerings to some primeval god. Pagan, perhaps, but evidently romantic and thrilling for the participants.

Next, the dance orchestra strikes up a tune; the Guest of Honour steps out onto the dance floor with the wife of the President, and the ball begins. The orchestra plays all evening and there is Scottish dancing to the pipes as well. The young girls who had dreamed in boarding school days of being swept away by a knight in shining armour (or by a Black Watch cadet) must have felt, as they whirled around the room in their beautiful ball dresses with partner after partner, that the dream had come true.

Whenever dinner or supper is served (and in the twenties it would be midnight or later), the pipe band appears to lead everyone into the dining room. There are traditional toasts in Gaelic, and the haggis is brought in on a board carried on the shoulders of two pipers. It is marched to the patron who draws his dirk and stabs it. A puff of steam rises from the dish. Thus "killed" the haggis is served to the guests and the dinner begins. After that, the dancing continues until dawn, when a breakfast is served.

This ball was the beginning of endless parties and dances in honour of the new debutantes during the entire winter and spring. It was part of the point that young people who had spent their adolescence at school should have opportunities, when approaching a marriageable age, to meet eligible members of the opposite sex. Girls often went to parties in groups, or were brought by a father or brother; if the latter, he would probably have been invited to the party. The hostess, however, made it a point to provide every girl with an escort to see her home. Continual chaperonage was no longer required, but girls were still not expected to be on the streets alone at night. Many men claim to have hated all this partying and having to escort girls whom they might not like but to whom they had to be nice. On the other hand, many of them found their future wives at such affairs. Debutantes after all, were being presented as available for marriage to suitable men. One woman remarked sardonically about the whole process, "We were put up for auction to the highest bidder, but it was so much fun we didn't think of that at the time." ◇

People gave "marvellous" parties, sometimes taking over an entire floor of a hotel. Orchestras were hired, either for home or hotel balls. Girls were wearing dresses above the knee in front and longer behind, and everybody was dancing the Charleston. "I remember one [ball] where every girl had a bunch of American Beauty roses at her place at the supper table. Some of the men were such wonderful dancers ... you'd just be in a sort of dream, waltzing around the ballroom." ◇

The parties were sometimes spectacular. One of my informants remembers the last party of the sort given at Ravenscrag, in the early l930s: "At supper I went to get my eggs and sausages as usual and was handed a bottle of champagne. I looked in surprise at the fellow serving it and he said, 'It's all yours.' Everybody was handed a bottle. Now you can imagine how the party picked up'! They found people under tables, beds, everywhere! Such goings-on! Lady Allan was very generous and gave parties for everyone, marvellous parties for a hundred or more guests." ◇

In addition, young people went to nightclubs—Ciro's and the Venetian Gardens, or to the *thés dansants* at all the hotels.

148

The dress style and the location of the St. Andrew's Ball have changed, but the ceremony is almost the same today as when this photo was taken in 1878 at the Windsor Hotel.

The members of the Montreal Hunt in action.

After McGill football games, girls would have "bids" to go to one of the hotels for tea and dancing at the Ritz or perhaps the Windsor, or the Mt. Royal's Normandie Roof. "If McGill won their game, there would be dancing on the tables at Ciro's." ◊

As though there were not enough social affairs in Montreal, the prominent young Montrealer would also attend parties in Quebec and Ottawa. As one lady says, "Ottawa was just a suburb of Montreal to us. It cost about $2.00 to go there by train, so people often went there for parties." ◊

Murray Ballantyne expresses the fun and pleasure of this round of social activities.

> Oh, the parties of the twenties! Never again can their like be seen in Canada. All the facilities were at hand. Houses were still large, and sometimes immense. Servants were taken for granted. Money was not worth thinking about. Everyone had time, and no one had worries. We dined and we dined. Even among ourselves in our parents' houses there were "white ties," good food, and the ordered procession of wines.... After dinner came ballet, theatre, concerts, or dancing. But only when midnight was approaching did the really big parties begin, when we would sweep up whatever artists had been performing and go on to supper. Well do I remember one night at our favourite house, when "Argentina," the dancer, was holding court in the ballroom, when very good bridge was being played in the library, and when one of Canada's greatest—and heaviest—industrialists was imitating the love dance of the elephant in the drawing room. And through it all passed footmen with inexhaustible champagne. We had parties, we had parties, endlessly we had parties, and never did we tire of them.

A woman who must have been very popular as a girl reports that according to her dance cards saved from the late 1920s, she attended forty balls in one season (that is, from September to May), many of them held in private homes, always considered the most elegant venue.

The heavy drinking implied in these accounts was a post-war phenomenon. Several people maintained that they had never had a drink until they were in their twenties and that it was not served to younger people. In fact, a good proportion of people appear to have been teetotalers. One woman recalls being at a party where someone had put sherry in the punch and being told by several of the boys, "Don't touch it! It has liquor in it!!" ◊ She was then in her early twenties.

There was an effort in 1918 to restrict the sale of liquor in Canada, by orders-in-council which were to be ratified by each province. Montreal in April 1919 went overwhelmingly "wet" as did most of Quebec. In any case, the return of the soldiers from World War I was believed by many to be at least one of the causes of a breakdown in the general disapproval of drinking which had characterized a large part of the Protestant community of Montreal prior to that time. "The boys came home after the war used to having the odd drink in the services and not used to being told what to do with their private lives. Then the six months of prohibition increased the drinking because if you got hold of a bottle, you'd finish it, since it was illegal to have it at all." ◊ A lady who was part of all this reports that after the war "everything was wide open. Our parents were too busy having fun themselves to pay much attention to us. A lot of people had drinking problems. Before that, if there was drinking at all, it was controlled. You might be served one cocktail by the butler and that was that. You weren't offered another. There might be wine at dinner, but you would get maybe two or three glasses all evening—not much. But after the war, men began to carry hip flasks and at dances at the Mount Royal or the Ritz there would be private rooms hired and some people would just stay there and drink all evening. It caused a lot of trouble—young men and even some girls having regularly to be carted off home from parties." ◊

Sports were another source of fun: for men as participants, and for women as spectators, although a few of the latter were riders or played golf or tennis. The Montreal Amateur Athletic Association was pivotal in the development of organized sport. At the turn of the century, the MAAA had 2,331 members, practically all of whom were British Canadians, and these members in turn organized, played with, and ran almost all the other sports clubs and teams in the city. The executive of the MAAA was composed of a small group of English, Irish, and Scottish Canadian business owners and professionals who were also active in the national sports organizations. As a result, the MAAA occupied a position of prestige and power out of proportion to its size in the organization of Canadian sport.

Curling was perhaps the first sport imported to Canada, or at least the first sport to organize itself into a club. The Royal Montreal Curling Club was, in fact, the oldest curling club on this continent. It was founded in 1809 by twenty "sporting merchants of Montreal, who had been curling on the St. Lawrence River behind Molson's Brewery," and of course the names of

151

the first members were entirely Scottish. Competitive curling was and remains it's principal activity, although the number of members has now grown to over three hundred and includes some people who rarely, if ever, play the game.

The Montreal Hunt Club, founded in 1829, became by the 1890s the apex of the Montreal social scene. It had everything to make it so. It was highly traditional, ceremonious, and aristocratic at a time when all these qualities were enjoyed and appreciated unabashedly. It was sponsored by wealthy Montrealers, and to become a member of the Hunt required proof of skill at riding and hunting, as well as evidence that the applicant would be socially agreeable. The Hunt Ball was one of the important places to make one's debut. The club sponsored a steeplechase, horse shows, and a hunt, with all its pageantry and glamour, three times a week from September to December. People who could attend three hunts a week either had a great deal of leisure or a clear set of priorities. The latter theory is suggested by W.W.Johnson, who stated in his *Sketches of the Late Depression* that, "The Stock Exchange held only a morning session on October 13, 1882, since there was a Hunt 'meeting' that afternoon."

The hunters rode to the locale in the pink coats and black boots they were entitled to wear if they had passed the probationary period of two or three years. Those members who had not yet qualified to wear the pink coat wore ordinary riding clothes and bowler hats. The hounds were loosed and the chase was on as soon as the hounds picked up the scent of the fox. The terrain was often very difficult and unpredictable. Both rider and mount needed to be in good shape to stay the course, and people began riding and jumping in June to get ready for the hunting season. When the fox was cornered, the hounds were trained to break his neck with one jerk. After that, there would be a Hunt breakfast served at the clubhouse. In the early days, people on the estates through which the hunt had passed sometimes provided a breakfast.

The role of women in the Hunt Club is not clear. Only their husbands were members; but they used the club for social events and some of them rode, side-saddle and in black habits, to the hounds. In 1914, when the daughter of a prominent citizen appeared on Sherbrooke Street riding astride, it was said that she caused more of a sensation locally than the assassination of the Archduke at Sarajevo. Gradually, however, women became more active, eventually riding and hunting on something like equal terms with the men.

*The Mount Royal Golf Club after it moved to Dixie,
circa 1900.*

A polo game in the Cartierville-Senneville area.

In 1900 the club house was on Côte Ste. Catherine Road, then quite rural, and for many members its chief attractions were the dining room, the quoits ground, bowling green, miniature golf course, the teas, and the annual Hunt Ball. By the 1920s the Montreal Hunt was well known in the United States and had visitors from Britain and Europe. Lord Minto was closely associated with it during his term of office as Governor General, and the Prince of Wales rode with the Hunt on two occasions in the 1920s. The list of members for 1919 could well serve as a social register for Montreal: Allan, Angus, Ballantyne, Cantlie, Cowans, Cape, Dawes, Drummond, Ewing, Gault, Greenshield, Holt, Lyman, Meredith, Meighen, Molson, MacDougall, Mackay, Marler, Ogilvie, Paterson, Porteous, Paton, Reford, Ramsay, Redpath, Ross,Shaugnessy, Savage, Smith, White, Williams-Taylor. All the ''best'' people belonged, about three hundred in all.

In tandem with riding and hunting were the polo games which were organized by the Montreal Hunt and Le Club de chasse (its French-Canadian equivalent). The first polo game in Canada was played near Montreal in 1902. The game proved so popular that matches were scheduled regularly and ''the idle rich used to go to polo games on Saturday afternoons,'' said one lady. ◊ By the 1920s the Hunt was moved to Fresnière (near Lachute) since Montreal had grown uncomfortably close to the Côte Ste. Catherine property. About this time and possibly following the example of Senator Forget, Major Hooper, and Charles McEachran, all of whom were enthusiastic riders with estates in the Cartierville-Senneville area of the northwest Island, a number of prominent Montrealers bought property in that area and raised and rode horses for shows, the hunt, and polo. It was a way of life. In Saraguay there were ten families who owned large adjoining properties. They turned their estates into polo fields, hunting woods, stables, and riding trails, and built swimming pools, tennis courts, and croquet grounds. As a community they played at all these things together with their numerous guests who were always delighted to be invited for a weekend. At the time there were still plenty of servants, grounds-keepers, grooms, and servants available to make possible a life of such leisure.

Only slightly less prominent socially was the Royal Montreal Golf Club, which originally played at Fletcher's Field and, like the Hunt, had to move further and further out as the city grew. This club also rested heavily on tradition and ceremony, sustained

154

by proper attire. Golf was invented in Scotland and the Scots of Montreal were the first to import it to the New World complete with Scottish traditions: an annual competition for a silver golf club with silver balls attached like those at St. Andrew's; the red jacket used in Scotland by golfers crossing common lands as a warning to the populace; and as the club's history concludes, "from the very early days in Montreal it was the Rules of Golf as promulgated by the Royal and Ancient [the St. Andrew's Club] which governed play in the new land."

The Royal Montreal Golf Club also had lavish social events. There was an annual "Beef and Greens" dinner meeting, and the sumptuous Golf Club Dinner in mid-winter. The menu of a seven-course meal complete with wines and whisky for each course was presented in broad Scotch: "Oysters cauld wi' drappie Yill" opened one dinner.

The first woman to be admitted to membership in the Royal Montreal Golf Club was Mrs. W.W. Watson—the first woman member,indeed, of any golf club in North America—in 1891. Eight years later the Ladies' Branch moved into its own club-house on the grounds at Dixie and had a membership almost as large as the men's—slightly over a hundred, although few of them played much golf in the beginning. For about twenty years there was what the historian calls a "waspish" relationship between the two branches of the club. The men felt that the ladies did not respect the rules limiting membership, or hours of play; while the ladies felt that they were never consulted about anything and not taken seriously.

By the 1920s there was cross-country skiing in the Laurentians. Although snowshoe and toboggan clubs had existed from the beginning of the nineteenth century, skiing became popular only after World War I. The extension of the railway north of Montreal to Ste. Agathe opened the Laurentians to tourism. Even before the war, a few Montreal English Protestants had summer camps in the area; and in 1911 the CPR began to promote the region for fishing and hunting. But the railway journey of three hours or more, with the prospect of travelling by buck-board from the station, had discouraged development of the area. The Laurentians really came into their own when skiing became popular. There being no tows or commercial slopes at the time, people skied cross-country, taking the train up on a Saturday or Sunday morning, with a packed lunch. They skied until noon, had lunch somewhere out of the wind, then skied to the nearest train station

Skiers preparing to board the ski-train in the 1920s.

to catch the late afternoon train back to Montreal. Some people had their own cottages. A member of one of Montreal's most prominent families describes winter week-ending: "In winter we went up to our cottage at Ivry to ski. We would leave from Place Viger station on a train at 4:00. We would be met by the farmer who cared for our place driving a sleigh with buffalo robes. He would have started the coal furnace and his daughter would have dinner ready or at least started. The food was ordered by Mother at Dionne's. Dionne's would deliver everything needed for the weekend to the train the morning before we left that afternoon. It would arrive at Ivry and be picked up by the farmer and delivered to the cottage. All very simple, much simpler than now when no such services are available." ◇

Who persuaded the Canadian National Railways to put on more trains is not certain, though it is said that Percy Douglas invited Sir Henry Thornton, then president, to observe the thousands of people trying to get on a train for the Laurentians on the weekends. In any case, the first CNR "ski specials" were operating by 1927; and soon the CPR was operating them as well. Eventually, there were as many as twenty-five ski specials, carrying 25,000 skiers every weekend. Everyone remembers these trips as at least half the fun. The trains had about ten coaches plus a baggage car for skiing gear and accident victims. Skiers travelled in groups. People sang, visited back and forth in the cars, ate, drank, played cards, gossiped, made dates, romantic or otherwise. "We sang, we danced in the aisles, we had a wonderful time. And it happened every weekend." ◇

Men's clubs played an important part in the business, as well as the social, life of Montreal. The oldest men's club is the St. James, founded in 1857 by Harrison Stephens, George Moffat, John Redpath, Peter McGill, Sir William Logan, and others. The Mount Royal Club, the most prestigious men's club, was founded in 1899 by a group of men who felt that the St. James was becoming "too crowded"—in other words, not exclusive enough. Its list of founders included Lord Strathcona, George A. Drummond, Senator Forget, R.B. Angus, Montagu Allan, Edward S. Clouston, Hugh Graham, Vincent Meredith, Hartland Macdougall, William Ogilvie, Hugh Paton, and James Ross—several of whom would within a few years have a title of some kind. It has continued to have a small membership, carefully selected. All the clubs are exclusive to some extent, requiring at least a proposer, a seconder and scrutiny by a membership committee.

In addition to special dinners and other social events sponsored by the men's clubs, members met there for lunch, where they might have a place permanently reserved at a table with men of similar interests or status. They often stopped off for drinks on their way home in the evening. This opportunity to know and talk on an informal basis with other men of influence was invaluable when a business deal was brewing or when a man wanted to get something done in the community. And of course, the more prestigious the members, the more prestigious the club, and the more valuable were the contacts it provided.

Dau's Blue Book of 1928, a compendium of the prominent families of Montreal and their clubs, lists 105 clubs which were predominantly or entirely Anglo-Protestant. Of these, 52 are sports clubs: tennis, fishing and game, snowshoe, golf, bowling, rowing clubs; the Royal St. Lawrence Yacht Club; the Montreal Amateur Athletic Association; and the Forest and Stream. There were clubs for people interested in art (the Art Association) or music (the Ladies Morning Musical Club), or in stamp and coin collecting. There were service clubs such as Rotary and Kiwanis. The St. James Literary Club, the various historical societies, and the Canadian Club discussed public affairs. Women belonged to the Themis Club. The University Club catered to university graduates, a select group in those days. All of the clubs had programs of entertainment, dinners, teas, lectures, trips, picnics, or sporting events. A prominent man in the community usually belonged to ten or more clubs, and his wife to four or more. The 1928 Blue Book reports that Col. Herbert Molson was a member of 24 different Montreal clubs; W.J. Morrice, of 26; Norman Dawes, of nineteen.

Should the clubs and private parties not be enough to fill one's social calendar, there were the militias. Since the days of the British garrisons, military men and their activities had brought glamour to Montreal. When the British left after Confederation, the militias were formed of volunteers as a reserve force for national defense, and for keeping order locally. In peace time, the militias assumed ceremonial obligations.

Among the militia regiments the Black Watch was socially the most prestigious, partly because of its close ties with Scotland and Scottish traditions. The Black Watch was in fact called out for national defense several times: during the Fenian raids; at the time of the Boer War; and in World War I. It was also called out to quell riots and control demonstrations. In 1903, it was

158

sent to Valleyfield to police a strike by construction workers who were building a new mill for the Montreal Cotton Company. According to the Black Watch history the necessity arose when the strikers attempted to intimidate workers in the existing mill in an effort to get them to join the strike. Clashes between the soldiers and the strikers lasted five days, during which nine members of the Regiment were injured. The Black Watch history does not mention casualties on the other side.

As for ceremonial functions, the militias paraded on all public occasions, such as a royal visit, a coronation, or the arrival of some important dignitary. The officers and band members of the Black Watch took part in the St. Andrew's Ball. In addition there were regular activities such as brigade drills, qualification course classes, summer camps, picnics, smokers, and dinners.

Officers of the Black Watch were drawn almost entirely from the Montreal Anglo-Protestant elite. Black Watch picnics took place at Ravenscrag. Sir Montagu Allan, who was an honorary lieutenant-colonel of the 1st Battalion, bore the expense of outfitting the band with new uniforms in 1911. Colonel G.S. Cantlie, a man whose entire life was spent in the Black Watch and was its Colonel for much of that time, formed an Honorary Members' Mess, "for the purpose of strengthening the Regiment." The twenty-five men invited to join were of Scottish birth or descent, and included Lord Strathcona, Lord Atholstan, R.B. Angus, Hugh Paton, R. Meighan and Lord Mount Stephen. As expected, these men who "formed a closely-knit exclusive little club within the Regimental structure," were a recurring source of financial support.

In 1921 the Presbyterian Church of St. Andrew and St. Paul became the regimental church of the Black Watch. This church was well-endowed and supported by its wealthy Scottish congregation. The regimental colours hang in the church still, and the church parade and service for the Black Watch occurs there once a year.

The militias' popularity tended to diminish in any period between wars, but was kept refreshed, in Montreal, by the number of young men who attended the Royal Military College in Kingston. The RMC was regarded by many as the best education available, and it was free of tuition; however, one had to agree to serve two years in the militia reserve after graduation. This was scarcely onerous, since a young man with a degree from RMC was commissioned automatically. Besides, a cadet in uniform or a young officer in one of the militias was much admired by the girls. One woman described the RMC balls as "pure glamour." ◊ Another said that when her daughter was proposing to have no cadets present at her wedding, "I said I wasn't sure I wanted to go through with it. A wedding without cadets was unthinkable." ◊

There were theatres, both live and cinematic, although most shows of either sort were imported, not local or even Canadian in origin. His Majesty's Theatre on Guy Street presented plays and concerts, mostly from England. The *haute monde* arrived for performances in evening dress and tails. The Orpheum Theatre, which began as a theatre featuring vaudeville, was by the 1920s a stock theatre, putting on twelve performances a week of popular plays of the day.

Many people loved this constant round of gaiety, sleeping late, dancing until dawn night after night, a frivolous life that caused few if any pangs of conscience even among Presbyterians. They were not people inclined toward profound or philosophical reading or discussion. Murray Ballantyne suggests that even when serious reading was done, it was as much in search of having an interesting point to make at dinner as in pursuit of knowledge or ideas. The expression that "I dined out for weeks on that story," is only half-facetious. With so many parties attended by the same people, good conversationalists were much in demand. Ballantyne writes:

> It may be asked if no doubts assailed my youthful and spoiled self-assurance. Did I never realize the vanity of it all, nor see how superficial we all were? Did I never wake in the morning weary with the whole silly show? Did I feel no remorse for time wasted, no responsibility to wrestle with the problems of the day? The answer, quite simply, is No.... I was still legally and psychologically a child, and I was living and moving in a typically immature era and set. We didn't even say "Après nous le déluge," because we didn't know any deluge was coming.... If I wondered "what" the world was, or "why" it was, it was principally to be prepared to talk well at somebody's dinner-table.

The leisure activities of Montreal's English-speaking elite in the 1920s demonstrate what a small, closed community it was. Members worked together, played together, and as we shall see later, carried on all community responsibilities together, as they had before the war.

160

*A parade of Royal Military College cadets along
Sherbrooke Street, circa 1925.*

*Garrison Church Parade, the Pipe Band of the
Royal Highlanders of Canada, 1927.*

This pattern of life could only exist as long as there were people willing to be servants: to dust, scrub and polish; to cook and serve the meals, and wash the linen; to wait up until the wee hours to help people into their coats and boots; to drive them home from the dinner parties at the great houses; and then be up at six the next morning to do it all over again. Interviews with both employers and servants reveal the full range of relationship from maltreatment to life-long involvement and mutual responsibility. It is useless to guess which was most common; but what we can say is that the nature of servitude encourages exploitation of the servant. If there are people who manage to overcome and rise above this built-in aspect of the relationship, it is to their credit, but does not change the fact. When employees can leave their place of employment when they please, this tendency is limited if not curbed. In Montreal in the 1920s, chronic unemployment and inadequate wages, besides the necessity of obtaining a good character reference for every job, meant that the freedom to quit was often freedom to starve.

As a rule, the servants who stayed for years or for life belonged to the servant class in Britain or had received training as servants there. They were usually of the higher status group: butler, steward, cook, nanny, housekeeper, valet, or lady's maid. If this kind of relationship went on long enough, it was common practice to care for the servant in his old age, by paying him a pension and, if necessary or desirable, housing and feeding him for the rest of his life. It was often necessary because such old retainers, having dedicated their lives to service to their employers and having little free time had few friends and often never married. In fact, most employers found it easier to deal with unmarried servants and discouraged romantic relationships.

The number of servants in a household varied, of course, with the wealth of the family. In the case of very large houses and great wealth, there might be twelve or thirteen, including typically a butler, a coachman, a footman, one or two gardeners, cook, upstairs and downstairs maids, kitchen maid, laundress, odd-jobs boy, and whatever nursery help was required. Six servants seemed to be the minimum to maintain a fair-sized household, whose owners did a great deal of entertaining, much of it lavish, yet did absolutely no physical drudgery or manual labour themselves. Whenever anything needed to be done for the physical well-being of the family members, someone was hired to do it. The six necessary servants were: a cook, a nurse (or governess);

two maids for cleaning, serving, polishing, and helping the cook; a laundress, and a coachman-groom,(or chauffeur when automobiles replaced horses).

Servants went noiselessly about the household doing their work. As Mrs. MacC. said, "You weren't aware of them at all except as you encountered them doing their work or if there was some difficulty." ◊ They did not intrude on the privacy of the family and the family largely ignored them, neither looking at them nor speaking to them except when necessary. But, of course, the servants noticed and heard everything. They were, as several people said, "expected to keep their mouths shut about what they saw and heard, and if they didn't they wouldn't last long. They would be sent packing without a character reference." ◊ One informant remembers that her mother invariably talked to the gardener through the kitchen screen door. As far as she can remember, he never crossed the threshold. ◊ It was partly a matter of privacy. As one lady commented, "It was actually easier to maintain family privacy when you had many servants than when you had only one or two. In the first case, they would have a floor or wing to themselves and you never saw them except going about their work. If there were only one or two, they would get lonely and so you had to spend more time talking to them or even including them in family activities." ◊

Servants and family members called each other names appropriate to their status. Butlers were called by their last names only: "Fletcher," or "Langley," for instance. A cook was "Mrs. Jones" (her own last name). Nurses or nannies were called just that, or "Miss" or "Mrs." Smith. The lower-level servants, maids, and footmen, were called by their given names: Rosa, Paul, or John. The master and mistress of the house were called by their titles, if they had any, and otherwise might be "Madame" or "Sir." Sometimes the employers preferred to be called "Mr. and Mrs. Smith." Even children were expected to observe such proprieties. A woman remembers: "When I was about eleven, my mother decided it was time I grew up. I had always called the butler 'Dick' because that is what my nurse called him, and he had called me by my first name also. The new rules were that I must now call him 'Johnson' and he must call me 'Miss.' I was furious because this put a distance between me and someone who had been my friend." ◊

Family privacy and social distance were maintained by such practices and by separate quarters, closed doors, and social non-recognition, on both sides. Social non-recognition is the failure of the family and guests to see or speak to a servant who enters a room about his or her business, never including him or her in the conversation or changing what is being said. The servant meanwhile, wears a blank, expressionless, but cheerful face, no matter what is said or what happens, appearing to be both deaf and blind. Thus, to an outsider, it would appear that these are non-persons who move about the room serving meals or dusting.

The higher echelons of servants—butlers, cooks, ladies' maids, nannies, stewards, valets—had a different relationship to the employer. They worked in personal service capacities on the family's side of the closed doors, and were privy to many family secrets. Trustworthiness was a necessity in their cases, and it was for this, as well as other reasons we have mentioned that the highly trained, discrete British servant was usually preferred for these positions. Servant and master more easily understood and trusted each other if backgrounds were similar.

The hours were long and indefinite. Servants were free when the work was done. Sometimes, in the summer they might have a couple of hours off in the afternoon between lunch and tea. On the other hand, they were expected to be on duty until the last guest had left and the last dish washed when a party was in progress. The next day would begin for kitchen maids at about 5:30 a.m. and for butlers or cooks about 6:00. An upper class lady reports that she first became class-conscious when a young girl of her own age was helping her into her boots at 2:00 a.m. at the end of a party. It suddenly struck her that this girl would be up at six the next morning to do another fifteen or more hours of hard labour. "I felt ashamed. I didn't need help with my boots." ◊

Their wages were incredibly low. As late as the 1920s, a laundress worked for a dollar a day and a maid of all work received ten to fifteen dollars per month plus room and board and might be expected to work fifteen or more hours a day. Paid vacations were unknown. As a rule, a servant had one afternoon off a week and a full day off every second Sunday. It is not surprising, then, even allowing for inflation over the past sixty years, that most of the people in prominent families could afford to live in this style. To ensure this, employers constantly discussed what they paid their servants, thus establishing a "going rate" which was understood by the whole community. Anyone who offered more faced ostracism. "Good cooks were in great demand because they could make or break your reputation as a hostess. So now and then Mrs. What's-her-name down the street would try to steal your cook by offering her a higher salary. A cousin of my mother's tried to steal my mother's cook that way and the two cousins didn't speak to each other for years. Offering more than the norm was regarded as 'infra dig.'"◊

Having servants to care for the children, clean the house, and perform the physical labours of entertaining gave upper class women a great deal of leisure time. However, it also deprived them of two of the few important roles then available to women: home-making and child care. One ex-member recalled: "When I was first married, and had a cook and servants to do all the work, I didn't know what I was going to do with myself. I thought I'd go mad. But then I got involved in the League work and that saved me."◊

The Junior League, founded in New York in 1901, was in its small way a rebellion on the part of wealthy Victorian and Edwardian women who were kept like ornaments in the homes and on the arms of their men. According to one of its founders the League represented an escape from "the boredom of a life with nothing useful in it." The purpose of the League was to train its members to become good citizens, responsible and well-informed through volunteer philanthropic community service of all sorts, from welfare cases to museums. The first Junior League in Canada was founded in Montreal, with 43 members, in 1913. Although it was active during the war, it was only in the twenties that the League hit its stride and became as important a part of Montreal life as the social round for the top-drawer women; for some, more important.

At the time a girl was ready to "come out" she was also ready to be proposed for membership in the Junior League. No one was supposed to *ask* to join. "Everybody" knew who was of the right age and station to be eligible. Not that social status is anywhere stated as a requirement. But the Junior League was from the beginning so clearly an organization for ladies of status and leisure, that there must have been few women brave enough to hope to get into the League without either. A member would propose the young lady, and she would be considered carefully. Candidates had to be at least seventeen years of age, but not more than thirty. Eleven members constituting a *secret* Committee of Admission held not less than two meetings each year to consider applications for membership and two negative votes were sufficient to disqualify any candidate. If she was invited to join the League, she must then agree to spend at least half a day a week on a charitable project assigned to her. The by-laws of 1920 required that she perform an average of three hours' work per week, or 105 hours between October and June, with records kept. During the summer, of course, she would be away.

A former president of the Junior League states that "the most important factor in deciding whether to invite a girl to join was whether she would be reliable and a conscientious worker." ◊ Girls who were assigned a job in a hospital, for example, and who did not turn up, were dropped. New members spent the first year on probation, during which time they had to attend weekly lectures on the social problems and the facilities available for solving them in Montreal. These courses were usually offered by a trained social worker. At the end of the year, the candidate had to pass an examination. If she failed she might try again; but she would not become a full member of the Junior League until she could pass her course.

Projects to which girls might be assigned could be projects initiated, financed, and manned by League members; or they might be projects supported by other community groups needing volunteer help. In 1921 the League founded the first free dental clinic (with Dr. Cyril Flanagan in charge). It operated the Griffintown Club for children in Point St. Charles. It established a housekeeper service to provide help in homes where the mother was ill and had no one to care for her children. Members worked in the Redpath Museum as trained guides or docents and helped with the children's art classes at the Montreal Museum of Fine Arts. They worked in the canteens, libraries, play therapy classes for children in the hospitals. They worked at the S.P.C.A. Clinic. They worked at the University Settlement, read to the blind, tutored children or any student who was temporarily unable to attend school, and provided services for the ill or disabled. Their activities ranged over the whole city, and their ingenuity in raising money and organizing to meet community needs suggests what a vast store of energy and ability was tapped by the League. That it served an important purpose for individual members is clear from their almost unanimous enthusiasm for the League. As one lady said, "The League saved us. We weren't allowed to work or go to University. My cousin was dying to go to Oxford and had passed the entrance exams while she was in boarding school in England. But her father said that she was to come home and "come out"', and the next year she married. That's the way it was. But the League was very serious in my day and we were told very clearly that as volunteers our responsibility was greater than if we were paid. If you didn't do your volunteer job, you were out. It made you feel useful and your work important." ◇

Not that the Junior League was the first group of women to be active in Montreal charities. The effort to meet community needs had often been initiated by women. The Female Benevolent Society (later known as the Ladies Benevolent Society of Montreal), founded in 1815 by Mrs. Benaiah Gibb, was the first private charitable organization in Canada. The Montreal Local Council of Women, founded in 1893, was an effort to foster coordination and cooperation among all women's organizations. Beginning with thirty groups, it had fifty affiliated societies by 1900. By the 1950s, there were 114, as well as two to three hundred individual members. Over the years hundreds of women's groups organized for specific purposes, such as the Protestant Orphans' Home, the Cottage Industrial Schools, the Montreal Diet Dispensary, the Montreal Day Nursery, the Society for the Protection of Women and Children, the Parks and Playgrounds Association, all worked together under the aegis of the Council of Women. In 1899, after an intensive study of the charity movement and of community needs, the MCW founded the Charity Organization Society, later to become the Family Welfare Association. This was thereafter the organization which collected and distributed funds for Protestant welfare. Responsibility for the Protestant poor traditionally had been assumed by the English elite through its various charitable organizations and churches. The Catholic charities, especially the St. Vincent de Paul society, handled needy cases among their parishioners, and the Baron de Hirsch Institute was responsible for Jewish welfare. In case of mixed marriages, the religion of the head of the household would determine which agency was responsible for the family. This traditional division was by the 1920s formalized in an agreement between the welfare agencies of the three religions.

It is clear, therefore, that the work of the Junior League was a continuation of a historical pattern. What was different about it was that it offered young women systematized training, standards of performance, and organized social pressure to take such activities seriously. It was the kind of charitable work for which they had been prepared in the private schools and by the example of their mothers.

McGill University Campus, circa 1900-1920.

Wealthy fraternity brothers gather to lay the cornerstone of a new Zeta Psi fraternity house, 1924.

After the war, the League bought a summer camp for the children of Griffintown. For women who had never seen poverty, work at the camp and in the homes of the poor was disturbing. "When the children arrived [at camp] the first thing we had to do was to go through their hair and get all the nits out of it; then give them toothbrushes—none of them had toothbrushes. Then we gave them baths. They smelled. Their homes smelled terrible, too. How could they not? They had no running water. Water had to be brought up to the flat from the faucet or well outside. Toilets didn't work, even if there was one in the flat, which there often wasn't. It was very upsetting to go in there and try to do something, but we were brought up to feel that this was the dues we owed to society." ◊

Some women made a full time job of their service; but, as one might expect, by no means all members of the Junior League were so dedicated. Minutes of meetings are full of the complaints of active members about others who did not show up on time for their work, about a dearth of volunteers, about inadequate attendance at meetings—all the usual headaches of any volunteer working organization.

These, then, were the activities in a young lady's life in the early 1920s. Aside from her Junior League or other volunteer community work, she enjoyed completely carefree pleasure, insofar as that is humanly possible. This represented little change from the pre-war pattern except that she had slightly more freedom from supervision and through the Junior League more training for community work than her mother had had. She would by the end of her "coming out" year be engaged to be married, it was devoutly hoped.

Young men of prominent families had traditionally attended McGill University, although a few went to Bishop's University in Lennoxville. And so did our generation of young men in the post-war period.

In the early twenties Sir Arthur Currie was Principal of McGill. His selection reflected both the continuation of the old values and the arrival of some new ideas. Stanley Frost notes that "McGill as a community believed as firmly in 1920 as in 1914 in the cause of British righteousness and the ancient loyalties due to the crown." At the same time, the commander of the Canadian Corps in World War I was much admired by the Montreal English elite. In forging the Canadian fighting forces into a distinct organization with its own commanding officers, cooperating with but not subordinated to British command, he had won the respect of the soldiers. He was instrumental in developing a sense of pride in Canada, both at home and at the front. Inviting a Canadian war hero to be principal of the university confirmed both the old British military connection and the emerging Canadian identity.

Although McGill was originally attended by and governed by members of the English Protestant upper class, by the 1920s it was known as the "Harvard of Canada," attracting students and professors from around the world. The student body came from middle class Montreal backgrounds, from farming families in the English communities surrounding the city, as well as from the rest of Canada and the British Empire. Increasingly, Jewish students began to enter McGill (in 1921 there were three Jewish fraternities on campus) and as immigration shifted from Britain to southern and eastern Europe, people of those backgrounds also enrolled. Some of these lived in the student residences, but most lived at home or in rooms in the "student ghetto" east of the university. Most male students worked their way through school; an opportunity offered by a school year which began the first week in October and was finished in mid-April.

The young men of the upper-class families joined fraternities, thus separating themselves from the rest of the students as they did from the other social strata in Montreal at large. The growth in the number of non-Anglo Protestant, non-elite students attending McGill after the war presented the challenge of new ideas which was not necessarily noticed by the upper class students. The out-of-town brothers of the same backgrounds who resided in the frat houses offered new social contacts, but hardly any new or radical views. When new ideas were encountered by this group they were often dismissed as "rubbish—certain to be ignored by anyone with sense." ◇

Professors, as well as students, wearing their academic gowns, walked to classes along the long line of elms planted by Principal Dawson almost seventy years earlier. The Arts Building had been enlarged since then and an assembly hall, Moyse Hall, added to it. The Roddick Gates had been built, and the road leading from the gates on Sherbrooke Street to the Arts building was paved, so that students' roadsters would not kick up too much dust or get stuck in the mire when it rained. Automobiles were becoming more and more in evidence, though only the wealthier McGill students had them.

170

In those days only four percent of the population attended university. The male student experience at McGill thus continued the privileged elite education pattern we have already discussed. One of these was the license accorded to young men in a male-dominated society to express aggression, get into mischief, be a nuisance. The "hazing" of freshmen, for example (a hangover, we may assume, from fagging or hazing in the private schools), continued through most of the 1920s. John Pratt wrote:

> ... whole classes of freshmen were kidnapped by the sophomore class after completing their day's work, and after their arms were tightly tied behind their backs, they were threaded into a couple of hundred feet of rope, like beads on a necklace.
>
> Hustled onto the lower campus, or up to the site of the Molson Stadium, they were divested of their jackets, and their shoes were thoroughly scrambled in a vast pile with all the laces tied in tight knots to every other lace handy. After their heads had been shaven completely bald, their waistcoats were put on back to front, their faces blackened with shoe polish, and they were rethreaded into the rope for a humiliating parade through the downtown streets of Montreal. The ceremony usually ended with the entire miserable bunch being forced to dance in a circle around a bemused traffic policeman at Peel and St. Catherine.

Memories of McGill graduates include law school dinners which ended with the dean bailing students out of jail at 3:00 a.m.; a Plumbers' Ball (an annual event for engineering students) which destroyed their own drafting tables; a Theatre Night (the annual Red and White Revue was then presented in His Majesty's Theatre on Guy Street) when students dumped a bag of flour from the balcony on the tuxedos and evening dresses of the patrons in the high-priced seats. Some of my informants say that flocks of pigeons were once released at a convocation. If McGill won a football or hockey match, the students customarily staged a victory parade which sometimes involved breaking a few store windows or derailing a street car. Protests against this behaviour and efforts of the university administration to control it seem to have been relatively mild. The community had indulged these young men's high jinks since the Victorian era under the assumption that "boys will be boys" and that they must "sow a few wild oats."

As one graduate of the time observed, "Different groups of students kept to themselves. They rarely knew what those *not* in their group were doing or thinking." ◊ There were several distin-

Redpath Library of McGill University, 1927.
Female students studied on the right side of the
dividing shelves; males on the left.

guishable groups: the fraternity men, the sports crowd, and the political group. The "politicals" belonged to the Student Christian Movement, or worked on the *McGill Daily*, or were active in the Debating Society. There were also the various ethnic clubs. There were the students who spent most of their time in music or drama, and put on the Red and White Revue. Exceptional people might belong to more than one of these groups, or at the other end of the scale, to none except their university classes. The great majority of the students at McGill, as elsewhere, were simply working toward a degree and enjoyed a social life on campus among like-minded fellows in medicine, engineering, architecture, or law.

The McGill campus of 1920s was a very lively place, full of ferment and new ideas. This was partly because of the returning veterans, who were much more serious and mature than the average student. Students and young faculty members drew their inspiration from ideas that were abroad outside the university. Revulsion against the horrors of World War I, and the failure of traditional beliefs which it represented, opened the door to rejection of the ruling group, which was blamed for the war. Socialism of various hues was believed to offer an alternative to the injustice and militarism of the capitalist system. The Student Christian Movement was an international student movement promoting peace, social justice, and equal opportunity. According to one ex-member of the McGill chapter, the SCM "sensitized many students to the inequities and injustices within Canadian society and between nations." ◊ The Labour Club offered more political and less religious discussions along the same lines. Fabian socialism and its application to Canada was being discussed by Frank R. Scott, Brooke Claxton, V.C. Wansborough, Jacques Bieler, and later, Eugene Forsey and King Gordon. Scott, A.J.M. Smith, A.M. Klein, and Leon Edel were espousing modernism in poetry and poking fun at Montreal's establishment and its sacred cows in the literary supplement of *The McGill Daily*. In short, the SCM and the other student groups just mentioned were questioning the legitimacy of the social elite and its way of life. Speaking of those days, a 1920s activist asked, "Have you ever noticed how many of the people who were in the SCM in the 1920s were important in the development of the CCF later?" ◊ When this observation was passed on to a person with upper class connections who had also been at McGill at the time, she commented, "Oh, really? I'm quite surprised to hear they were doing anything of importance. They seemed at the time to be such dim lights, taking themselves so seriously. No sense of humour at all." ◇

Their fathers on McGill's Board of Governors were somewhat more wary. According to one report, the Labour Club in 1926 put up notices on the three university announcement boards, to the effect that the socialist Scott Nearing was to speak to the McGill Labour Club. The governors ordered the notices removed. So Phil Matthams took the notice down and in its place put up another typewritten notice which said, in effect, "The three notices which appeared on the McGill notice boards announcing that Mr. Scott Nearing would speak on the 27th of April, 1926 to the Labour Club at such and such an address have been removed by order of the Board of Governors." ◇ Although this event went unnoticed among the fraternity students, almost all of them remember another action of the same Phil Matthams. He refused to stand up when "God Save the King" was played. A man who was a fraternity boy at the time says, "That was really something that nobody could understand. We wondered whether he did it for notoriety or what. We thought he had gone too far for a loyal Canadian. Some of us took him up behind the stadium and shaved his hair off." ◇

Thus armed with a firm sense of the irrelevancy of social action, the fraternity crowd continued to enjoy its student days. Among fraternities, there were rich ones and not so rich ones. Mr. R., a student in the 1920s, explained that at that time there was a real reason for fraternities because there were no residences; and outside of the theological colleges, "where was the out-of-towner going to stay other than a boarding house? At least in a fraternity, if he could afford it, he had a room. There was a caretaking couple, the boarders were fed three meals a day and lunch was the big event. The town members would come in for lunch. It was our club." ◇

Fraternities tended to have reputations for particular activities and therefore to choose members who could support their specialties. "Our particular fraternity was known as a sports frat. We had as many as fifteen members on one team or another. New members were told by the senior members of the fraternities that part of your time in university was to contribute to the university. You were supposed to get involved in something, whether the *Daily*, a team, or whatever you had interest or talent for. Of course, we tended to favour athletes as members, but not entirely." ◇

174

Girls, the few who belonged to the socially prominent families and attended classes at McGill, were much involved in fraternity life, as were many girls who were not at McGill. "My life at McGill was just nothing but a series of parties. I don't think I even read a newspaper in those days. I was just so busy going out, going to football games, to tea dances. We really had a glorious time. It was right at the peak of fraternity life. The Alpha Delts, the Zetes had houses especially built for them. The others which didn't have such wealthy alumni just took over the old houses along University Street. Football was important and there were teas in all the fraternities after games. Everybody came down from the game in Molson Stadium and streamed into the fraternity houses." ◊

And so these young men and women, themselves only as old as their century, carried out the expectations of their aristocratic rearing. Privileged, but with a sense of *noblesse oblige*, financially secure, surrounded by close friends and relatives of like mind, they enjoyed it all and naturally believed that it would be hard to improve on things as they were. The *status quo* was in their sacred trust, and they intended to pass it on as they had received it.

CHAPTER 8

Entering the Business World

Having finished McGill, the young men of prominent families entering the business world in the middle or late 1920s would find the Bank of Montreal and the Canadian Pacific Railway still cornerstones of the wealth and power of English Montrealers. Few of them could have guessed that these bulwarks were being threatened by developments elsewhere.

If a young man wanted to start a new business, the procedure had not changed. The former president of a well-known Montreal construction company described the steps by which his own firm was started: first, Mr. C. made a bid on a construction job and won; second, he hired enough workers to do the job; third, he went to the Bank of Montreal, whose general manager was a relative of Mr. C.'s, and got a loan of $25,000. It was so simple in this case because Mr. C. had a good reputation in Montreal. "That's crucial. The business community was small and everybody was likely to know each other. In general, to start a business people try to get backing from friends—it is easier than to get backing from the banks. Trust is tremendously important either for starting a new business or negotiating a merger. Your reputation in the community as reliable, competent, able, and honest pretty well determines whether you will get a chance to succeed." ◊

St. James Street was still the financial capital of Canada; but the manner of maintaining that financial control had changed. The McGill graduate entering the business world often found that trying to start a new enterprise had become much more difficult than it had been for his father. The law, accounting, or investment brokerage firms now opened the way to make his fortune. By the 1920s the wealth and power of the Montreal group already had passed from the old entrepreneurs who built factories, stores, and railways to their sons, the financiers, who bought and sold established companies like commodities. Between 1900 and 1908 there were eight mergers, involving fifty-seven firms. During the peak years, 1909 to 1912, fifty-eight industrial mergers involving 275 individual firms occurred in Canada. Many of the important ones were engineered from Montreal: Stelco, for example, the CPR's consolidation of the Montreal Rolling Mills, the Canada Screw Company, the Hamilton Iron and Steel Company, Pillow-Hersey, the Hodgson Iron and Tube Works, Dominion Wire, and others. In the first decade of the century, iron and steel and their manufactures became the most important industry in Canada. Stelco was a "spin-off" industry of the railways and was one of the first firms to be organized and run, not by manufacturers, but by financial interests. Its board of directors included William Molson, Peter Randolph, Andrew Allan, and Sir Edward Clouston of the Bank of Montreal. Another example is the Dominion Textile Company, a merger of four textile companies, put together by Sir Herbert Holt and a syndicate of sixteen men. Holt's merger of three other companies into the Montreal Light, Heat and Power Company was called the "Octopus" because it managed to buy out all its rivals except the Shawinigan Water and Power company.

Mergers require specialized financial services. In a typical case, an accounting firm will consider and advise the company wishing to take over (or merge with) other firms about the economic prospects, the tax results, the values of the combined assets, and the validity of the securities. The accountants provide a plan, a statement of the financial prospects of the combined companies. When this has been done, if the parent company wishes to proceed, the lawyers will turn the package of companies into a legally viable structure and draw up the necessary agreements to be signed by all parties. The shares of the new company are turned over to an investment firm or underwriter, which agrees to market the shares. When a city can provide this kind of sophistocated infra-structure, then all major firms must move there in order to have the advantage of such services. The principal financial institutions which arose after 1900 or were already in place by that time in Montreal were the trust companies, accounting, investment, and legal firms, and the Stock Exchange. The financial institutions and the mergers they underwrote were extremely profitable, turning a few men into multi-millionaires, and giving them increasingly awesome power over the economic life of the country. There were some men in the twenties who were as rich and powerful or more so than the turn-of-the-century magnates: Sir Herbert Holt, J.W. McConnell, I.W. Killam, the Websters, for example.

Trust companies arose about the turn of the century as adjuncts and partners of the chartered banks. They served the fiduciary functions of managing funds on behalf of a third person. They were usually established by banks, and worked very closely with them, supporting and sometimes performing activities, such as real estate transactions and inheritances which would be legally difficult for banks to do. The Bank of Montreal has such a relationship with the Royal Trust. The Royal Trust was founded in 1892 and nine of the members of its first board of directors were also members of the Bank of Montreal board. A similar relationship existed between the Royal Bank and the Montreal Trust.

The Montreal Stock Exchange, begun in 1832, was by the late 1920s the largest on the continent, outside New York City, in value of the securities listed. A man whose father was a member of the Exchange, and who himself later obtained a seat, describes it as "so select a club that unless you had connections you couldn't get in. It had only sixty members. You didn't need qualifications—just connections." ◊ In the early days the activities of the exchange and the bucket shops and other informal brokerage arrangements that were associated with it were as questionable, by current standards, as some early business practices and for the same reasons—greed, ingenuity, and a lack of rules. Tom Naylor, business historian, says that "It was a standard technique of the brokerage firms of the day when manipulating bank stock to get together and sell large amounts of a particular stock which they did not own in the expectation that the effect would be to depress its value, at which point the brokers would buy cheap and fill the sale orders they had already contracted to fulfill." In addition, according to the *Monetary Times*, brokers often publicized fraudulent quotations so that they could make the stock go up or down, and collaborated with promoters in manipulating the price of watered stock and disposing of it.

By the 1920s, however, the Montreal Stock Exchange was trying to cut down the competition from such unscrupulous brokers and by various internal regulations to eliminate the kind of trading which was likely to lose the confidence of the public. Requirements were established for being listed on the Exchange, most of which concerned the reliability of the company, its assets, audits, etc. It was not until 1930, however, that the Quebec Security Frauds Prevention Act required the registration of all brokers doing business, and required two audits a year of brokerage accounts, one of them on a date not known in advance. The enforcement of these provisions was left in the hands of the Governing Committee of the Stock Exchange. Ironically, its effort to become respectable contributed to the decline of the Montreal Exchange and the rise of the Toronto Exchange. At the same time that Montreal was moving toward conservative brokerage practices, gold mining stocks, many of them "penny mines" of unknown value, were being listed on the regular exchange in Toronto. Speculative money flowed into the unrestricted Toronto market. As an investment broker explained, "The stock market by definition is a place where people gather to trade with each other and, particularly in the days before World War II when telephone and telegraph communications were nothing like as good as they are now, people who wanted to trade in mining stocks had to be where the trading in mines was. This began the move to Toronto." ◊ In the 1930s even though most nations had abandoned the gold standard, gold mining stocks remained active and strong. The Toronto market grew; the Montreal market shrank.

Given these changes in the nature of business opportunities, the McGill graduate of the 1920s was likely to go into law, accounting, or investments. That was where the action was. He would go into the family firm as a matter of course, or be helped by his father or other family connections to get a position in another firm. This was not new. In his study of two generations of Canadian industrialists and businessmen, T.W. Acheson found that in 1910 three-quarters of this elite were sons of leading professionals and businessmen. In the Montreal and Ottawa areas, at the same period, "a third of the leading industrialists began their careers in firms belonging to close relatives." This proportion was likely to have been even higher by 1920, since moving up in the world was becoming more difficult as control at the top narrowed to fewer men with greater power.

Young men, particularly in the upper social echelons, were usually advised and assisted by their fathers in choosing a career. A young man did what his father thought best, and what was best was work in which Father had the power to help him succeed. Men who entered the legal profession in this time recall a typical reason: "My father always told me that wealthy and powerful men were lawyers," ◇ or "I went into law because my father was a lawyer and he could help me." ◇ Another man who had been unable or unwilling to get through law school remembers his father saying: "If you will just get through at no matter what level, you'll be set for life. A job in my law firm is waiting for you." ◇

Family influence was exerted to find positions for young people at all social and economic levels. The difference was only in the amount of influence the father or relative could exert. One of the wealthiest and most powerful Scots in Montreal wrote a letter on behalf of his son to a Montreal manufacturing concern in 1898:

> I am obliged by your letter of 10th instant offering to take my son ... into service of your company with the view to his qualifying himself to assume a trusted position therein and on condition of his acquiring a portion of the capital stock so as to interest him in the process of the concern and to cause him to regard it as a permanent occupation.
>
> I approve the conditions, and on his behalf accept the terms. The payment of $20,000 for 40,000 of the common stocks at $0.50 to be placed in his name, will be at your disposal when called for. ◇

Other young men, by contrast, might find the absence of family support a hindrance to beginning their careers. A man whose father died when the son was a boy and whose family was not wealthy said that he had "to beg on bended knee until I found somebody to take me on as a student in his firm." ◇ His straitened circumstances were a serious disqualification, since he would be expected to work without pay in the law firm during his three years in the McGill law school. To be taken on as a "student" by a law firm was not only required by McGill; it also was a foot in the door when the student had finished his degree. This experience varied considerably with the man to whom the young man was articled. For one it was a waste of time, because the senior partner to whom he was assigned "was only interested in politics and had no time for me." ◇ For another, "It was a wonderful training and Mr. P. was my mentor and friend for life." ◇ Whatever that experience, the student in a law firm, an accounting firm, or investment firm, and even the young man being groomed to "assume a trusted position," had to serve his time being "a dog's body," just doing what nobody else wanted to do, the dirty work. It was part of the system, like being a new boy at boarding school. Everyone had to prove that he could accept authority and be willing to spend some time working and earning his way up. He had to be able to take orders before he was ready to give them.

Once student days were over and the degree earned, it was time to get a paying job. If a job was not waiting in his father's firm, the next-best bet was the firm where the young man had been a student or apprentice. One of Montreal's most prominent lawyers, descended from one of the oldest families, got his first job this way at a salary of $50 per month, as did two fellow students at the same firm. "Years later, the three of us who had gone to Selwyn House together, then to Bishop's College School, to the Royal Military College, and to McGill Law School and who had been students in the firm at the same time took it over. We became the senior partners." ◊

A man who chose a career with one of the largest life insurance companies in North America started as an investment clerk in 1927 and rose to be vice-president in charge of investments. Early in his career he profited by the network of financiers who were dominant by the 1920s. He was sent by his company to investigate conditions in countries where Sun Life was considering investing money, and in the process he came to know top bankers and investment counsellors in London, New York, Johannesburg, and other financial centres. Through these connections he developed ancillary interests and work. Sun Life owned a company in Cork which distributed electricity, and operated street cars and buses. He was on the board of that company for about thirty years and was president for eight years. He was on the board of a construction company which was building a hotel financed by Sun Life, and this led to a position on the Board of Sheraton Canada as the Canadian representative. "All the rest of the directors were American. The president of Sheraton would call me frequently on all sorts of questions relating to Canada. I found it a very interesting association." ◊

The young man who had a job felt fortunate, especially if he had no affluent father to ensure his future. However, his income was likely to be low for many years. Most men interviewed state with some wonderment that their beginning salaries were anywhere from $50 to $125 per month and that they might stay there for years. Low salaries for white collar workers, like low wages for manual labourers, were one of the personnel policies of Montreal businessmen. As one elderly man, a retired executive of a very large, international firm, commented, "People in those days, particularly people like Herbert Holt, seemed never to be able to learn that they ought to pay people a living wage. It was always their idea to get labour, like materials, at the cheapest possible price." ◊

Herbert Holt's attitude toward wages has a venerable history. George Simpson's biographer reports that when Simpson came out from Scotland to be governor of the Hudson's Bay Company in 1820, one of his first acts was to cut wages. He believed that paying high wages made men slothful and insolent, and he cut the already-low wages of the ordinary employee by fifty percent. And quite recently a taxi driver in Montreal echoed a belief that the same point of view is still operative when he commented, in picking up a fare from an imposing house in upper Westmount, "The people in that house have more money than they can spend, but they think money would corrupt me." ◊

In an era when employees were often ill-educated, when the paternal authority of the employer was unquestioned, employees often were treated like wayward children who must be protected from their own weaknesses. A retired officer of Sun Life asserts that "T.B. Macaulay, the President, paid himself $100,000 a year, but he didn't feel he needed to pay anyone else, not even the vice-presidents. He really thought he was the company. Everybody felt that they were underpaid and morale was not good." ◊

Although everything cost less in those days, nobody felt that it was easy to live on such incomes. Some men had to live with their parents until they could earn more. Others had to postpone marriage; it was not unusual for a young man to wait seven to ten years before he could afford to start a family.

Some financial institutions wrote into the contracts of white-collar workers that they could not marry until their salaries reached $125 a month. The idea, according to men to whom this happened, was that a man who married and began to take on family responsibilities might be more tempted than a single man to abscond with funds! A man who was a clerk in a railway office in the 1920s bought furniture at sales from time to time while he and his prospective bride waited seven years to have enough income to marry. They laugh now about their dismay on discovering that "the sofa we had bought was too big for the living room of any house or apartment we could afford to rent. We finally rented a place for $25 per month, but it took so much of our wages that we managed to pay it only by saving on everything else and doing without a lot of things. But we managed." ◇

The residue of this kind of power over the lives of others can still be seen in people, now long retired, who were in their first jobs during the 1920s. Although people who achieved high office in their companies, such as the Sun Life vice-president quoted above, are fairly outspoken, people in less powerful positions remain nervous about discussing even well-known facts about their former place of employment. One ex-employee of Sir Herbert Holt's Montreal Light, Heat, and Power Company said that because that firm required of all business office employees that they take an oath of secrecy every year, and jobs were hard to get, it is still hard to talk about the place. ◇

A man who had discussed the old restrictions on employee marriage said anxiously at the end of the interview, "I certainly hope you are not going to use my name. I wouldn't want to lose my pension." ◇ The same uneasiness seemed to be present in the statement of a woman who once had been the executive secretary of an important Montreal institution. Her boss is long dead and she is in her eighties, yet she asserted that ex-employees have a continuing obligation to be loyal to the organization for which they have worked, and to say nothing about their working experience without the permission of the current head of the organization—a man she doesn't know, personally. ◇ Of course, young men from wealthy families usually had an additional stipend from their fathers and did not have to live on such salaries.

If a young man was a member of a prominent family or slated for other reasons for high position, he would now be expected to join one of the prestigious clubs as part of his work. A senior partner of a large law firm said to a junior partner, "It would be a good idea if you would join the Mount Royal Club. I already belong to the St. James Club and the other senior partner is not up to it, since he is getting along in years, so its your turn to do this." ◇ Another businessman recalls that at the turn of the century "The Royal Montreal Curling Club was the most prestigious club for men in the city. You had to belong to it if you were in business." ◇ And even in 1949 a rising young executive with the CPR was told by his superior, "You'd better join the Curling Club." ◇ This last association is visible on the walls of the Curling Club, where pictures of past presidents show a predominance of Canadian Pacific officers, with Sun Life officials a close second.

Once in the club, the neophyte faced the usual hurdles to becoming acceptable. Young, too ambitious, or too eager members were soon put in their places. One of the traditions of the Mount Royal Club on which youngsters occasionally tripped themselves up was that certain men sat at certain tables. In particular, there was a central table where the most important business leaders in the city sat at lunch. Woe betide any upstart who tried to sit there! A member of the club entitled to sit at this table told of a young newcomer who was seated there by the steward on a day when the club was particularly crowded. He was ignored after introductions all around, but finally everyone at the table had finished lunch except the newcomer and the head of a very large Montreal company. Whereupon the young man said, "I've been admiring your suit. Could you tell me who your tailor is? I'd like one exactly like it." Clearly the older man did not like the question, but he answered affably, "Well, I'll tell you. I happened to be in Chicago between trains, and having a few hours to kill and needing a new suit, I walked over to Sears Roebuck, went into the basement, and that's where I found this suit." ◊

Having survived such humiliation and learned the unwritten club rules, the young man would be expected through his social contacts with other club members to build his firm's and his own reputation for competence, dependability, and good-fellowship. Future business deals might well depend on his success in that task. As a member of the Mount Royal Club said, "It is where trust is built up. Men learn in clubs who is reliable and who isn't." ◊

There were many signs in the 1920s that the wealth and power of the Montreal financial interests were past the zenith. Political and economic enemies were coalescing to reduce their power and this was evident in the changed relationship of the Montreal group to the Dominion government. In the Confederation era, as we have seen, the Montreal business magnates dominated Canada politically as well as economically. During the 1880s, the St. Lawrence region, of which Montreal was the heart, had eighteen members of the elite who held political office in the Dominion government as compared to twelve from the Maritimes and eight from the Lake Peninsula (Toronto) area. Equally important, however, was the indirect power exerted by rich Montrealers at a time when patronage and bribery were the accepted practice in politics. As Sir John Willison said of the

Macdonald government, "It carried out a great constructive Canadian policy by bad political methods and gross corruption in the constituencies." The fifteen-year reign of the Liberal party after its victory at the polls in 1896 brought about a decline in the Montreal Tories' influence. They were stigmatized by the scandals of the defeated Macdonald government, while the patronage regarded by everyone, including Laurier, as the spoils of victory, went to Liberal supporters—primarily, in Quebec, to French Canadians.

The leader of the opposition, Robert Borden, was trying in 1908 to 1910 to rebuild the Tory party, to give it a new image, and to defeat Laurier. Montreal businesses, such as the CPR and the Montreal Star, still contributed almost all the Conservative Party funds ($300,000 in 1904, for example). At the same time, the hue and cry about the monopolistic position, the wealth and the corruption of the Montreal barons had rendered their support embarrassing (however necessary) to the politicians. In an effort to free himself from this dependence, Borden courted "progressive" businessmen like Sir Herbert Ames of Montreal and Joseph Flavelle, and those provincial premiers who were Conservatives.

Borden won the 1911 election. During World War I, he formed the Union Government, in which elections were set aside for the duration of the War and Liberals were invited to form a coalition. The Union Government, however, fell apart shortly after the war, partly because the introduction of conscription in late 1917 outraged the French Canadians and threw them solidly into the Liberal camp. There they remained, nationally, for many years.

Mackenzie King, trying to reconstitute the Liberal Party after the Union experiment had seriously weakened it, faced a delicate situation. He depended on the Liberal stronghold of Quebec for political success. The problem of assuring the French voters that the Liberals offered them an effective voice was complicated by dissensions among the Quebec Liberals themselves. The right wing was led by the premier, Sir Lomer Gouin, a director of the Bank of Montreal who was regarded as a representative of St. James Street. Ernest Lapointe was leader of the moderate, anti-big-business Liberals and became King's right hand man on Quebec issues. Meanwhile, the Progressive Party, a new militant farmers' party, had been organized specifically to fight for the western farmers' interests against eastern power—that is, against "St. James Street"—and had done surprisingly well.

King's first cabinet in 1921 included two members of the right wing: Gouin and Raoul Dandurand, the latter a director of the Montreal Trust. Five other Quebec representatives were of the moderate wing of the Liberal party. King wrote in his diary after the days of pressure which achieved this result, "A very strenuous day, but felt I had fought a good fight. Stood my ground firm against handing over Canada's future to the financial magnates of Montreal."

The English-speaking Montreal business community, although largely Conservative, acquired some influence over the Canadian government through French Liberals, whom they kept informed of their interests by electing them to boards of English Montreal firms. It was a far cry from the days when George Stephen had direct access to his good friend John A. Macdonald and M.H. Gault had a seat in Parliament.

A lawyer, member of the elite, whose practice involved provincial politics stated "What political power the English had was as a result of tradition: the practice of alternating mayors; the reserving of the post of provincial finance minister for an Anglophone. Even seats in the national assembly, judgeships and seats on the Bar were distributed with a quota for the English." ◊ These traditions were weakening after 1920. That of rotation of mayors had already been lost in Montreal after the election of Martin. W.S. Johnson, a young lawyer interested in city politics, wrote in March, 1926: "The difficulty has been of late years that Médéric Martin, by raising the 'race cry' has made it practically impossible to have an English mayor. It is childish, small-minded, narrow and mean of those who would thus shut the English minority out from the natural ambition to have an English mayor once every few years."

This did not mean the group had become politically impotent. As an ex-president of the Montreal Board of Trade pointed out, "Businessmen always could and did work through the Montreal Board of Trade, which was then almost entirely Anglo, and when they sent a delegation to the City Council or the mayor, they were listened to." ◊ As for the federal government, he pointed out that businesses as a rule gave sixty percent of their political contribution to the party in power in Ottawa; forty per cent to the Opposition, and in every government there is at least one cabinet minister chosen because he represents the interests of business. "The government depends as much on business as business does on government. They really can't afford to ignore

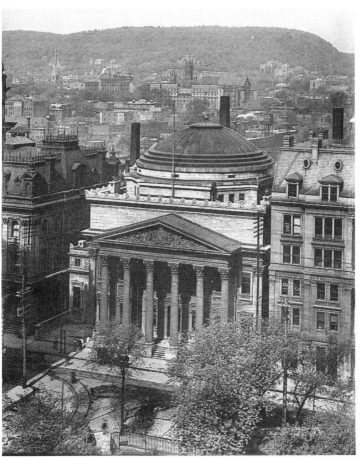

Bank of Montreal head office from 1847 to 1960.

us."◇ In addition, personal connections between members of the political and the financial elites were also exploited for special interests.

The waning power of the old Anglo-Montreal families could be seen in what was happening to the two pillars of their strength: the Bank of Montreal and the Canadian Pacific Railway. The loss of power in Ottawa of Montreal big business interests was partly due to nation-wide opposition and resentment against the policies and power of these two companies.

Farmers claimed that the Bank of Montreal was unwilling to provide the loans they needed on terms they could afford. Young aspiring industrialists complained that the bank's lending policies were so strict as to discourage new business ventures. Both believed that investment money needed in Canada was being loaned abroad. As Canada's leading bank for so many years, the bank was blamed for many economic ills; as we have seen, national coalitions had been formed to curb its power. Indeed, there is evidence that with the years the Bank of Montreal had become even more conservative in its lending policies and less concerned with service to the small businessman, farmer or other customers than in the past.

Repeatedly the presidents of the Bank of Montreal excused their conservative lending policies to stockholders. Such policies, they said, were due to the dependence of the Dominion government on the bank as its agent and chief source of financial aid. The needs of the government for large sums periodically meant that the bank had to maintain strong liquid reserves. To do this it had to restrict its domestic commercial business, particularly to western farmers, who needed large seasonal loans but could not always guarantee repayment on demand. On the other hand, call loans in the New York money market could be (and were) called in on short notice by the bank, without disturbing the Canadian financial and monetary situation. Outside the annual stockholders' meetings, these explanations seem to have fallen on deaf ears.

Illustrating lost opportunities caused by conservative lending policies is the story of E.P. Taylor, who, as a young man just starting out, proposed to organize a fleet of taxis equipped with meters—a new invention. His first business, the Yellow Bus Line in Ottawa, consisting of two buses driven by Taylor and a friend, had just been sold. On the strength of this beginning, he approached J.K.L. Ross in Montreal for backing of the new enterprise. Ross was not impressed and said, "Come back when you have more of a track record." Although not on the board of the Bank of Montreal, Ross was a director of the CPR and was famous for giving away millions of his own money for philanthropy and high living. However, when it came to business deals, it appears that he was as cautious as the rest of his neighbours. Taylor became one of Canada's richest men without Montreal's financial assistance.

In the first quarter of the twentieth century, banks, like most other enterprises in Canada were involved in mergers and takeovers, leading to an even greater concentration of wealth in a few hands. In 1875 there were 36 banks in Canada, of which the Bank of Montreal was clearly the largest with 18 percent of the total assets. By 1927, there were only 10, and the financial resources of the Bank of Montreal represented 26 percent of the total bank assets in the country. The Royal Bank was in about the same position; and the Bank of Commerce assets accounted for 17 percent. These three banks accounted for about 70 percent of all bank resources.

As these figures show, the Royal Bank was steadily overtaking the Bank of Montreal in assets and activity. It was founded in Halifax in 1902 and moved its head office to Montreal in 1905. After Herbert Holt became president of the Royal Bank in 1908 it grew rapidly by taking over other banks and financial institutions. It had amalgamated by 1918 with twelve other banks. By 1925 the total had reached sixteen. By 1919 the Royal Bank had grown from 25 branches in 1894 to 662, including 74 international branches in France, Argentina, Cuba, Brazil, Russia, the West Indies, the U.S. and England. In 1927 it had 900 branches. It was paying a 12 percent dividend. Its board of directors, unlike that of the Bank of Montreal, came from across Canada. In that year, only six of twenty-four directors, including the president and two vice-presidents, were residents of Montreal. These were Sir Herbert Holt, C.E. Neill, Hugh Paton, A.J. Brown, G.H. Duggan, and Robert Adair. At the Bank of Montreal, on the other hand, fifteen of the eighteen members of the Board were Montreal residents. The Royal Bank had the benefit of diverse points of view and experience. It was less likely that fresh ideas or initiative would appear at a board meeting made up almost entirely of Old Family Square Milers.

The Royal Bank had inaugurated a more aggressive as well as a more liberal stance. It "did an unheard of thing and organized

Canadian Pacific Railway's Windsor Station and head office, in the 1920s.

an advertising department of its own," at a time when "it was considered beneath the dignity of a bank to advertise, except in the most general terms." The ad department not only bought space in newspapers and periodicals, and produced Royal Bank calendars and posters; it also produced a booklet for distribution to potential immigrants entitled *Canada - The Land of Opportunity*. The booklet's purpose, according to C.E. Bourne, the bank's first advertising manager, was "to make friends with him (the immigrant) before he lands in Canada, to associate in his mind this Bank with Canada, so that when he does arrive, he will instinctively come to us to conduct his banking business."

School saving plans, in which the Royal Bank cooperated with schools in teaching children how to save and how to deposit their money were introduced. A *Monthly Letter* reviewing trade and business conditions in Canada and in other countries where the Royal operated first appeared in April, 1920 and attracted considerable attention. Equally important was the bank's customer relations, which according to one lady, were excellent. She had heard many people in different towns and cities in those days remark that they liked to deal with The Royal Bank because of the courteous treatment accorded them by the Staff.

The Bank of Montreal was not quick to meet this challenge to its old, entrenched business style. A man who was involved in public relations with the Bank of Montreal during this period recalls that although the Bank had been willing to take risks in the 1880s in building the CPR, by the 1920s it was "smug and complacent." He reports that the Royal Bank officers are said to have remarked that "the best business agents we have are in the head office of the Bank of Montreal," because people finding no support for or interest in their ventures at the Bank of Montreal, came to the Royal Bank where lending policies were more open and liberal. This employee, running across these complaints in the course of his duties, tried to call the competitive rise of the Royal Bank to the attention of the Bank of Montreal officials. "But they were blind. Their reaction to unpleasant problems was to refuse to deal with them, to put them in a drawer and hope they would go away. They regarded people in the Royal Bank as upstarts, not worth worrying about. They would say to me, 'I'm sure there is something in what you say,' but their manner belied any such possibility." ◊

By 1926, belatedly, the president of the Bank of Montreal, Sir Vincent Meredith, and its general manager, Sir Frederick

Williams-Taylor, began to try to change that bank's public image. A series of booklets including weekly crop reports, a business summary, discussion of scientific farming methods, and a description of Canada intended to lure both immigrants and investors, were published. Williams-Taylor explained to shareholders that the publications were intended to create goodwill and to demonstrate that "the Bank is keenly interested in the public welfare and in furthering the general interests of this country."

The Canadian Pacific Railway, the other Montreal enterprise basic to the dominance of the Anglo-Protestant elite, prospered during the years from 1900 to 1914. The men at the helm became millionaires many times over, and stockholders made good returns on their investment. The railway's net earnings rose year by year, growing from $13,005,000 in 1901 to a pre-war high of $46,246,000 in 1913. The company began to exploit the mineral resources included in its land grants, to form or get control of mining subsidiaries, ocean shipping companies, telegraph facilities, rolling stock and steel factories. But by the end of World War I the Canadian Pacific was struggling to maintain its position. As it had grown, its enemies had also multiplied and with the Conservatives out of power during most of the pre-war period, the government was no longer on the side of the railway. The Western critics of the CPR monopoly, Liberals, Toronto entrepreneurs, small manufacturers, all envied and resented the profits pouring into Eastern railway coffers. Meanwhile, the principal competing lines, the Grand Trunk, the Grand Trunk Pacific, and the Canadian Northern (as well as numbers of small lines scattered about the country, some publicly, and some privately owned) were about to go bankrupt. Government efforts to control railway fares and rates at a time of rapid inflation, though aimed at the CPR, succeeded only in driving the weaker lines out of business.

Borden appointed a railway commission in 1916 to investigate the bankrupt rail lines, and to make proposals as to what should be done with them. Shaughnessy, then president of the CPR, proposed to the commission that all the lines be unified under the management of the Canadian Pacific. Indicative of the political motive behind the commission was its response to the Shaughnessy plan. They rejected it strongly on the grounds that the Canadian people had already spent or guaranteed hundreds of millions of dollars, "largely with the object of breaking a private monopoly and they would never consent to the re-establishment of a still greater monopoly, even if the Government were a partner in the concern."

The commission recommended that the government should take over the Grand Trunk and the Canadian Northern railways and, with the National Transcontinental and the Intercolonial which the government already owned, should reorganize them into a nationalized trans-continental railway in competition with the CPR. The Canadian National Railways, organized by 1922, with Sir Henry Thornton, an Anglo-American, imported from London as president, were to be a "commercial enterprise" independent of political influence. However, since the CNR was from its inception totally dependent on the government for financing and often was unable to pay its own expenses, it could hardly be either commercial or independent. Never having to make a profit, to be accountable to shareholders or to raise its own capital, the CNR represented competition which the business community of Montreal regarded as grossly unfair. Newman believes that when the Bank of Commerce in Toronto became a major financial agent in the formation of the Canadian National Railways, the first business exodus from Montreal occurred.

Meanwhile, in the Rouyn-Noranda district of northern Quebec, high grade gold ore deposits had been discovered. A senior partner in a prominent Montreal law firm, who helped organize several mining companies in the course of his career, asserts that the CPR board of directors refused to build a rail line to connect Montreal with Noranda; the money was therefore sought elsewhere, and the line to the newly discovered gold mines was connected to Toronto, even though the mines were located in Quebec. "The thinking of the directors of the CPR permeated the whole business community. Gold mining was just a speculation they didn't want to get involved in. So, the Toronto Exchange took over the Standard Mining Exchange. They had a big market. Our boys got smaller and smaller. And so, bit by bit, beginning in the thirties, Toronto grew up. And the directors of the CPR, I think, can be charged with the fuse that sparked that growth. We're finished now." ◊

The railway of which this informant speaks was the Nippissing Central line of the Temiscaming and Northern Ontario Railway, owned by the province of Ontario. In fact, the story of Rouyn-Noranda and the opening up of the rich mine fields of northwestern Quebec affords an interesting illustration of Toronto's rising ability to compete with Montreal as a commercial and financial centre, with American financial assistance. It is also the story of faltering leadership by the Montreal group.

193

The Canadian Pacific staff and management, unlike the board, perhaps were quite aware of the significance of the mineral and gold strikes in the Rouyn-Noranda district. As early as May 14, 1923 F.L. Wanklyn, the general executive assistant, urged Premier Taschereau to build both a road and a bridge connecting with the CPR terminus at Angliers and an extension of the CPR line from the Des Quinze River to Rouyn. This, he argued, was in the interest of Montreal and the province of Quebec: that if these connecting transportation links were not built, the mining traffic would go to Toronto and Ontario. Wanklyn made the same representations to J.E. Perrault, minister of Colonization, Mines and Fisheries in Quebec. Throughout 1923, G.G. Ommanney, CPR's development engineer, and D. Hillman, the district engineer, reported that the Rouyn area was destined to become a rich mining area. Their reports were duly reported and apparently appreciated by Wanklyn. In September, the news of the proposal of the T&NO (Temiscaming and Northern Ontario railway) to run a line into the new gold fields was reported in the *Financial Times*. Wanklyn wrote Taschereau in alarm asking whether the province proposed to subsidize this railroad, and again pointed out that such a plan "would very adversely affect our joint interests in the development of traffic on the Interprovincial and James Bay Railway [a CPR line] and in our effort to retain the business arising in the new mining districts for the benefit of this Province." Both in this letter and in a subsequent meeting with Taschereau, Wanklyn asked formally whether the provincial government would assist, i.e. subsidize, the extension of the I&JB from Angliers to the new mining districts. Taschereau seems to have been encouraging but non-committal.

In Oct. 1924, to the dismay of CPR officers, the Montreal Board of Trade's transportation bureau reported that their investigation of the Rouyn mine claims led them to oppose a railway extension. Wanklyn wrote to Grant Hall, CPR vice-president,

> This, of course, would to some extent influence the Provincial Cabinet in considering any application for substantial cash subsidy to encourage the construction of this railway extension, and I think it might be worthwhile to find out exactly what influences in the Board of Trade is [*sic*] taking the view expressed in the newspaper article and their reasons for doing so.

Approaches were made, but the Board of Trade proved adamant, reportedly convinced that the district of Rouyn was "not sufficiently developed at present to justify the expense of a road, the burden of which rests on the country as a whole.'' A man who was a member of the Board of Trade at that time said, ''I went up there in the 1930s, myself, to investigate. There was nothing there. They were just penny mines.'' ◊

Whether this tipped the balance, or whether it was purely political horse-trading to save the province money, Perrault by February of the following year was declaring to the Reform Club that ''We had hoped that the Canadian Pacific would have extended its line from Angliers to Rouyn, thereby developing simultaneously both mining and colonization.'' Wanklyn reiterated that ''the only basis on which we could under present conditions consider extending our line into the Rouyn district would be by receiving from the Government in connection with such extension assistance similar to that given in connection with the building of the existing Angliers line.'' In July 1925, Taschereau announced that the CNR would operate an extension from O'Brien to Rouyn. The line was actually to be built by a newly formed private railway, rumoured to be backed by New York financiers, and leased by the CNR. The Quebec government proposed to pay $50,000 a year for five years to cover deficits. Such insurance against deficit could amount to $250,000 against the $360,000 subsidy requested by the CPR.

In the event, the CNR did run a line into Rouyn; but it was a circuitous route east to Quebec City and west again to Montreal, a trip much longer and less efficient than the trip to Montreal directly along the CPR route. And of course when the T&NO arrived in the gold fields shortly after the CNR spur, the ore traffic and its profits went to Toronto, just as the CPR officials had foreseen. The rail project apparently failed over the subsidy issue; in fact, there is no evidence that the provincial government and the CPR ever made a serious effort to negotiate terms. Both sides seem to have been straining at a gnat; such mutual unwillingness to risk $360,000 on a project worth $2,500,000 which both thought important is hard to understand. A lifelong employee of the CPR offered some explanations. He pointed out that the Canadian Pacific officers have always taken a federal, not a provincial view. They work out carefully what they think a venture is worth, and after that ''there's no bargaining. I imagine that they felt that if this was in the interest of Quebec and Montreal, primarily, then those people should support it and back it. Otherwise the CPR wasn't interested. With the lack of support of the Montreal Board of Trade, the officers of the time probably saw no point to it. Of course, Montreal has never tried to be a mining town. We always regarded gold as ephemeral and looked down our noses at penny stocks. That was good enough for Toronto, but not for Montreal.'' ◊

The CPR's refusal to risk money in the gold fields, even when their engineers were urging it, seems a symptom of entrepreneurial timidity or complacency or both, weaknesses that were perhaps widespread in Montreal at the time. The Board of Trade, which also opposed the gold venture, represented the entire business community and was almost entirely English, so it seems fair to say that Montreal businessmen in general were unwilling to take a risk on the Rouyn-Noranda-Val d'Or mines. As one of them not connected with CPR said, ''What did we know about mining? It seemed to us folly to invest in something we had had no experience with.'' ◊ The financing and development of the Rouyn-Noranda operation and of many other gold and metal discoveries made later and acquired by the Noranda company were provided by American financiers. There were a few Canadians involved in the technical and managerial work, but Noah Timmins of Montreal, president of Hollinger Consolidated Gold Mines, was the only Montrealer of note involved in the promotion, and he only joined three years after the company began operations. Noranda's head office was in Toronto and as time passed, more of the directors were from Toronto and fewer were Americans.

Another example of faltering business leadership was Edward Beatty's ill-conceived effort to solve the post-war financial problems of the railway by encouraging immigration. The policy had worked well early in the century, but by the 1920s most of the best land in the west was already settled, while across the country unemployment was chronic after the war. MacKenzie King's government had severely restricted immigration in the immediate post-war period because of the high level of unemployment. Nonetheless, Beatty believed that the growing deficit of the railways could be liquidated only by increasing the population of the West, and thereby the railway traffic. ''The gates of Canada should be opened once more, not only to the British, French and American immigrant, but also to the Scandinavian and the more desirable type of Continental.'' When in 1925 the King government did re-open Canada to immigrants, the railways on their own brought in 200,000 central and eastern Europeans to Canada. As things turned out, this policy added to the unemployment problem, particularly during the 1930s, without appreciably benefiting the CPR. It suggests a lack of vision and imagination both in the government and in the management of the railway.

The Canadian Pacific Railways responded to the organization of the Canadian National Railways in two ways: first, through a fierce competition in service and second, through Beatty's ten-year campaign to persuade the government that Canada could not afford two transcontinental railways, did not need them, and that the two lines should be merged under the experienced CPR management. The first response proved expensive for both lines and for the country, while Beatty's proposals for unification under CPR management ignored the political fact that the CNR was formed partly to break the CPR dominance of the country's transportation system. Beatty blamed the all-out competition on the CNR officers who, he believed, intended to surpass the CPR in every way, "to reduce it to a condition of inferiority." Thornton believed that as long as the Canadian National Railways appeared to be inferior to the CPR it could neither attract customers nor hold the loyalty of its employees. Parity or, if possible, superiority therefore became his objective. Beatty's reaction was to fight back on every front.

The competition between the CPR and the new CNR involved building rival hotels, expanding their branch lines into new territory, competing over terminal facilities, and offering extraordinary services. The CNR refused to give running rights over their rails from Moncton to Halifax to the CPR or to jointly build with CPR the Lord Nelson Hotel in Halifax. Instead, the CPR built the Lord Nelson, the CNR built its own hotel, and two tracks were run into an area barely supporting one. In Saskatchewan, Alberta, and British Columbia, as the 1932 Royal Commission on Railways reported, "the construction programme [of new branch lines] of one company was responded to by an equal or greater programme of construction of the other." Two terminals were built in Montreal within a few blocks of each other. Not only was there duplication in the operation of passenger trains, but practically identical schedules were adopted when a "staggered" service would have been more useful. Tickets delivered to homes, costly advertising, and over-luxurious services were other results of the competition.

Such competition increased the operating costs of both railways, making it even harder to make ends meet. The boom of the 1927-1929 years obscured the facts, briefly, but the Crash in October, 1929 made the situation glaringly evident. The CPR was fighting for its life. Barely solvent, it had to forgo its customary 10-percent dividend and even dividends on its preferred stock during most of the Depression. The CNR, although it improved its position during the twenties and had offered surprisingly good service in a short time, was in an even worse financial position. Sir Henry Thornton told the Duff Commission in 1932 that even in 1929, the net income of CNR had been $13 million short of paying the interest due to the public, while in 1930 revenues dropped an additional $46 million. The railway was clearly insolvent; but, of course, its shortfalls were picked up by the Government. According to his biographer, Thornton was made the scapegoat in an impossible situation. He was blamed by the Duff Commission for the problems of a set of bankrupt railways which had to survive with disheartened and disgruntled personnel in competition with a highly efficient private railway of many years' experience. D'Arcy Marsh suggests that Thornton was destroyed by political enemies of the nationalized railway and by business competitors in Montreal. However that may have been, Thornton's departure from the Montreal scene did not mean the disappearance of the CNR. The combination of the Depression, the competition of the nationalized railway, and technological advances in automotive transport spelled the end of the CPR monopoly and its dominance in national affairs.

Between the first and second world wars net dollar earnings of the Canadian Pacific exceeded the 1913 total only in 1928, and the operating ratio (the ratio of expenses to revenues) rose steadily, never falling below 77 and climbing to 92 in 1947—compared to 60.7 in 1901. Professor and statistician Lorne McDougall says of the inter-war period: "Within fifteen years it [the CPR] had been pushed out of its role as the leading railway in the country. Its earning power had been undercut; its very existence challenged."

This is perhaps too dramatic a statement. Both lines lost passenger traffic as the automobile and the airplane encroached on railway travel. However, both lines did well in freight revenues and the steamship, telecommunication, mineral development and other investment interests of the Canadian Pacific produced sufficient profits to make it still one of Canada's most solid companies. What it lost was its dominance based on a monopoly position in the West and its government support. Its policies were no longer capable of shaping the nation.

Another old policy was storing up future trouble for Montreal's English-Scottish business leaders: their relationship to their labouring employees. We have seen that wages in Montreal were lower than in other comparable cities, a situation which naturally led to labour organization and labour protest. In Montreal, however, labour agitation was almost completely ineffectual, until after World War II. The *Labour Gazette* reports major strikes year after year in all Montreal industries between 1900 and 1929; but they rarely accomplished anything. Most of the time the workers, afraid of losing their jobs, returned to work without having gained anything. In the twenties, companies commonly brought in scabs to replace strikers, and when this led to violence, the militia or the police was brought in to restore order on the picketline.

During World War I labour peace was bought by patriotic appeals, with the tacit understanding that wages held down for the sake of the war effort would be improved afterwards. The cost of living rose by 50 percent during the war, an intolerable increase for families already living at or below the poverty line. At the same time, workers were aware that fortunes had been made by their employers during the war. Not only did the workers' situation not improve when the war ended, it became even worse, as war industries closed and workers were laid off. Even where this was not the case, wages remained at or below pre-war levels. Montreal witnessed the bitterest labour disputes in its history. More than 13,000 workers in 1919 and 10,000 in 1920 were on strike in Montreal.

Quebec was second only to British Columbia as the major centre of industrial unrest in the ten years after World War I, primarily because such a high proportion of its labour force was employed in low-wage industries such as textiles, tobacco, boot and shoe manufacturing, and the needle trades. These industries hired largely unskilled labour. Not many of the workers were British Protestant. We have already seen that by 1900 the British workers were foremen and supervisors, or in the skilled trades as machinists, welders, carpenters, fitters, pattern designers. They worked on the railroads and in heavy industries such as iron and steel, or established small businesses: cabinetmaking, electrical repairs, upholstering, typesetting and printing. The practical training in a skill possessed by most of the immigrants from Scotland was one of their advantages over other groups in the early days and may account for their rapid rise to the top, in the various trades and in supervisory positions. Such people were encouraged to immigrate; and Montreal employers advertised jobs available in British papers. The importation of skilled labour reduced advancement opportunities for Montreal workers. This, and the over-supply of unskilled labour, kept wages low and unemployment constant.

Partly because of this over-supply, the right to bargain collectively, to be represented by a certified union for contract negotiations, to strike if this process failed was not really won until World War II. Employers insisted on their absolute right to set wages and conditions of work, and believed that the cheaper they could get labour, the better businessmen they were. They were outraged by strikes and in this they were supported by all levels of government and by the Catholic Church in Quebec, all of which saw strikes as a threat to the social order. In the ensuing confrontations between employers and employees, and between skilled and unskilled workers, there was an element not present in the rest of North America where the same struggle was occurring. In Quebec, the unskilled and most underpaid workers were likely to be French Catholics and the employers easily identified as English (although many of the low-wage industries were in fact owned by Jews, Greeks, or French Canadians). Resentments between workers and owners were thus doubly grounded.

Nonetheless, in the 1920s, Montreal was still the arena in which competing national business interests struggled against each other. A young man just getting a start in a legal firm describes the heady experience of being where the action was. "I cashed two of the biggest cheques that had ever cleared a Canadian bank at the time. One was for $45 million and the other was about the same size. I had to take them down to the Royal Bank on November 30, 1927 (I'll never forget), and they were waiting for those cheques because they couldn't close their books before receiving them without going bankrupt. That's the way things were when Montreal was the real financial centre of the country. The Toronto firm, Wood Gundy, for instance, was an underwriter as big as any on the continent, and it was based in Montreal. People who worked for Wood Gundy became heads of firms of their own." ◇

Every major company had its head office in Montreal. By the 1920s, this fact, combined with the mergers, was bringing enterprising younger men into the city from the Maritimes, Ontario, the West, and the United States. The Killams,

McConnells, Websters, Nesbitts, Neills, Stewarts, Birks, Morgans, Culvers, and others were replacing the Allans, Anguses, Rosses (James), Drummonds, Ogilvies, and Van Hornes. The old families might call the newcomers "upstarts" but a woman whose husband was one of the new group says, "The old families were on their way out. We were really running things. We were the new Montrealers." ◊ A business executive commented that "Old money always thinks New Money is made up of charlatans and upstarts. New Money always thinks Old Money is becoming senile and has lost its grip. The fact is, I think most people thought of the CNR people as just a bunch of civil servants, not to be taken seriously." ◊

Symbolizing this competition, in the social and business life of Montreal of the 1920s, was the personal rivalry between Sir Edward Beatty of the Canadian Pacific and Sir Henry Thornton of the Canadian National Railways. Thornton was adored by the young group, "but none of us liked Beatty." ◊ A charming, competent man, Thornton was an American who had lived and worked some years in England and had been knighted for his work with the British railways. He was also a big spender. He loved entertaining and considered it part of his work. He was modern. He divorced his wife and remarried shortly afterward, at a time when this was still somewhat scandalous in Montreal.

The older business leaders liked and trusted Beatty. A serious, hard-working Canadian and a bachelor of simple tastes, he had worked his way up in the Canadian Pacific and had all the sound principles which made him one of them. They disapproved of Thornton, partly because he was profligate, partly because he had the easy self-confidence and optimism of an American; but most of all because he represented unfair competition which threatened the Canadian Pacific, a cornerstone of their world.

Each group had its own clique of close friends, but business rivalry didn't prevent their mixing socially and being friendly. They attended each other's parties and married into each other's families, but a retired member of the Stock Exchange says, "I don't think there was any love lost between them." ◊ The new people flirted with each other's wives, danced the Charleston, played tennis on J.W. McConnell's private court, carried on love affairs, fished for salmon on their private rivers, smoked too much, drank too much, travelled first class on luxury liners to Europe. The new group was more open about business matters than the old and women sometimes overheard men talking about business, even at parties. On one occasion an important bank official, far gone in drink, muttered disparaging remarks to a lovely lady about the management of a stock brokerage firm which was in arrears to his bank. This was regarded, however, as a major and, for guests who were involved in the financial difficulty, an unforgivable indiscretion. They also made the socio-political gaffes that Old Montrealers had learned not to make, such as that of the bank president who announced at a public dinner that as long as he was president there would be no French Canadians on his board of directors. People who had been competing to buy out a firm met over cocktails or dinner and made witty verses about being winners or losers. As long as everybody was really winning in the late 1920s, what was a million dollars among friends?

As time went by, the more successful and likeable newcomers were taken in by the older group and became indistinguishable from them. The New Montrealers were soon the Old Montrealers; nothing had changed very much.

At the bridge between the two groups stands the figure of Sir Herbert Holt. Holt is always used by other businessmen as *the* example of wicked business practices; indeed, he seems to have combined the ruthlessness of the nineteenth century entrepreneurs with the methods of the twentieth century financier. He was one of the wealthiest and most powerful men of his time. He played both sides of the street, working as a young engineer for both the CPR and the rival railways built by Mackenzie and Mann. He was a director of the CPR and president of the Royal Bank and the Montreal Trust; was a governor of both the Royal Victoria Hospital and its social and medical competitor, the Montreal General. One man said, ''Everybody respected his business ability, but nobody like him personally.'' ◊ However unpopular he may have been, Holt was a man to be feared. He became a member of the Mount Royal Club. Not content with having ''arrived'', he soon made himself powerful enough to ''pill'' anyone who had ever crossed him. The story is that he was prepared to pill Max Aitken, who lived across the street from the club and had applied for membership. When Aitken got word that Holt was going to blackball him, he withdrew his application and shortly afterward moved to England, where he later became Lord Beaverbrook. ◊

This was the business and social milieu into which young members of the Old Family elite were taking their places. Now that the men were established in jobs (or positions) they were marrying. Their brides usually were girls they had known since childhood in the Square Mile. Once married, however, they bought and moved to their own houses, usually west of the Square Mile. This was a new development. There were no small houses in the centre of the city, except one or two terraces like Chelsea Place or Richelieu Place. "So, when we married we moved out because family fortunes weren't so great that each child could start out living in the style of his parents, unless the parent died. We inherited later and meanwhile had to live more simply. By the time we inherited we were established in other places such as Senneville or Westmount." ◇

Perhaps the most important cause of the exodus was the advent of the automobile as a major form of transportation. The automobile made it feasible to live outside the city and commute. In the downtown, there were not enough paved streets or parking spaces, while the noise and fumes of traffic were becoming a problem. A special committee of the National Association of Building Owners and Managers investigated the situation in 1929 and concluded that the era of the big private mansions was past. Accordingly, the Montreal city council passed a by-law which permitted limited and controlled commercialization, small shops, hotels, clubs, banks, museums and the like along the once-residential Sherbrooke Street. The Square Mile was beginning to break up.

Young people moved to new terrace houses on parts of the "priest's farm," an area of eastern Westmount originally belonging to the Sulpician Seminary and sold to developers in the late 1920s. Some went further west to Roslyn or Grosvenor Avenues. By the beginning of the second World War, Westmount had a population of 25,000, was 88 percent English-speaking and 70 per cent of British origin. It was self-governing, and had its own public parks, playgrounds, schools, public library, and police and fire departments, as well as its own commercial section, hospital and other services. In that sense, it was more like a small town than a true suburb. It had been founded, according to John I. Cooper, by people who wanted to have more political involvement in their municipal government than was possible for the English population in French Montreal.

The Town of Mount Royal began to develop as a predominantly English-speaking suburb after the completion of the railway tunnel under Mount Royal in the centre of Montreal Island.

This brought the area on the northern plain into easy reach of the city. Montreal West, which had hitherto been only a CPR railway junction and a summer resort, began to grow and became an English middle-class suburb. Other young couples moved to the country. The estates they bought in Senneville, Saraguay, Cartierville, and Hudson on the west end of the island soon became worthy of any landed gentry in England or Scotland.

Michael Bliss maintains that the Canadian businessman, in the period 1880 to 1914, was in a constant state of anxiety because he was besieged by enemies on all sides. There were political uncertainties and the opposition of labour and farmers. Worst of all, however, was the tension provoked by other members of his own group—his business competitors. Bliss says that unrestrained competition in the formative years of Canadian business was ''too destructive to be tolerated'' and goes on to suggest that ''this.. anxiety has in many cases driven entrepreneurs on to build great industrial empires, thus forestalling all future anxieties incident to competition (monopoly being the obvious answer...)'' It appears that the same, or worse pressures continued into the twenties.

Sir Edward Beatty would have agreed. Throughout his term of office as president of the CPR, he stated publicly his view that government interference with business was a cause of economic troubles. His prime example was, naturally, the agitation against the transportation monopolies which had resulted in the building of thousands of miles of unnecessary rail lines. He laid the blame for this not on western farmers but on business pressure groups. In a speech to the Canadian Chamber of Commerce in 1936, he said, ''Has not the growing attempt to make the government all-powerful in its control and direction of our daily life been largely stimulated by the jealousies of groups of businessmen, one against the other?''

The merger movement was another response to competition, an effort to achieve monopoly and thereby reduce anxiety, a defensive retreat from risk-taking. It is also worth noting that clubs tend also to reduce at least the most ruthless of competition. Taking a man into your club disarms him to some extent. It implies that he will show some loyalty, consideration and at least good manners toward you as a fellow club member.

The justification for free enterprise and for the fortunes made by risk-takers was put forcibly by a man who heads his own multinational firm and still exhibits the spirit of the tycoon when

204

he points out that "business contributes to everybody's welfare by providing jobs and wages and products or services people need or want to buy. And to stay in business, the operators have to make a profit. You have to make money for a lot of people who aren't wage-earners or the investment money will go elsewhere." ◊

Yet for some members of the inheriting generation growing up with the century this sense of purpose, however self-serving it may be, seemed to have evaporated. As one retired businessman observed, "The sons, nephews and such in many family firms were just coming into their offices to collect their cheques periodically, and that was it." ◊ Some young men were doing nothing to earn their money. They had neither the vision and creative leadership, nor the aggressive entrepreneurship necessary for building a city, a nation, or a fortune. Eventually a family fortune is exhausted by growing numbers of family members unless the business on which it is based also continues to grow. Yet, several informants mentioned that as they grew up they were told that they were privileged never to have to work; that their financial position was one of "permanent security." Thus parents placed the capstone on the edifice of aristocratic expectation which a lifetime of training had built for their sons and daughters.

CHAPTER 9

Providing for the Community

Services

When the young women of the Square Mile had made their debuts and joined the Junior League; when the young men had finished their education at McGill; when they had married, taken up a career or job, and in general reached adult status, then they were likely to become involved in the operation and support of the community institutions. These included besides the economic or business organizations we have discussed, the schools, churches, hospitals, social welfare, and recreational organizations, charities, museums, libraries, orchestras and anything else that was needed. Here the principle of *noblesse oblige* they had learned from childhood came into practice: the men made the major decisions and provided the money; the women carried out the practical work of canvassing, of hospital auxiliary, church and school bazaars, of home visits to the poor, and summer camps for children.

At a time when governments were minimally involved in public welfare, before there was unemployment insurance or Medicare in Canada, one of the responsibilities of Anglo-Protestant Montreal businessmen was to provide guidance and help to their ethnic community members as the Laird had done in the Old Country, and as the Catholic Church did for the French Canadian. Sir Joseph Hickson, Sir Hugh Allan and his son Montagu, William Dow, George Mackenzie, Henry Morgan generously supported St. Andrew's; Lord Strathcona, Lord Mount Stephen, John Greenshields, James Cantlie, Robert Meighen, were equally supportive members of St. Paul's. Lord Strathcona and Lord Mount Stephen gave millions to the Royal Victoria Hospital; Sir William MacDonald endowed McGill University; the Molsons gave to the Montreal General Hospital and McGill. The same men gave large sums to Montreal charities. They also controlled these institutions in their roles as members of the boards of directors. At the time, directors took personal financial responsibility for the institutions or organizations they governed. For example, McGill University was able to count on its governors to meet its deficits, and since 1854 it had been a tradition that the Master of the Hunt, if necessary, was liable for overruns at the Montreal Hunt Club. This was true of all English institutions, but as a current governor of McGill remarked,''the graduated income tax put an end to that. Nowadays, only corporations have that kind of money.'' ◇

It is evident that when a man was invited to be a director or governor of his club or his church, the Montreal Foundling Home, or the Royal Victoria Hospital, and he might be on all of them, it was a serious financial responsibility as well as an honour and a recognition of his ability. The practice, quite general at the time, of a son inheriting his father's position on a board, or of directors appointing their own successors, makes practical sense, in these circumstances. There was no point in appointing or electing a poor man. It follows from this, of course, that being asked to serve on a board was a mark of social distinction and that philanthropy was proof of high social standing. Competition for status may have been as important a motive as *noblesse oblige*, though not often mentioned.

Young members of the elite might inherit positions on the boards of directors of these institutions, or they might serve as volunteers in the actual work, or in fund-raising activities. Roles were passed on from generation to generation in the same family. ''My mother used to leave the house about 11:00 a.m. to go on her charitable rounds. She was on the board of the Protestant Orphan Home, of the Lying-in and the Montreal General Hospitals. I was a director in all the same organizations in my turn.'' ◇

A man might be asked by his firm to take on a charity fund drive. As one man explained, ''You get involved in charities because somebody knows you and asks you to do it, and you were brought up to feel that you owe something to the community.'' ◇ A man was asked to go on the board of the Verdun Protestant Hospital and stayed with it for years. He says, ''And let's face it, you don't hurt the firm you work for if you do some of these things. In the process you meet people, and if you do a good job of the charity you may attract clients. The board, on the other hand, wants people who can attract money and whose names enhance the reputation of the board. It's reciprocal.'' ◊

In these institutions all social classes of Anglo-Protestants met in a common task. Each institution was a microcosm of the whole community—directed and funded by the elite, executed by the middle class and the resulting service rendered to all, although not necessarily on an equal basis.

The young board members were not immediately in charge, of course. As newcomers to any particular charitable or cultural organization, they were expected to serve their time, learning how things were done before making suggestions. It was the new boy experience all over again—one they fully understood and, by now, appreciated. In general, they found the organizations they joined encrusted with tradition. The older members of the board, whether their parents or their parents' friends, had developed and inherited from *their* parents rather clear-cut and efficient, if authoritarian, procedures.

The Montreal English community abounds in stories of how these community institutions were run. Even if some are apocryphal, they have sufficient consistency to suggest an element of truth. In any case, minutes of meetings of such organizations give precious little information about what was actually said. They consist of motions proposed and passed or tabled, rarely defeated. Anyone who has attended such meetings knows that frequently this is all that did happen, the decisions having already been made in private conversations among the officers before the official or public meeting began. The motions represented the consensus reached. If there was likely to be opposition it was, if possible, cooled out in advance, perhaps over lunch at the St. James Club, or by a series of telephone or personal calls. There was as little discussion as possible at the meeting itself. Movers and seconders merely explained the advisability of a given action, proceeding as quickly and smoothly as possible to the vote, which was in the circumstances nearly always favourable.

McGill University was one of the centerpieces, a linchpin in the whole English Montreal community. Its significance in the network of institutions run by the powerful group of English Montrealers is illustrated by the charter of the Royal Victoria Hospital. The governors were to include the presidents of the Board of Trade, of the Canadian Pacific Railway, and the Bank

208

of Montreal, as well as the Principal and the Dean of Medicine of McGill. Sir Edward Beatty was chancellor of McGill during the 1920s. He was also chairman of the board and president of the Canadian Pacific Railroad and a director of the Bank of Montreal. The CPR, the Bank of Montreal, and the Royal Victoria Hospital were popularly known as "the three powerful interlocking directorates." Not only was Beatty involved at the top of all three as well as at McGill, but the board of each of the three organizations had representatives of the others. Besides Beatty, McGill's board of governors in the 1920's included Sir Vincent Meredith, chairman of the board of the Bank of Montreal, president of the Royal Victoria Hospital, and director of the Canadian Pacific Railway; and R.B. Angus, founder and director of the CPR, president of the Bank of Montreal, and former president of the Royal Victoria Hospital. By the 1927-28 McGill session, there were three Molsons on the board, two of whom, Herbert and Fred, were directors of the Bank of Montreal. The Molsons were also important benefactors and directors of the Montreal General Hospital. Another governor, Sir Herbert Holt, was president of the Royal Bank, of the Montreal Light, Heat and Power, and a director of many other companies. Every important English institution in Montreal was run by this small group, and McGill was their university.

Sir William Macdonald, president of Macdonald Tobacco Company who had a reputation for being tight-fisted in his dealings with employees, paid for the major scientific research laboratories and buildings at McGill: the Physics building, the Engineering building, and the Chemistry building. In addition, he endowed chairs in agriculture and chemistry and provided for the operating costs of the Department of Architecture. In his history of the university, Stanley Frost says that Macdonald "almost single-handedly financed and maintained the science departments … on a scale which gave them first-class potential throughout the world."

The major teaching hospitals founded and funded by private English benefactors, the Montreal General, the Royal Victoria and the Children's Memorial made McGill University one of the foremost medical centers in the world. Important research resulted from this support. Edward Archibald's work on pulmonary tuberculosis and J.S.L. Browne's work in endocrinology are examples, as well as Professor J.B. Collip's discovery, with Banting and Best, of insulin. Even earlier, Sir William Osler had done outstanding work in pathology. Ernest Rutherford won a Nobel prize in chemistry in 1908 for pioneering work begun at McGill on the internal energy of the atom. Science and medicine were the fields of knowledge which were expanding most rapidly at the time. For businessmen who were supplying the funds, these areas were attractive because of their possible application to practical problems.

What started as financial necessity became a means of control by a small elite group. In fact, it may have served this additional purpose from the beginning, under the assumption that "he who pays the piper calls the tune." When the Montreal Hunt was incorporated in 1903, it was understood that the first trustees (John Crawford, Hugh Paton, A. Baumgarten, Montagu Allan, George Hooper, Charles McEachran, Robert Craig, Charles Cassils, Markland Molson, Albert Ogilvie and Bartlett McLennan) being a "self-perpetuating body ... could secure continuity of policy, and guarantee that the Hunt would remain in *the control of the hunting* [rather than the social] *members*."

As another example of the autocratic control exerted by the elite, Reginald Dawson, a young man just starting an accounting business ran for the office of mayor of an English suburb many years ago at the urging of a group of local citizens. His opponent was a member of the Old Guard which had been running the affairs of the municipality for years. The young man lost, but afterwards, "a powerful member of the winning clique called on me and told me, shaking his finger in my face, that I was never to run again. I replied that I had not intended to, but that now I would." Dawson later ran for office again and won. He served as the mayor of the Town of Mount Royal for thirty-seven years.

A clergyman in one of the summer resorts frequented by a number of wealthy and powerful men made the mistake one Sunday of holding forth from the pulpit on the evils of money and power. That afternoon the minister was invited to tea on the veranda of the summer cottage of one of these men, where were assembled several of the host's friends. It was made abundantly clear over the teacups that these men had not come on holiday to be lectured and that if he persisted in delivering such sermons they had ways of removing him from his post. The sermons returned to happier themes. ◊

A woman who was head of an important social agency which depended on Junior League volunteers for some of the work said, "They put you down whenever they got the chance, but that

210

didn't bother me. We needed their help." ◇ A minister's wife hated her role because as she said, "There were rich people in the parish who generally took care of fund drives for the church, but who made it clear that being a minister's wife didn't entitle me to be treated as an equal. Not that I wanted into their circle, but I hated to feel that they looked down on me." ◇

Dr. Wendell MacLeod recalls "the lag in the adaptation of hospitals to the swell of democratic sensitivity and the movement for reform which followed the First World War," which he observed as a medical student working in the Royal Vic:

> There were great discrepancies in many aspects of patient care between the public wards and the private rooms. We were upset about the low salaries and miserable conditions under which the Irish and Scottish immigrant maids lived in garret-like rooms under the hospital roof.... And there were the imperious manners and caustic tempers of some of the staff in their treatment of orderlies, public ward patients and sometimes students. At a theatre clinic for students in the out-patient department in 1928, for example, a senior physician was interrogating a Chinese dishwasher with leukemia. When the patient, who knew little English, made no reply, the teacher raised his voice, and finally bellowed at him. The man cowered in fear. Many of us were incensed.

A nurse at the Royal Victoria Hospital during the same period confirmed MacLeod's observations. "The chief doctors wore their cutaway coats and stripped trousers on their rounds. They were the lords of creation. When they spoke, everybody was supposed to jump." ◇ A retired doctor, now in his eighties, who possesses a manner suggesting he was one of these, presented another perspective on the matter. "The practice of medicine is not a democratic process. Like most activities that involve life and death decisions, often on the spur of the moment, they require authority vested in an expert or a designated leader who can count on instant obedience in a crisis. You don't have time for committee meetings." ◇

The Protestant School Board was supported through the taxes of non-Catholic Montrealers with a share of school taxes also levied on business. Local school boards, as well as the central board, had by-laws requiring public elections to fill vacancies. However, the school boards usually selected candidates they knew personally and declared them elected, there being no opposing candidate. Before World War II, Home and School Associations were never consulted nor their opinions considered in school board decisions. They were informed of what the board felt they might do for the benefit of the school in the way of financial contributions or services. Furthermore, parents could not even telephone directly to the school their children attended. It was not listed in the telephone directory. They could only leave a message with the Protestant School Board of Greater Montreal to be relayed to the school.

Shopkeepers of those days provided extraordinary service. Everything was delivered and picked up for return if unsatisfactory. One woman remembered that when unexpected guests were arriving and she had nothing for breakfast she called the grocery store with whom she usually did business just at closing time and explained her predicament. The owner of the quite large and well-known establishment offered to bring her order up himself on his way home. Everyone remembers being met at the door of Ogilvy's and Morgan's department stores and in Birks' jewelry store by the proprietor himself. In cutaway coat and morning trousers he would bow and call the important customers by name,"Good morning, Mrs. _____, and how are you today?" As part of this highly personalized service, retail establishments and services offered unlimited credit to those customers who they thought could pay their bills. This proved to be their undoing in some cases because both men and women believe that there were people, women particularly, who, finding their allowances or *dots* did not permit them to keep up with their friends, ran up huge bills. Women's lack of any responsibility for financial matters, in the presence of the fierce status competition in the Square Mile at the time, lends some credence to the report. The shopkeeper or dressmaker was reluctant to press for payment for fear of being blackballed by the friends of the lady-in-arrears. It is said that some shops were actually driven into bankruptcy. These must have been exceptions, however, since I was told repeatedly that Scots are trained never to use credit at all, although they think the English did.

The story of a dressmaker to whom large sums were owed illustrates the point. The daughter of the indebted family was to be married and the dressmaker was commissioned to make the wedding dress. She did, but on the day before the wedding she announced that she would not deliver the dress until the arrears were paid. They were.

These stories give us some insight into the relationship between the Montreal elite group and the English-speaking middle class. In general, it was one of inter-dependence. The middle class needed the patronage of the wealthy, and relied on that group to finance the necessary institutions of the English community, at the price of enduring constant social disparagement and snobbery, and of largely relinquishing the right to make decisions in their major institutions.

Organized charity, as practiced in Montreal in the 1920s, provides a good view, not only of the controlling role of the benefactors, but also some of the values they brought to bear on the community, and their relations to the poor. The conditions of the Montreal poor, whether English- or French-speaking, were appalling. Terry Copp quotes a housing official from Philadelphia who visited Montreal in 1912 and told the Canadian Club that in the slums he had found "whole families living in single rooms—in some eight beds in a room; rooms without windows, rooms where the plumbing was defective and the floor covered with filth.... I went in one property here and found something I had never seen before: I saw toilets, old open toilets, seven of them in one narrow little court surrounded by houses occupied by ten families.... You must remember that children are born and develop there."

In 1900 Sir Herbert Ames, in *The City Below the Hill*, called attention to the fact that Montreal contained the greatest poverty of any comparable city in North America. The working members of slum families—men, women and children—together earned less than the minimum needed for subsistence. The wages paid in Montreal were, on average, lower than in Toronto, New York, or Chicago. The infant mortality rate was the highest on the continent. This had changed little by the 1920s and Montreal continued to have the highest infant mortality rate and be the most unhealthy city in North America. Even in 1927 when the causes of tuberculosis (if not the cure) had been identified, and when most other cities had begun to drastically reduce their death rate from the disease, Montreal's mortality rate from tuberculosis was three times that of Toronto—"chiefly because of ignorance, and apathy, and an unwillingness to appropriate sufficient money to really cope" with the problem, according to a medical observer at the time.

Mortality rates from all diseases, infant and adult, were very high, but these rates were not equally distributed. For example, the St. Denis Ward in 1921, a lower-class, largely French-Canadian district, had 202 deaths per 100,000 from tuberculosis alone

213

as compared to 50 per 100,000 in the wards of St. Andrew and St. George which included the Square Mile. Nonetheless, there was hardly a family among the elite group that had not had a member with the disease at some time. The mortality rate does not describe the incidence of the disease and it was probably more widespread than these figures suggest. The upper-class group was in a position to provide the conditions of rest, fresh air, uncontaminated food and isolation of the patient which gave the best chances of recovery. This alone, plus better medical care, would reduce the death rate and perhaps the incidence also.

The businessmen of the Anglo-Protestant community organized to make public the situation and, if possible, to do something about it. In 1924 they formed the Montreal Anti-Tuberculosis and General Health League, headed by Sir Arthur Currie. Lord Atholstan, a member of this group, donated $100,000 to the Royal Edward and Bruchési Institutes to open two new clinics, one in the east-end Hochelaga Ward and the other in St. Henri, both working-class districts of mixed ethnicity.

In 1927 the League commissioned "A Survey of Public Health Activities," to publicize the known facts. The general conclusion of the survey was that "Montreal's official and voluntary services measure only about two thirds of the best examples of such services in other cities of comparable size." Much of this failure was laid at the door of the municipal authorities. According to Copp, the city in 1927 expended only 39 cents per capita on public health as compared to an average public expenditure of 78 cents in the twelve largest American cities. Even when funds from the private sector were added, Montreal's expenditures only averaged 69 cents per person. Although the Survey recommended that the city should appropriate funds to bring costs to 91 cents per capita, such expenditures never rose above 64 cents throughout the 1930s—still much lower than elsewhere in North America in cities of comparable size.

There were three kinds of institutions working with needy or dependent British immigrants or the poor of British origin: national or ethnic support organizations such as the St. Andrew's Society, St. George's Society, St. David's and St. Patrick's Societies, church organizations, and agencies such as the Charity Organization Society. By 1921 the English, Scottish, Irish, and Welsh citizens of Montreal were coordinating their work and their charitable donations through a Montreal Council of Social Agencies for planning and a Financial Federation, for fund-raising.

Under their aegis were the social agencies actually engaged in work in the field: the Family Welfare Association, the University Settlements, Child Welfare, hospitals, orphanages, and others. The Presbyterian Church and the Church of England had their own social services; both specialized in welcoming immigrants, and in offering temporary monetary relief and housing to British and Canadian people of their own faith.

From the earliest organized charity efforts in the nineteenth century, charity had been distributed on the basis of whether the person was "deserving" or not. Men who had been in jail, alcoholics, and those who refused to work were not considered deserving and little charity came their way. In fact, not until the YMCA and the Protestant House of Industry and Refuge were founded in 1865, was there any assistance for men at all. In a male-dominated society, it was taken for granted that women and children were not capable of taking care of themselves. They were the first of the "deserving." Determining who was eligible for assistance in a community where immigration was high and the majority of the population was below the poverty line posed some problems, but largely for the private social agencies. The churches and the national societies took care of their own; and since they were small enough and were mixed as to social class, the donors were likely to know the poor in their midst and have some idea of their character and circumstances. However, if the needy person did not attend church (even though nominally a member) he was not "deserving." Church charity always had a moral tone. Charity was a Christian obligation, but the poor had an obligation also to improve themselves and the Christian way of life was offered, along with fuel, food, or clothing as a solution to their poverty.

The notion that poverty was an individual problem, caused by personal failings, existed not only in Montreal but in the rest of Protestant Canada, in the U.S., and England in the Victorian period. However, it persisted longer in Montreal than elsewhere. An American social worker named Francis MacLean was brought to Montreal in 1900 as general secretary for the newly formed Charity Organization Society. A year later he reported that outdoor relief in Montreal was backward, compared to most North American cities, and involved "forcing applicants to stand up before a board of eight or ten men and state their wants, one by one, while two or three hundred applicants wait their turn." The board met only once a week and no relief could be given out between meetings. When the board agreed that a case deserved assistance, the relief was totally indiscriminate. No matter what the problem, MacLean reported, "whether there be one or six in the family, the family will receive a package of groceries a week and a quarter ton of coal or a quarter cord of wood each three weeks." When the Meurling Refuge was opened by the city of Montreal in 1912, men were eligible only if not intoxicated and possessing no more than 25 cents. Here a man could receive a bath, a medical examination, coffee or soup and bread. He could sleep on an iron bed with metal mattress equipped with two blankets, two sheets, one pillow and one pillow-case. His clothing was fumigated, and his working capacity ascertained "in order to find out the impostors who are in the habit of living at the expense of the community; this is a protection for the honest pauper." The refuge was intended, according to its first director, to be sufficiently unpleasant as to "repel everyone, not in extremity, from accepting it" and should "also ensure a distinct moral and physical improvement on the part of those forced to have recourse to it." The Charity Organization, founded in 1900 by wealthy Anglo-Protestant businessmen and their wives, was described as a "direct import from Britain" by the Ville Marie Social Services Annual Report for 1978-79. This fact may help to explain the slowness in Montreal to accept new ideas on the nature and treatment of poverty. Once again, traditional views came from Britain.

By 1920, however, The Charity Organization Society (COS), the forerunner of the Montreal Council of Social Agencies, began to conclude that the cause of poverty was social rather than individual in nature. In 1919, Lady Drummond, president of the Society since the death of her husband, Sir George, presented a report which placed an emphasis on the social nature of the problems faced by the Society's clients. Unemployment and sickness accounted for 60 percent of the "disabilities" causing poverty. Twenty-two per cent of the clients' homes contained dark rooms (inner rooms without windows); 15 percent had damp rooms (basement rooms subject to flooding or poor drainage); 32 per cent had unsanitary plumbing, and 40 percent had no bathrooms. The Annual Report for the following year said: "The plain fact is that so far as the dependent poor are concerned, the sufferings of the poor themselves and the economic loss to the community are occasioned in great measure by conditions outside the control of the individual, conditions that only an intelligent and aroused public opinion can effect [sic]."

216

By the time, then, that the young men and women of the upper crust were beginning to take on responsibility for charity, the idea that poverty might be social rather than personal in origin had dawned on Montrealers. But it was to be many years before it had much effect on the distribution of charity in the city. Shortly after the war Howard Falk was to head the new McGill School of Social Work, and the newly formed Montreal Council of Social Agencies asked him to investigate and report on its eighty member agencies. Falk's report was devastating. He bore down heavily on the selfishness of the business man and his wife who used charity as a social stepping stone and on social workers who were afraid to speak out against the abuses they saw every day and which required legal or social remedies. However, another survey of all Protestant and non-sectarian groups giving relief, made five years later by Frances O'Neill, showed that little had changed since Falk's report.

Although these attitudes and even the methods of providing relief and other social services by Anglo-Protestant institutions in Montreal differed little from those of the rest of English-speaking Protestant North America, there was one important difference. Among French-Canadian Catholics in Quebec charity was traditionally provided first by the family and second by the Catholic church through its hospitals, orphanages, and parish charities. The provincial and municipal governments therefore took less responsibility for social welfare than civil authorities did elsewhere. This, in turn, laid a heavier burden on the private institutions and on the individuals who were the major source of their funds.

The introduction of the Public Charities Act in 1921 recognized that private charities could no longer meet the needs created by industrialization and urbanization. The Act provided that the burden of the various types of public assistance should be divided evenly among the Quebec government, the municipality, and the charitable institution. It was the first Quebec law providing for government intervention into the field of private welfare agencies. Ontario, since 1851, had passed many such laws governing various social services. There, traditionally, a major share in responsibility for health and welfare services was passed on to the municipalities. In Quebec, on the other hand, the financial burden of municipalities with respect to social assistance before 1921 was confined to the upkeep of prisoners, half of the maintenance of mentally-ill indigents, and part of the cost of child detention in reform or industrial schools. The provincial Boucher Report commented "Thus, for nearly two centuries, social assistance consisted only of assistance in kind and in services provided by individuals and families and of fairly arbitrary aid granted by the State."

In spite of the provisions of the Public Charities Act, less than six per cent of the total revenue of the Federated Charities in 1930 was provided by the Province of Quebec and the City of Montreal—considerably less than in Toronto, Winnipeg, or Halifax. Perhaps of necessity, throughout the 1920s, 97 cents of every dollar subscribed to the Federated Charities in Montreal was actually used for charity. It was "a record of economy in management which for a city of its size cannot be equalled on the American continent," according to N.R. Crump, in a radio address made in 1930. Furthermore, during the same period the number of different business firms and individuals contributing to the Federated Charities grew from 7,000 to more than 50,000. Crump, not a native Montrealer, concluded "I do not know of a city in Canada which enjoys and has earned such a reputation for consistent and generous support of measures of community welfare." Since the church was the principal initiator and support of Catholic charities, this statement particularly applied to the Protestant and Jewish community appeals.

Political solutions to poverty were suspect in the era of "Bolshevism" and were likely to be regarded as "socialistic". A former member of the Junior League said: "It never occurred to me, and I never heard it discussed in the League, that you could change the conditions of the poor, by working politically. The only way we thought you could do it was by raising money and getting in there and doing the work." ◊ This is hardly surprising. Most young women of the social elite in those days still lacked an awareness of public issues. Besides, many upper class Montrealers, especially after the election of Médéric Martin regarded politics as "dirty." As one lady recalls, "We had the same kind of attitude toward the provincial government that we now have to the city government, that it was just a group of people lining their own pockets and not too interested in good government. The real government was in Ottawa, at least for my generation. The city government was even then just awful. Look at all the mayors we had: Martin, Houde, Reynaud—just a bunch of scoundrels."

A businessman who was a young engineer in 1922 supports this view of the provincial government. At the time he had prepared a bid for a provincial government contract which was accepted by the Minister of Roads because it was the lowest bid. His boss went to Quebec City to clinch the deal, but "when Mr. C came back he didn't have the contract which had been offered. He had refused to sign it when he found that he would have had to bribe half the government officials in order to get it. He then said that he wanted me to remember and pass it down the line that we would never again offer a bid to the provincial government on anything. And we never have." ◊

As the suburbs of Westmount, the Town of Mount Royal and of Montreal West grew, the withdrawal of the upper class Anglo-Protestant from Montreal politics was almost complete. The governments of these small municipalities were run and controlled by their wealthy citizens in the time-honoured way, and their finances waxed as those of the City of Montreal waned. As we know, this exodus was begun by the generation who came of age and married in the 1920s.

Cultural Activities

Before the 1930s, the Anglo-Protestant businessmen initiated, organized, and funded much of the art, music and theatre in Montreal. Their efforts and financial support were of great importance in the establishment of Montreal Museum of Fine Arts, the Montreal Symphony Orchestra, the Ladies Morning Musical Club, many of the city's architectural monuments, and other artistic and intellectual organizations of which the city is now proud. Their British origins and international travels gave the Montreal businessmen at least an image of what a truly civilized city and country needed in the way of cultural institutions and opportunities. In their capacities as community and national leaders (if not always as connoisseurs), they accepted cultural improvement as another of their responsibilities.

The state of the Arts in Montreal through the 1920s demonstrated that a great many of the city's patrons, whether financial supporters or appreciators, supported by their patronage old values and traditional forms drawn from British or European concepts of the arts, and had little interest in Canadian arts and letters, or in "modernism." There were, as we shall see, some important exceptions to this. Sir George Drummond and Sir William Van Horne, for example, accumulated fine art collections that included impressionists and post-impressionists (although William Watson, the art dealer, reports that when he tried to interest Van Horne in some modern *Canadian* paintings, the latter called them "trash").

Some young Montrealers whose ties with Britain were non-existent or becoming tenuous were eager for new directions: the "modernism" that was already established in Europe. In painting, the Impressionists had been followed by the Fauves and Cubists; in music, Hindemith and Bartok were producing strange dissonance; in literature, James Joyce and T.S. Eliot had broken loose from old forms and were exploring the darker, pessimistic emotions; in architecture, Gropius and Le Corbusier were erecting structures without ornamentation. Modernism is a complex concept; but, basically it was an effort to express and come to terms with the experience of living in a world of constant change, where technology and science were destroying old absolutes and substituting relativism and uncertainty. In the arts, modernism exalted the individual artist and declared his opinion equal to (or better than) that of traditional authority as represented by academies, critics, and the public. It rejected the past and believed in a future of unlimited possibilities based on the freedom of the artist to explore everything without hindrance, as science was doing. Art was seen as its own excuse for being and owed nothing to society. By extension, this rejection of authority in the arts could include all established authority. The response to such a challenge was predictable among people whose interests lay with tradition and authoritarian structures. They instinctively recognized the threat such ideas represented to the order they believed to be essential to their welfare and that of society.

The attachment to Victorian traditions lasted longer in Canada than elsewhere. It has been said that the Atlantic barrier slowed the spread of the revolutionary attacks on tradition which produced modernism in Europe, and that Canada was slower than the U.S. to respond to these ideas because it was still absorbed in pushing back its frontier, a process already completed south of the border. E.K. Brown, writing in 1944, analyzed Canada's tardiness as a result of four restraining forces: economics, colonialism, the frontier mentality, and puritanism. Economic forces are the most obvious. The art market was too small and too scattered geographically to be profitable. As for colonialism as an obstacle, Brown stated that "A great art is fostered by artists and audience possessing in common a passionate and peculiar interest in the kind of life that exists in the country where they live," whereas "most Canadians continue to be culturally colonial ... they set

their great good place somewhere beyond their own borders...."
The frontier mentality is revealed in the admiration for the practical, for "the man who can run a factory, or invent a gadget, or save a life by surgical genius," this being the kind of activity which is needed for building the material structure of a nation. Canadian puritanism has the effect of enforcing moral orthodoxy and, like the frontier mind, it does not believe that art is of any importance; or as Brown puts it, both believe that "life devoted to one of the arts is a life misused: the aesthetic life is not a form of the good life."

These attitudes were all strong in the Montreal of the 1920s, and however widespread they may have been in Canada generally, they persisted even longer in Montreal. We can guess this by comparing the development of the arts in Montreal with that of Toronto, its nearest competitor in every way.

A practical problem in Montreal was that the money to support art was in the hands of the English, but only the French population was large enough to support it as consumers or audiences. Even when the population of the city was almost evenly divided between English and French, the Anglophone population (people who speak English) included Jews, Italians, Greeks, Germans, Russians, and many other ethnic groups. Each of these had its own artistic heritage, and was not necessarily interested in the output of the others. This meant that the potential audience for British or English-Canadian literature or theatre was small indeed. In the late 1920s, although some of the young adult members of the upper class who were taking their places as the leaders of English cultural institutions in Montreal were somewhat interested in modernism and Canadian art and letters, their parents were still the financial patrons and were quite clear about what *they* liked: "pastness in general" and British "pastness" in particular.

Evidence of this preference can be seen in the records of the topics and books discussed in the prestigious St. James Literary Society. Founded in 1899 for the purpose of promoting interest in literature and public issues, it met once a week from October to April. Its membership included many prominent people such as Sir Edward Beatty and Sir Henry Thornton, Sir Arthur Currie, and Justice R.A.E. Greenshields. Speakers were brought in from Ottawa, Toronto, Boston, and New York, as well as from Montreal. During the period 1899 to 1943, scarcely a dozen evenings were devoted to Canadian culture. There were thirty-five talks on art in all its forms; but Canadian art was not discussed until 1924, when on March 18 Carless Williams gave a talk on the "Arts and Crafts of Canada." Robert Pilot presented a "Short History of Landscape Painting" in 1929, and on March 10, 1932 W.M. Barnes discussed "Art in Canada." The next talk on the subject was by Arthur Lismer in 1943. During the same period there were eight evenings devoted to British art of various kinds. Fiction was discussed on thirty-two evenings, but English-Canadian fiction was discussed only once. Poetry was discussed on thirty-seven occasions up to 1943, but Canadian poetry or poets only six times. By comparison, biography and non-fiction, politics, history, current events and social issues accounted for about three hundred and fifty evenings between 1900 and 1943. The subjects most frequently discussed in these categories were British, followed distantly by American, with Canadian topics discussed about as often as Greek, Russian or Chinese. The neglect of literature, especially Canadian literature, by this literary club suggests a general lack of interest in the subject. Lorne Pierce, speaking to the St. James Literary Society in 1929, lamented the fact that Canadian literature was not appreciated even in the universities, where Canadian history had finally been included in the curriculum, but not Canadian literature. "If the Academy of France crowns a score of the great names of Quebec, if the American Academy of Arts and Letters, and the Royal Society of Literature elect our writers as members and Fellows, can we not say that they are deserving, in some respects at least?"

The Canadian Club of Montreal was founded in 1897 for the purpose of "fostering patriotism by encouraging the study of institutions, history, arts, literature and resources of Canada and an appreciation of matters of interest to Canadians." It also had a membership largely from the business community. Its officers during this period were Henry Morgan, Brooke Claxton, W.F. Macklaier, P.S. Fisher, H.G. Hanson, and J.A. Lalanne. A perusal of the Dau's Blue Book of 1928 listing prominent Montrealers reveals that very few of them belonged to the Canadian Club although many were members of the St. James Literary Society. Even fewer belonged to both. This again reflects the split in the English business community that had become obvious in the postwar period. The wealthy Old Guard members, who were primarily interested in British and European arts, letters, history, and institutions, joined the St. James Literary Society, while the rising new rich and the middle class were interested in Canadian issues and joined the Canadian Club.

The Canadian Club had equally distinguished speakers from around the world, and their topics were more than twice as likely to concern Canadian issues than those of any other country. Between 1926 and 1930, for example, British topics were discussed only slightly more often than that of other non-Canadian nations. In spite of the Club's stated purpose, however, art and literature were rarely mentioned. Its speakers spoke on national and international politics, economics, and social policy.

With such lack of interest among the literate members of English Montreal (and in Canada, generally, according to most critics), it is not surprising that many Canadian writers emigrated to the United States, England, or France, as did Bliss Carmen; or wrote for English or American audiences as did Thomas Haliburton, Morley Callaghan, and Mazo de la Roche. At McGill, on the other hand, a group of poets who were students and young instructors in the early 1920s were fighting the battle for Canadianism and modernism. A.J.M Smith, F.R. Scott, Leon Edel, Leo Kennedy, A.M.Klein, Lew Schwartz, Graeme Taylor, John Glassco, Lancelot Hogben, and perhaps a dozen others were writing verse on Canadian themes, inspired by such modernist poets as T.S. Eliot and Ezra Pound. This, and the fact that their poems debunked the *status quo* and deflated the pompous, caused them considerable trouble on campus. These writers had been publishing in the literary supplement of the *McGill Daily,* but when the *Daily* withdrew its support for the supplement, they founded and published The *McGill Fortnightly Review*, the earliest and perhaps the most influential of the '' little magazines'' in Canada. Collard quotes Leon Edel about this movement:

> We were called bohemians, rebels, Communists, smart-alecks. But we were read ... No one would have foretold that on the national literary scene we were, in effect, bringing the ''modern movement'' to McGill—to Canada.... It took time for the pioneering to be recognized.

The economic problems that beset the publication of novels, plays, or poetry in English were even more acute in the case of theatre. Few communities were large enough to support a permanent theatre. Toronto was first off the mark, with the Margaret Eaton School of Literature and Expression and its playhouse donated by Timothy Eaton in 1905. This was followed by the Arts and Letters Club Players in 1908, and by the Hart House Theatre in 1919. Toronto was already the capital of English-language theatre in the 1920s and 30s.

During the twenties, professional theatre in Montreal was "branch plant," with plays and actors imported, and productions assembled here. At His Majesty's on Guy Street and at the Orpheum touring companies performed and the great English and American actors of the age appeared—Sarah Bernhardt, Sir Harry Lauder, Sir John Martin-Harvey, and George Arliss, for example. More rarely, a Canadian actor, such as Matthew Lang, performed. The plays and musicals were mostly set in Britain or the United States. The Dumbells, headed by Red Newman, continued as a peacetime revue and was one of the few shows to be concerned with Canadian themes. Local productions were amateur affairs performed in church basements and high school auditoriums. Such were the Trinity Players, for example, a group connected with and playing in Trinity Anglican Church in Westmount.

The first indigenous English theatre company in Montreal, the Montreal Repertory Theatre, was established in 1929 by Martha Allan, of the Allan Shipping Line family. She had had some training and experience in theatre in Paris and at the Pasadena Playhouse in California, and returned to Montreal with the intention of starting a community theatre. The MRT survived until after World War II, largely as the result of Martha Allan's determination and energy. She was a dynamic, forceful, and talented woman and because of her connections, the MRT became a project of the upper class English Montrealers. At first the MRT was an adult continuation of the amateur theatricals the prominent families had got together in their homes or summer cottages. The MRT rehearsed in the coach house of Ravenscrag and performed at the Ritz-Carlton or the Windsor Hotel ballrooms, at McGill's Moyse Hall, or Westmount's Victoria Hall. Martha Allan telephoned people she knew for whatever she needed: actors, costumes, props, a hall, money—and got it. As one accountant turned amateur actor commented, "There was no refusing Martha Allan!" ◊ Later, the MRT began to attract trained actors, good directors and reached a level of professionalism. A number of its actors went on to international fame. One of them who was part of the company in the days before the MRT found a permanent home on Guy Street, was impressed by the audience. "It was a snobbish group that supported it. At its peak we had 1500 subscribers, including all the powerful and rich families. Socially prominent people just flocked to see it. I think they came because they knew the cast, the director, had helped it financially and lent their drapes for the scenery. It was their theatre put on by their friends and relatives." ◇

When Martha Allan died in 1942, the MRT continued for a few years under the direction of Doreen Lewis. But after the theatre on Guy Street burned down in March 1952, the MRT never quite got on its feet again. There were other attempts to establish professional English theatre in Montreal, but most of them were short-lived during this period.

The MRT had its own playwriting groups, and the Junior League since 1920 had produced plays and musicals by local writers. The McGill Red and White Revue presented annually musicals written by students, some of whom went on to write for the professional stage. These local playwrights wrote what Montreal audiences liked: light-hearted comedy and singable tunes. Montrealers shared with other English Canadians of the period a distaste for heavy and serious drama. As long as they could get the kind of fare they liked (which Brown would say reflected their puritanism and colonialism), they supported it. Theatre professionals with other ideas had to leave to earn a living. The *New York Dramatic Mirror* noted about this time that there were enough Canadian-born actors, actresses, playwrights and theatre managers in New York to establish a Canadian national theatre. They included Marie Dressler, Beatrice Lillie, Mary Pickford, among others.

Painting and music were two areas where the French and English Montrealers might have cooperated to overcome the problem of limited audiences and patronage that bedevilled literature and theatre. But even in these areas where language was not a barrier to artistic communication, Montreal lagged behind Toronto in development and support, particularly of new ideas and forms. Partly this may have been because Montreal's two linguistic groups rarely worked very well together on anything. They usually had very different ideas about how things should be done. The result was, as one woman remarked, that "the social leaders among the French would sometimes join us in organizing something like the Art Institute or on a League project, but as soon as they had learned how to do it, they would break away and start their own organization." ◇ This statement was supported by a French-Canadian lady. "We French would go down there 'chez les Anglais' but we never felt comfortable on the committees of the museum, the orchestra and those things that had been founded and run by the English." ◇

The history of the Montreal Art Association (later the Montreal Museum of Fine Arts) during the period 1900 to 1950 not only shows the struggle between different tastes in art within the English community, but also shows that the financial contributions and most of the effort to promote art in Montreal were made by the upper-class Anglo-Protestants.

The first art classes were held in 1868 and the first building housing the Montreal Art Association was built in 1879 in Phillips Square on land bequeathed by Benaiah Gibb. Gibb's bequest also included some paintings and $8,000. The first sizeable endowment fund for the acquisition of pictures was made in 1892 by John Tempest, followed by the Learmont bequest of 108 pictures and objects, including a Rembrandt drawing. James Ross, one of the richest men in Montreal at the time, paid for about a quarter of the cost of the handsome new Museum of Fine Arts built in 1912, and when he died the following year he left the Museum $100,000. From then on, many bequests were made to the Museum by prominent Montreal businessmen, all British Protestants, with the exception of Senator L.J. Forget who donated Van der Helst's "Portrait of a Gentleman." There were two paintings from Sir George Drummond's collection (one of them, Daubigny's "Return of the Flock," may have been partly responsible for starting a local Barbizon school vogue), and 154 paintings donated by Lord Strathcona. The Morrice family gave some paintings done by James Wilson Morrice and, much later, Sir William Van Horne's daughter gave the Museum 103 paintings from her father's valuable collection. A few Montreal collectors were knowledgeable about art and collected artists then considered modern. Sir George Drummond's collection, distributed among family members, included a Renoir, a Corot, and a Turner. Sir William Van Horne's collection was regarded as probably the best in Canada and comparable to collections in England or the United States.

When a collector bought a new painting, it was customary to invite people to tea to see the new acquisition. Acquiring art became part of the social competition. All too often this led, among people who knew little about art, to a dismal sameness in Montreal décor. As one Montrealer whose father had been an important art patron remarked, "I cannot bear what I call 'signs of respectability and having arrived' shown by Montrealers of my childhood. That included those awful pictures of that Dutch school. *Every* house had the same pictures of the rear ends of sheep at dusk." ◊

William Watson, who had succeeded John Ogilvy in Montreal's earliest commercial gallery, tried to promote Canadian artists and collected a number of paintings by Coburn, Cullen, Morrice, Suzor-Côté, Paul Caron, Henri Julien, and others who have since become internationally known. However, what he *sold* were French, Dutch, and English paintings in the romantic and neo-classical styles. He observed that although in 1912 he was beginning to sell Canadian paintings and bronzes, "I still had to go to Europe every year for the inevitable quota of Dutch School unabashed 'pretty pictures' or quite obviously be unable to continue in business."

By the 1920s the Montreal Art Association was housed in the impressive Montreal Museum of Fine Arts on Sherbrooke Street. Its construction had been financed entirely by member's subscriptions. The officers of the Art Association were the same men who ran everything else, and their taste in art dominated. The new building and its growing acquisitions represented the enshrinement of Victorian and Old World tastes. There was no public involvement; the Museum was a private institution. "You had to be elected to be a member. It was all just very old Montreal, and the councillors ran it as though it was their private domain— which it was. They had paid for it, built the building, and contributed all the art that it contained." ◊

In 1917 Cleveland Morgan, whose family owned Henry Morgan and Company, a large St. Catherine Street department store, became chairman of the Museum committee and "dedicated his life" to developing the collection of *objets d'art* and Canadiana. One woman who worked with him in later years said that Morgan had no training that she knew of (in fact, nobody at the Museum had any training); but he had "great knowledge of art objects and good taste," ◊ and that in a very gentlemanly way he cultivated people who had things he wanted for the Museum. Miss Mabel Molson, for example, was persuaded over tea, and through a graceful little exchange of notes, to donate many valuable items to the Museum. Morgan was acting curator during many years.

In spite of many complaints that "people passing by would not know what was inside" the Sherbrooke Street building, annual reports of the Art Association show that during the 1920s around 60,000 people visited the Museum galleries each year. Most of them came on Sunday, when the Museum was open free of charge. The free Sundays had required contributions sufficient to replace the Orkney legacy, which would be forfeited should the Association permit the galleries to be opened on Sunday. In 1922, eighty-three people, all Anglo-Protestant Montrealers, gave $42,475 to make this possible. In addition, many of these same people regularly contributed $1,000 to $10,000 per year and made good any deficits the Association suffered.

The art classes sponsored by the Art Association developed and encouraged many Canadian artists, some of whom, such as John Lyman and Robert Pilot, later studied in Europe and became modernists. The Association had an annual Spring Exhibition at which they offered the Jessie Dow prizes in oils and in water colors, for the purpose of encouraging Canadian artists. William Brymner, who was for many years in charge of the Art school, won prizes at these exhibitions, as did Maurice Cullen, Marc-Auréle Suzor-Côté, and F.S. Coburn—all Canadians. In 1919 there was an exhibition of Tom Thomson, whose painting "In the Northland" was purchased for presentation to the Museum by Dr. Francis Shepherd, Sir V. Meredith, Mrs. H. Molson, and others on the board . Other members banded together to buy a Phillipe Hébert sculpture in 1924. It is, therefore, not true to say that all Montreal patrons rejected or failed to encourage Canadian artists. The young art students, however, were subject to malicious attacks by pre-war Montreal critics, and William Brymner was very important in shielding and encouraging his pupils to carry on in spite of that.

In Toronto, the Group of Seven painters had banded together to try to "make a Canadian statement in Canadian terms" and to escape from a "foreign-begotten technique." They painted Canadian landscapes depicting the harsh colours, the tortured forms, and the vast emptiness of the less pastoral parts of the country. They attracted much attention and support in Toronto and by the early 1920s were exhibiting annually in the Toronto Art Gallery. By contrast, the Group of Seven did not have its first exhibition at the Montreal Art Association galleries until May 1930. In the same year, Dr. Shepherd gave funds for purchase of Canadian paintings, and Watson was able to have successful exhibitions of Maurice Cullen and William Brymner.

Modernism took much longer to win acceptance. The jurists for the Museum's Spring Exhibitions were usually "academic," as supporters of the traditional, École des beaux-arts and Royal Academy standards were called. The Royal Academy placed strong emphasis on portraits and the human figure, the depiction

228

of which was required to be anatomically accurate. To illustrate this concern, Marian Scott says that once, while viewing the paintings hung for a Spring Exhibition, she was joined by Dr.Charles Martin, president of the Art Association, who had "academic" views on art. One of the paintings which had been accepted for the competition was a back view of a nude figure. Marian remembers that "Dr. Martin looked at it and then said to me, 'Do you realize that the back in that painting is one vertebra short?'" He felt that because of this flaw, the painting should not have been accepted for the exhibition.

Under such definitions, modernists, whether Canadian or not, need not apply. It was a long, hard struggle for recognition. Marian Scott recalls that there were few opportunities for non-academic Montreal painters to exhibit. "The big exhibitions were the Royal Canadian Academy and the Spring Exhibition at the Museum and most of us were refused at those."

This situation led in 1943 to a boycott of the exhibition by the Contemporary Arts Society. Founded in 1939, the C.A.S, included the leading modern artists in Montreal: John Lyman, Goodridge Roberts, Clarence Gagnon, Paul-Émile Borduas, Louis Muhlstock, Fritz Brandtner, Marian Scott, Philip Surrey, and others. These artists, both French and English, and all with national (some with international) reputations, complained in a letter to the Art Association: "It was ... a great disappointment to us to learn that (once again) this year's jury was entirely academic, all its members but one viewing modern art unfavorably and several of them being outspoken opponents of it." It was only after a second year's boycott of the Spring Exhibition by the C.A.S. that the Art Association agreed to split the jury into two panels, one academic and the other non-academic. Modernism at last had a hearing.

The struggle for recognition had been bitter, and Montreal modernist painters sometimes felt that their biggest obstacle was symbolized by the only art museum in the city. Some, however, now say that they are grateful to the Museum because "anyone who showed talent could get a scholarship to pay his fees if he couldn't pay." Philip Surrey points out that the Spring Exhibition was one of the most important in Canada to which artists across Canada contributed. The museum also put on two-man exhibitions in Gallery 12 which attracted considerable attention. "That was very nice for young painters. It didn't cost anything and was a break that you don't get anymore." ◊

Although there seemed few if any French-English barriers to cooperation among artists themselves, the Art Association was an English institution in which French Montrealers participated very little. Musical organizations, wherein ethnicity would seem also to matter little, have a mixed record in this respect.

Instrumental music began in Montreal, as in the rest of Canada, with the brass and pipe bands (usually military) which performed for parades, dances, and Sunday afternoon concerts. The other major form of musical expression was choral and vocal, supported mainly by the Roman Catholic and Anglican churches. H. Kallman, music critic and historian, believes that the "rising merchant class and its twin attitudes of commercialism and puritanism" actually resulted in a decline in the artistic level which existed in the eighteenth century, when a combination of the military and the church actively supported music. In any case, Canadian music since then has suffered from insufficient patronage.

A number of musical organizations had already come and gone in Montreal before the 1920s, notably the Montreal Oratorio Society, the Montreal Philharmonic Society, and the Montreal Opera Company. The difficulties experienced by masters at L.C.C. and Selwyn House in having music treated seriously in those schools are worth recalling; music was simply not a priority of support by the elite—especially the male elite. However, it must be noted that certain individual members did what they could, although they got little credit for doing so. Frank Meighen contributed $100,000 of his own money (a large sum in 1913) to cover the deficits of the Montreal Opera Company. With such exceptions, the support of music in Montreal was always uncertain. In the twenties, young people in the English community in Montreal who were interested in music would have found the Elgar Choir, founded in 1923 by amalgamation of the Elgar Women's Choir and the Apollo Glee Club, presenting an average of three concerts a year, accompanied by the Montreal Elgar Orchestra. The Montreal String Quartette was performing between 1925 and 1928 and the Ladies' Morning Musical Club held concerts several times a year, but only for club members and only for women. The Montreal Symphony Orchestra, the third organization under this name to have been formed since 1894, was under the direction of J.J. Gagnier.

The history of the present-day Montreal Symphony Orchestra is interesting because it illustrates the difficulty of sustaining uninterrupted growth of musical organizations. It also demonstrates the particular kind of difficulty which English and French of Montreal had in working together. The history of the Ladies' Morning Musical Club, on the other hand, shows that it was possible for the two groups to cooperate and for their organization to enjoy steady, sustained progress.

When Gagnier took over the Montreal Symphony Orchestra in 1927, none had existed since 1919 when the last organization of that name had given its last concert. The new orchestra lasted only two years. In 1930 a group of musicians, thrown out of work by the Depression and by the "talking pictures" which made live music unnecessary in the theatres, approached Douglas Clarke of the McGill Faculty of Music and asked him to form an orchestra. Four years later, in the depths of the Depression, a French-Canadian group headed by Mme. Athanase David, founded a rival orchestra, called the Société des concerts symphoniques de Montréal (SCSM). The principal reason for this development was that the Montreal Orchestra was inflexibly tied to the English-speaking milieu. The English dominance may have been reinforced by the personality of Douglas Clarke, an Englishman who "did not succeed in identifying with Canada, regarding himself as an Englishman residing abroad." There was a struggle between English and French members of the board, the latter, led by Mme. David, demanding a greater role in the choosing of programs and soloists, which they regarded as excessively English. The management repeatedly refused to give a reasonable place to Quebec soloists, conductors and composers, even though some of these were winners of the Prix d'Europe or holders of grants from the Quebec government. At one point, the Honorable Athanase David, who as provincial secretary was responsible for the arts and humanities in Quebec, offered the Orchestra a subsidy to encourage it to invite Quebec artists. The subsidy was refused. The Davids and their supporters withdrew and formed the SCSM. From 1934 to 1941, Montreal had two symphony orchestras made up of almost the same musicians, a luxury the city could ill afford. The SCSM received its official charter in 1939. With the withdrawal of Mme. David's support, the illness of Douglas Clarke, and the outbreak of World War II, the Montreal Orchestra was disbanded and the SCSM carried on, changing its name in 1953 to the bilingual Orchestre symphonique de Montréal/Montreal Symphony Orchestra.

In contrast to the checkered career of the MSO, is the history of Ladies' Morning Musical Club, one of the oldest musical institutions in Canada. In 1892 Mary Bell organized a club for women who were amateur musicians and who wanted an opportunity to perform and to hear each other play. Later, non-playing members were invited. The next stage was to invite professional musicians who happened to be visiting the city to perform for the members. Finally, the Club organized a regular program with invited musicians and season subscriptions, as it still does. In spite of its reputation locally as an exclusive, socially-conscious club, the LMMC has always been at the leading edge of musical exploration and encouragement of young musicians. For example, it presented excerpts from Debussy's *Pelléas et Mélisande* in 1917, twenty-seven years before its Canadian premiere. It took an early interest in contemporary composers such as Bloch, Hindemith, Medtner and Reger and although world-renowned musicians (Walter Gieseking, Vladimir Horowitz, Glenn Gould, Maureen Forrester, and chamber music groups such as the Amadeus Quartet) performed for them they were always on the lookout for new, unrecognized talent. The LMMC also offers financial assistance to Canadian music students: the Mary Bell scholarship, the Cécile Léger award, and the Kerry-Lindsay award. It has always had both French and English members, and a record of sustained ethnic harmony and support by its female benefactors which a committee member attributes to the fact that ''music has always been more important than nationalistic competition'' to the members, perhaps because it was started by musicians. ◇

Architecture faced not only the same conservatism in the taste of its patrons as did the other visual arts, but the ethnic competition as well. We have already seen that the homes of the elite were inspired by the grandeur of the European past. In addition to this influence, the churches of Montreal expressed religious and social differences between the French and English. Protestant churches were a little plainer than Catholic and were planned more for congregational interaction than for ritual. However, when the congregation was of sufficiently high status, the churches were traditional in design. Thus, Christ Church (Anglican) and the Church of St. Andrew and St. Paul (Presbyterian) are Gothic-Revival churches. In fact, Gothic became so defined as ''English'' in Montreal that when Bishop Bourget wanted to build a Roman Catholic cathedral, in the early 1850s he waited nearly twenty-five years until he found an architect who would build a non-Gothic one. What he had in mind was something he knew no Protestant church would build: a replica, on a reduced scale, of St. Peter's in Rome. As such in 1875, St. James Cathedral (Mary, Queen of the World) was begun. Since 1894 it has stood in the heart of English Montreal as a monument to and reminder of the power of Roman Catholicism in Quebec.

The social aim of banks, office and municipal buildings is to give the impression of solidity, security and power. The forms which had represented these attributes in the past—in Greece, Rome, France or Britain—were used in another age to evoke confidence and willingness to invest money or votes. The Bauhaus group in Germany, generally regarded as the originators of modern architecture, began erecting the austere, glass, steel, and concrete structures in Germany in the 1920s, as did Le Corbusier in France. The migration of Walter Gropius and Mies Van der Rohe, of the Bauhaus, to the United States in the 1930s brought the full force of these new architectural ideas to North America, although Frank Lloyd Wright had been developing an American modern style earlier. Even in the 1940s, Canadian architectural students had to go to Boston, New York, or Chicago to see modern architecture. The first modern building in Montreal was the Town of Mount Royal Post Office built in 1949 by Ray Affleck. Throughout the twenties and thirties, office and public buildings, churches and mansions in Montreal continued to be built according to the tastes of a bygone era.

The struggle for recognition by Montreal's artists, writers, musicians, and architects who were trying to make a uniquely Canadian, modern artistic statement, demonstrates the rigidity and tradition-bound nature of the community. The opposition of the Montreal English patrons to change and their continued identification with Britain extended to writers as well as artists, as we saw earlier in connection with the *McGill Fortnightly Review*. In 1929, Lorne Pierce warned that Canadians needed to study intently the literary interpreters and spokesmen of Canada, ''as an act of self-preservation. The pressure of old and mighty civilizations tend to reduce so small and scattered a people to spiritual and aesthetic vassalage.'' The message went unheeded.

This, then, was the Montreal social, business, and cultural milieu which the young men and women whose lives we have been following inherited in the late 1920s. They were preparing to take charge of community and business leadership positions under precarious conditions. The old Montreal English business leaders had many enemies. They were resented by rising young industrialists, and competing businessmen, particularly in Ontario, because of their unwillingness to provide loans, to share control, or to assist people outside their elite circle. Western farmers, who always blamed all their problems on Eastern interests, had formed a political party to fight them. French Canadians resented the haughtiness, and the indifference or opposition of the Anglo-Protestants to the concerns of the Quebec majority. Women, the poor, the middle class, and the workers resented (however much they may have needed) the exclusive responsibility assumed by Montreal businessmen. The responsibility implied superiority. Their refusal to pay adequate wages and their suppression of labour protest were storing up trouble. Many of the immigrants who came to Montreal from Europe after the war owed no allegiance to the British Empire, which in any case had ceased to be Canada's chief trading partner and financial market. French-Canadians by the thousands were moving from the country to Montreal and the city was increasingly French-speaking. Médéric Martin had forced the English to take a smaller role in municipal politics, while their ability to influence the federal government had also diminished. Women were quietly but steadily challenging male supremacy. The young, educated English middle class, the intellectuals, and the artists, were restive and had the means and ability to publicize their thoughts about a system they saw as unjust, corrupt and crumbling.

Behind these developments were economic and technological changes which had world-wide import: the meteoric rise of the industrial wealth and power of the United States, the relative decline of Britain and the Empire as a political, economic and military force; the increasing secularization in which science was replacing religion as the explanation of and solution for man's problems; the radio, telephone, automobile, and airplane which collapsed distances and exposed everyone to ideas of equality and of relativism that further eroded the old values. The generation born early in this century was ill-prepared to lead in an era of such rapid change. In fact, the failure of Montreal's business leaders to heed all these changes and threats to their position seems either blind or heroic. Their defenses were those of the over-confident. As one man said, ''In general, we took then, as we do now, a very practical view of things. In business, especially if you are successful, you know and expect that others will try to compete with you and even defeat you. People will be envious and cause trouble if they can. So, you just try to make a practical assessment of whether an opponent has the power to do you any harm, and if he does, you fight him with whatever means you have. If he can't, you ignore him.'' ◊ In the soaring prosperity of the late 1920s it was easy to underestimate the enemy. Those caught up in the boom saw only the promise of endless golden tomorrows.

PART III

FACING ADVERSITY

CHAPTER 10

Economic Catastrophe

The fever of speculation which gripped the world during the late 1920s can only be compared to gold fever, which can make otherwise sensible people believe, and act on the belief, that they can become immensely wealthy overnight with nothing but luck on their side. As the prosperity of 1927-1929 grew into a boom, men and women with no previous experience and little knowledge of the business world began to play the stock market or to make extra money selling stocks. They bought on the margin; with very little down payment (5 to 10 percent in Montreal), they could purchase large amounts of stock, borrowing the balance from the broker. If the price of the shares went up, as they mostly did for two or three years, the investor could pay off the loan from earnings. If prices dropped, he and the broker were in trouble. But in the late 1920s prices of stocks soared, it seemed that nobody could lose, and the excitement became a frenzy.

At luncheon parties, well-to-do women would be asking each other what the price of nickel was, or excusing themselves to telephone their brokers for advice about buying more of some stock that was rising. It was on the top of everybody's mind. Then, after a few falters in September, called at the time "readjustment of the market," there came the Crash of October 24, 1929. It caught everybody by surprise. Most small investors had insufficient capital to back their marginal purchases. The New York Stock Exchange, by far the largest on the continent, led the collapse of stock values, and the panic that resulted on Wall Street reverberated around the world. By the time the news reached

Montreal in the early afternoon of that "Black Thursday," New York police were having difficulty controlling the pushing, shoving, screaming crowds trying to get into the Stock Exchange building to find out what was happening to their life savings. From inside the building could be heard the shouting and groaning of the harassed traders. The slide continued and the volume of shares traded reached unprecedented proportions. Mercifully, the market closed at three o'clock, but lights burned all that night as tellers calculated the day's activities. Ticker-tape messages were going out to stock holders to cover their margins "or your stocks will be sold tomorrow morning at the opening price." ◇

In Montreal, the news of the happenings on Wall Street did not arrive on the ticker-tape until the afternoon and full realization not until the next day. The Montreal Stock Exchange was like a club, having only sixty members, all of whom knew each other and were known personally to the biggest Montreal investors. Lacking the anonymity and impersonality of the New York exchange, Montreal's crash seemed, for a few hours, unreal and unbelievable. The whole reaction was somewhat slower and more muted. There was mounting fear, however, as the ticker-tape reported that stocks owned by Montrealers were dropping to half their value of a few days previously on the New York exchange.

Although there was a slight upswing on Friday, it was not nearly enough to make up for Thursday's losses. The following Monday was an even greater disaster than the week before. Once again Brazilian Traction and International Nickel led the way, the first falling by more than 11 points, the second by nearly 8. Consolidated Smelting, a stock valued at 575 earlier in the year, dropped to 300. Stocks fell again on Tuesday and the volume of turnover was the greatest in the history of the Montreal market. As prices dropped, people rushed to sell what they had, before it lost all value. Brokers who had lent money to buyers on the margin were sending out urgent requests to cover these loans. People who did not have the money to pay up had to let the broker sell at what he could get—and keep the proceeds. Investors were crowding into brokers' offices with their jewelry, deeds to property, and other collateral to cover their marginal purchases. A trader who had equities worth nearly $6,000,000 watched their value melt away to two million. An investor who began with $100,000 and ran it up in the prosperous days to $1,750,000 saw the value of his holdings drop to $400,000. Another man had a panic call from his broker to cover his margin on a particular stock. He hurried to his safety deposit box at the bank to get out 5,000 shares of a second stock which he intended to sell to cover the cost of the threatened stock. By the time he appeared at his broker's office the price of the second stock had dropped so low as to be insufficient to cover the call on the first. Within ten days, the small investor had been relegated to the sidelines. When the last drastic break in shares prices occurred in mid-November, even many big investors had lost everything. "People who had been well-to-do woke up to discover they had nothing." ◇ They had lost not only their money, but their jewelry, art collections, country homes, city homes, their yachts, their cars. "I knew a man who had three Cadillacs and lost them all." ◇ Mr. MacD. said, "What I remember vividly about the Depression was that if you had any money you could pick up the most beautiful and valuable things for very little. People who had been very wealthy were selling all their possessions for what they could get. You could go into those great mansions and buy Persian rugs, antique furniture, heirloom silver, art objects from all over the world." ◇ It took a year or two for people to realize that the collapse of the stock market signalled the start of a worldwide Depression that was to continue for years—for so long and of such wretchedness that it changed forever the attitudes of a generation as decisively as had the first World War. By 1932 the number of business failures and the resulting unemployment were resulting in bread lines and suicides. Even previously wealthy people lost their jobs, their capital, or both. In some cases the interest and dividends on which they had expected to live out their lives were not being paid by companies on the verge of bankruptcy. Kenneth Molson was an example of the last. Having retired early from his active involvement in the Molson enterprises, he saw his income melt away at an age when it was too late to start over. He committed suicide. Coroner's reports show a rise in suicides in Montreal from 49 in 1929 to 74 in 1933 and 75 in 1934, an increase of about 50 percent. The *Montreal Star* reported on February 26, 1935 that there had been nine suicides in the preceding nine days. However, this was unusual as the *Star* also said that there had been only one in the morgue report for January. For those who lived through these years in Montreal, suicides of people they knew or at least "you knew the names" were a persistent and shattering part of the experience.

The Montreal Board of Trade reported that in 1930 Quebec had 960 business failures, compared to 715 in Ontario. In 1926 there were only 646 bankruptcies in Quebec. The separate stock issues listed on the Montreal Stock Exchange dropped steadily, from 176 in 1931 to 159 in 1934. It was not only the increased number of failures that mattered; some of the bankruptcies involved the most solid and prestigious companies. A titled lady whose diary never mentions anything very serious outside her own daily life mentioned the Depression just twice: once when a friend committed suicide, and again when McDougall-Cowans failed. It was one of the largest brokerage firms in the city. In October, 1931 she wrote: "Everybody is talking about the bankruptcy of McDougall-Cowans. People are in a panic." ◊

Because of unwise investments in common stocks by T. B. Macaulay, president of Sun Life Assurance Company, "the Sun Life nearly failed in the Depression," says an ex-officer, "and the impact for people who lived through that was that for the rest of their lives they were too conservative. It made an enormous impact on subsequent presidents of Sun Life." ◊

Canada suffered inordinately during the Depression, and Montreal more than most cities. The reasons were to be found in certain rigidities in the design of the Canadian economy, some of which we have already discussed, which were to become nearly fatal in the conditions of the 1930s. First, there were the results of the National Policy. The economy had been designed to depend on the exploitation of certain natural resources (of which wheat and pulp and paper were the most important) and the exchange of these for manufactured goods and services. The huge amounts of capital in these export industries (including transportation) could not be transferred to other uses. Furthermore, over one fifth of the capital invested in private industry was bonded debt, and in 1930 about 40 percent of all the capital invested in Canadian business (excluding farms) and government securities was owned abroad. The interest on these capital borrowings could only be paid through the exports of goods and services. When the prices of exports fell, the cost to the Canadian public in interest charges rose. This cost doubled between 1928-29 and 1932-33, taking less than one sixth of the total receipts from exports in the first period and one third in the later. The entire National Policy had been designed for prosperity, and depended upon the availability of extensive virgin resources and expanding foreign markets. In bad times it proved disastrous. World prices for wheat and newsprint fell early; and since Canada produced 40 percent of the world exports of wheat and 65 percent of the

242

world's newsprint, the decline in prices was catastrophic. Wheat in Saskatchewan, which had sold for $1.65 in 1929, sold for 30 cents in 1931, and the price of newsprint had dropped by 40 percent. An early result of the drop in income which these events represented was that construction virtually ceased. No building, public, industrial, or private, not immediately needed or already contracted was undertaken. Another rigidity here came into play. The wages of skilled labour were relatively fixed and when volume of work was reduced, the easiest solution to the financial problem of owners and managers was to reduce the work force. Construction stoppage also reduced the market for many subsidiary industries and metalworkers, bricklayers, electricians, machinists, and other skilled and semi-skilled labourers also were laid off. In the descending spiral of dropping purchasing power, even producers of essentials such as food and clothing found their markets shrinking. The result was widespread unemployment. By 1933, 826,000 persons—nearly 25 percent of the labour force—were unemployed. These were, of course, largely residents of the cities. Finally, true to the long-standing policy of protective tariffs for certain manufactured goods, the tariffs were raised early in the Depression, thus shielding manufactured goods from the drop in world prices and preventing any alleviating drop in such prices for the Canadian consumer.

By the time of the Depression Canadian industry, commerce, and finance had become highly monopolistic. Mergers and take-overs had meant that a few enterprises dominated the field. This meant that prices could be maintained, even in a Depression, if the producer elected to sell less at the same price, reducing the work force to accomplish the same profit.

The burden of the Depression fell, then, on the unemployed workers, the farmers and other primary producers, the investors in common stocks, those dependent on equity income, and the non-protected producers of manufactured products. Employed wage-earners and persons receiving salaries, or people with enough excess wealth to cover their losses on the stock market or whose business enjoyed a monopoly or a protective tariff suffered little and might even have improved their positions. In trying to meet the emergency, the government was singularly inept, partly because it was so deeply wedded to the old Montreal-inspired financial and commercial policies. As the Rowell-Sirois report commented: "When a realization of the far-reaching effects of the altered circumstances was demanded, there was but faith in the speedy return of the old conditions of prosperity."

Relief, or as it had previously been regarded, public charity, was a municipal and provincial responsibility, but during the Depression neither of these levels of government had the revenues, or the ability to raise sufficient taxes to pay the huge amounts of direct relief that became necessary in lieu of any other means of dealing with unemployment and destitution. The Dominion government provided the difference, as a temporary measure, carefully phrased as due to "extraordinary conditions" and as an assistance only, in no way constituting an infringement of provincial responsibilities. In fact, the federal authority provided about 40 percent of the total expenditures on relief during the years from 1930 to 1939.

Although Quebec was near the Canadian average in terms of the ratio of total relief costs to total provincial income, Montreal was in a much worse situation than most other Canadian cities. In the first place, it was the largest urban concentration in the country. Secondly, in its role as entrepôt to the wheat exporting industry it was as dependent as the wheat farmer himself on prosperity in the West. At the same time, Montreal's specialization around transportation and finance left little room for self-sufficiency or alternate employment for individuals. Thirdly, during the prosperous days of the National Policy, Montreal had been steadily receiving large numbers of unskilled people from the surrounding countryside. When the Depression hit, "unemployment in Montreal and the satellite industrial towns of the area became one of the outstanding economic and human problems of the time, and seriously threatened the solvency of local finances," according to the Rowell-Sirois report.

Finally, Quebec munipalities, in the division of powers with the Province, were required to assume a much larger share of the relief expenditures than elsewhere in Canada: 28 percent of such costs as compared to 15 percent in the rest of Canada. Montreal had to borrow almost the entire amount of relief costs during the Depression, since it was impossible to raise taxes enough to cover it. The municipal debt rose from $252 million in 1930 to $345 million in 1937. Most of this went to direct relief, since public works proved too costly and often wasteful of the money. By the 1940s the city was bankrupt.

Some people blamed the situation on the immigrants. Without so many foreigners, there would be enough jobs to go around for the native-born, they thought. They urged deportation of jobless foreigners, and Canada as a whole deported over 30,000 immigrants during the Depression. The Dominion government established camps for homeless, single unemployed men, several of which were just outside Montreal. Canadian historian Donald Creighton estimates that since Canada had imported large numbers of unskilled workers for farms, railways, mines, and lumber camps, the ratio of single, unemployed men was greater in this country than in any other Western nation. They were the first to lose their jobs and made up the bulk of the single, homeless men in the relief camps or riding the freight trains aimlessly from one city to another looking for work.

Within the city, the Anglo-Protestant community tried to help through its own institutions such as the Family Welfare Association, the Salvation Army, and its church groups. The Family Welfare Association cared for 2,700 cases of Protestant families on relief in 1931, ranging over most of the central part of Montreal from Côte St. Paul, Verdun, and Point St. Charles to Maisonneuve and Rosemount. For this work the Agency had a budget of $290,242 raised primarily from private contributions. It received grants from the province of $5,000, the City of Montreal of $2,000, and Westmount gave $100, or a total of $7,100 public assistance—a pittance compared to the size of the task.

In the working-class district of Verdun, for which separate records were kept, the caseload of the FWA grew from 68 in 1927 to a high of 928 families in 1931. From September 1930 to December 1931 the FWA dealt with all Protestant relief in Verdun and spent: $44,850.54 on aid to families whose head was unemployed out of a total budget of $64,313.36. Besides being involved in financial and personal assistance to needy Protestant families through such official municipal organizations, the Anglo-Protestant upper class tried to help in other ways. The curate of Christ Church Cathedral established a soup kitchen behind the church hall. "Every day, a long line-up of homeless, wandering, unemployed men were fed and he did his best to find jobs for them and sometimes he succeeded." ◇ Although the salaries of ministers of the Anglican Church were not cut across the board, there were rectors in the industrial parishes who voluntarily took cuts in pay because their parishioners had had their wages cut. The Montreal Parks and Playground Association, which had been organized by members of the prominent families in 1900, set up the Community Garden League. "We took by gift, loan or rental, every bit of vacant land within the immediate community of

Montreal, and we turned it into garden plots for destitute families. The Association supplied plowing in the Spring, laid down water in the summer, lent garden implements to anyone who wanted to take up a garden plot. The provincial department of agriculture sent seeds in bulk and Montreal garden clubs packaged them in lots of a proper size for each plot. The plots were large enough so that a family could raise all the vegetables and some fruits they would need for a year. Instruction in gardening was part of the project and when people became expert enough, a cannery was set up, tins were supplied, and the gardeners canned what they grew. It was a real cooperative project. The Montreal Council of Social Agencies put up the money, the CPR handed over all the land below the tracks on their right of way, volunteers did the work." ◊

The Salvation Army and the Old Brewery Mission sold meal tickets to householders for distribution to the constant stream of men who came to their door or approached them on the street, asking for food or money to buy food. Each ticket was good for a meal at the headquarters of the Army or the Mission. It seems to have been the wealthier people who bought these meal tickets. One rarely hears of their feeding people at the door and they bought meal tickets partly as a defensive measure. "We were told that if once we started offering people food, we would be inundated." ◊ People of more modest means often did give everyone who came to the door something to eat, even if not a complete meal. One woman told me, "We didn't have much money ourselves. My husband was out of work for a year and a half, but I felt that as long as I had food, I couldn't turn anybody away." ◊ Of course, the modest home of someone unknown would not be as likely to attract large numbers of hungry people as would the homes of the wealthy. Some men and women were too proud to stand in lines for a cup of soup. "When the snows of the winter melted down on the streets, hundreds of these tickets would be uncovered." ◊ But most were not so proud and it was reported that the Vitré Street refuge alone served 6,000 meals a day to the unemployed.

Charitable efforts of this kind, although helpful in individual cases, could not touch the problems of a Depression in which Canada, with the rest of the world, floundered helplessly, unable or unwilling to take the drastic measures which might alleviate the distress. The individual was on his own, and his strategies of survival were infinitely varied. Everyone had to take stock of

246

his situation and use what resources he had, and accounts of the Depression in Montreal demonstrate the range of human ingenuity. The suffering of the poor was extreme, and if not dwelt on here, it is only because this is the story of people who had expected never to know deprivation.

Some people actually enjoyed the period. Anyone who kept his job or his salary, or had not lost his capital in speculative ventures, might actually have found his situation improved. After the first shock, some formerly affluent families began to enjoy the challenge of keeping up as much as possible of the old life without money. Women took in boarders in the huge houses in the Square Mile. Others got jobs. Because of the Depression, families who might have objected to their daughters' working no longer had a choice. Daughters had to work if they could find jobs. "My friends and I worked in Eaton's or Morgan's selling clothes to friends of our mothers who still had some money." ◊ Mrs. D. recalls that "for a while my $12 a week was all my mother and I had, since my father had died and our capital had vanished. But she liked people, and so started taking in paying guests. I know a lot of people who did that." ◊

They tried to keep up the old pleasures. "None of us sewed," one lady said, "so we scrounged around until we found a little dressmaker. You had to have new clothes if you were going to a ball. We found a little French girl who made dresses in her home in a tiny room with a curtain over a door in one wall. She was good and we all went to her." ◊ And they discovered simple pastimes such as folk dancing, pot-luck suppers, and parties where only coffee or tea were served. "Only one of us still had a car, so a whole bunch would take off in it for a weekend, taking a picnic. We had as good a time as we had had before the Depression." ◊

Social shocks followed financial ones. For some people, even of this privileged background, the Depression meant giving up their way of life and even their friends. A man from a well-to-do family, himself a prominent stock broker, moved to a "sort of shack on the lakeshore. I was down to my last $9,000 and just had to start rebuilding my business little by little." ◊ A woman who had always had an automobile and a chauffeur now walked or took the streetcar. As she was walking along Sherbrooke Street one afternoon a friend passed in her chauffeur-driven car and looked away without even a nod. "She cut me dead." ◊ Some found their world turned upside down. Those who had had money had lost it, and those who had had none now had it. "You were surprised to discover what resentment the new rich had built up towards people who had had money when they didn't. Some of them were quite nasty." ◊ Many people who had enjoyed a social life that depended on servants now did their own work and did little or no entertaining.

A common element in the experience of Montrealers was the support family members gave each other, which often made the difference. Families pulled together. At all income levels there was usually a member of the family whom the crash had not seriously affected. "They would do things for the rest, like send down some presentable clothes when needed, or if there was an illness they would pay the hospital bills. The family had been central before and it remained a solid core." ◊ Anyone who had a piece of luck shared it. Unmarried children of whatever age lived at home; married children moved back. A woman whose father was one of the wealthiest men in the city had had to give up the house they had bought in Westmount because her husband, just starting his first job in a brokerage firm, was making just enough to scrape along. They managed by moving into her mother-in-law's house and occupying what had once been the nursery on the fourth floor. "We lived up there for five years, during which time I had two children," she remembers. ◊

Another member of one of Montreal's oldest and wealthiest families was unemployed for a year and a half, during which time his wife gave birth to their first child. They got along through help of the family. "We used to say that we had two good meals a week: a chicken sent from my family in Cartierville and a roast beef from my wife's family." ◊ In this family, however, both the wife and the husband had a small stipend from their respective families and although the Depression meant a reduced style of life, it did not seriously threaten them.

Most well-to-do Montrealers agree that the old ostentatious lifestyle disappeared with the Depression. Daughters who would have spent all their time between entertainments and the Junior League were working for a living. Although some new money was being made, these newcomers found it indiscreet to try to carry on in quite the old style. One woman had her moment of revelation in the early morning hours, after dinner and the theatre. She and her friends, in evening dress, laughing and chattering decided to go for a sandwich to Ben's Delicatessen in downtown Montreal. As they approached it, "a little knot of men who had been crouched on the sidewalk in a corner out of the wind turned and just looked at us. They didn't look angry or anything, and they didn't approach us. But I knew they were hungry and homeless. I felt uncomfortable and embarrassed at our insensitivity." ◊

The men on the bread lines and in the camps for the unemployed, the masses of men riding the freight cars from city to city, could not be ignored even by those who were comfortable in the Depression. A prominent lady from an old Montreal family remembered going to a restaurant on Dominion Square for toast and tea, and being seated by a window. "I will never forget looking up and seeing seven or eight haggard faces looking in, and I knew that those people were hungry. And I will never forget the sound of the aimless shuffle of people walking who have no destination. How could anyone have lived through that and not have their whole perception of society and the ordering of it affected?" ◊

Hugh MacLennan, in *The Watch That Ends The Night*, has offered his own impressions:

> The unemployed used to flow in two rivers along St. Catherine Street, and I used to see eddies of them stopping in front of shop windows to stare at the goods they could not buy.... I remember how silent the unemployed were when they emerged after a snowfall to clean the streets, often without mittens on their hands, and how pitiful their cheap worn shoes looked as the snow wet them and turned the unpolished leather gray. And above all do I remember my own guilt as I saw them, for I had work and they had none.

The Vitré Street shelter and the Meurling Refuge offered a place to get out of the cold and to sleep. The Vitré shelter was closed in 1933 because the authorities feared that, so congregated, the men would be easy targets for communist propaganda. In the summer, the unemployed slept under newspapers in Fletcher's Field on the eastern slopes of Mount Royal. Libby Park, an activist in the thirties, writes "In the moonlight, it looked like a huge graveyard with flat white tombstones." On November 11, 1931 the *Star* reported that an unidentified unemployed man was found dead of starvation near the Town of Mount Royal. On the society page of the same issue was an account of a coming-out party of a local debutante at the Ritz-Carlton, with the old Montreal names and their new Paris-designed ball dresses described in glowing detail.

CHAPTER 11

Ideological Conflict

The Crash of 1929 was blamed squarely on capitalism. Economists discovered business cycles which were posited as inevitable in a capitalist system. The younger generation, the purveyors of the social gospel, the socialists, and the communists began to question the very basis of Canadian society, and everywhere except in the conservative press, the cry was raised that the economic failure was caused by greed for profits. Sir Edward Beatty took this result for granted when he said publicly, "We had every reason to know that, should speculation go wild and end in disaster, we, the business men would be blamed.... Nothing was more certain than that a speculative boom ending in a speculative crash would provoke an endless series of charges that big business had robbed the poor."

In the inter-war period, Canada's most active social protest groups were in the West. As far back as 1918 the Interprovincial Western Labour Conference meeting in Calgary had proclaimed the principle of industrial rather than craft organization of workers into One Big Union. The participants made no secret of their hopes that this would lead to a socialist state in Canada.

In May 1919, the Trades and Labour Council in Winnipeg called for a general strike in support of the metal and building trades who were demanding higher wages and union recognition. On June 19, pistol-brandishing Mounties in Winnipeg charged into a crowd of people who were peacefully marching to protest the arrest of the strike leaders. Hundreds were injured and one man was killed in the mêlée. It was Canada's first general strike. Not surprisingly, governments and many citizens felt that this was the beginning of a Bolshevik revolution in Canada. Not only was the RCMP sent in to break up this strike and arrest strike leaders, but Arthur Meighen, then Acting Minister of Justice, amended section 98 of the Criminal Code to enlarge the definitions of sedition and conspiracy and to increase penalties. He also changed the Immigration Act to permit the deportation of British-born immigrants suspected of sedition. Under the new law, a number of trade-union organizers from Britain, prominent in the union movements of Western Canada, were deported. These events became a legend of martyrdom in Canada.

Montreal and the province of Quebec, on the other hand, were citadels of entrenched conservatism, perhaps even of reactionary ideals. It hardly seems necessary to demonstrate that Montreal's English community, particularly that part that represented the Canadian capitalist leadership was solidly opposed to any basic change to the system as it existed. The virulence with which unionization efforts and strikes were put down, the resistance even to paying a living wage demonstrated by Montreal entrepreneurs, is clear evidence. The English business interests were supported in this attitude by the French-Canadian elite, particularly the bishops of the Roman Catholic Church and the politicians, and for much the same reasons. Both groups saw Bolshevism, socialism, and indeed most social reform, as a threat to their power positions. In addition, they saw these ideas as a denial of their fundamental values: the English belief in free enterprise and parliamentary democracy; the French belief in family, church, and rural cultural traditions; and the belief of both cultures in Christian religious principles as the basis of the social order. The French-Canadian worker was largely unskilled and ill-educated. As a result, he was the most ill-paid, over-worked, badly-housed, unhealthy worker in Canada. The worker of British origins in Montreal, though usually more skilled, was only slightly better off. Both had every reason when the Depression hit to welcome and lead movements that promised an amelioration of their condition. But between 1919 and 1921 the Church had organized French workers into Catholic trade unions on the Christian principles of brotherhood between employer and employee, and had pronounced strikes to be dangerous and un-Christian. Priests constantly warned of the dangers of communism and the views of labour radicals, thus heading off militancy in that quarter. Canadian workers of British origin were dominated by international trades unions which opposed political action, tended to cooperate with employers, and often restricted membership to safeguard the jobs and statuses of skilled workers. Constant defeat at the hands of authorities, competition between Canadian and American unions, and lack of leadership had discouraged workers. The result was that it was the middle class, largely of the British Protestant community, joined by Jewish and other immigrant anglophones, which in Montreal began and supported the movement for changes which they believed would yield greater equality and social justice for workers.

As the Depression deepened, and Quebec's unemployment rate rose to nearly 30 percent, and the shuffling, grey figures of the unemployed became a persistent aspect of Montreal streets, the young people who had come of age in the twenties and thirties began to feel uneasy, even if they were not suffering personally. How could this be happening? What had gone wrong? What could be done?

By 1935, there were dozens of organizations which invited national and international speakers to discuss the Depression and related social issues and offer answers to these questions. The American Presbyterian church attracted large audiences on Sunday evenings to hear Richard Roberts or Lynn Harold Hough discuss Christian action in the face of social evils. The People's Forum held meetings in the Unitarian Church on Sherbrooke Street, where Dr. Harry Ward and Emma Goldman spoke on Marxist solutions. Frank Scott and Eugene Forsey frequently proposed democratic socialism in public lectures. Stanley Ryerson, Louis Kon, and Fred Rose spoke at meetings of the Friends of the Soviet Union, the Workers' Unity League, or the League Against War and Fascism extolling the virtues of life in the Soviet Union, where no unemployment existed. Many of the social-protest organizations were inspired and organized by the Communist Party of Canada (CPC). Outlawed in 1930, it operated thereafter through "front" organizations, notably the Canadian Labour Defense League, the Workers' Unity League and such pro-Soviet groups.

F.R. Scott had added a concern with social evils and social change to his concern for a modern, purely Canadian literary expression in his poetry. For him, as for many others, the Depression revealed serious flaws in the capitalist system. It had a built-in tendency, he thought, to exploit the weak and the poor and to rank profits above human needs. Capitalism could not be patched up; it had to be replaced by a socialist economy planned to meet the needs of all citizens. When Scott met Frank Underhill in 1931, the two formed the League for Social Reconstruction,

252

which organized discussion groups across the country to consider and propose solutions for Canadian social and economic problems. The Cooperative Commonwealth Federation, a socialist political party, was an outgrowth of the LSR and Scott was its national chairman for a number of years.

The two principal foci for social protest and new solutions, during the thirties, were the CCF and the CPC. The latter was led by a mixture of European immigrants and native Anglo-Protestant Canadians. Some were of working class backgrounds, some were middle class. The CCF leadership was almost entirely Anglo-Protestant, middle to upper class, and well educated. The two groups had no connection with each other and in fact were more often at odds than not, disagreeing on both goals and methods. But to the general public they were birds of a feather. "Our parents could never understand the distinction between socialism and communism. To them, both were 'Bolshevism' which had been the Evil stalking the world since the Russian Revolution," said the daughter of a prominent businessman of the period. ◇

A crucial part of the battle waged against their own elite by the Anglo-Protestant middle class occurred at McGill University. The newspapers of the period were constantly reporting activities and speeches of McGill professors which eventually gave the university a reputation among conservative members of the public as a "hotbed of radicalism." They were, nearly all, men who had been influenced by the Christian social gospel message and were involved in the League for Social Reconstruction.

Eugene Forsey, a professor of economics wrote, with Scott, *Social Planning for Canada*, the LSR manifesto. Forsey also contributed to *Towards the Christian Revolution*, a work linking Christian values to socialism to which five McGill professors contributed. He was a frequent public speaker who made no bones about his belief in socialism. J. King Gordon, of McGill's United Theological College, was part of the group that founded the LSR. He was also a member of the Montreal Presbytery of the United Church whose bulletin reported on minimum wages in Quebec, women's wages, the textile industry, and unemployment relief. The *Star* of December 16, 1932 reported that Professor Gordon, in a speech to the West-End Protective Association, had advocated complete overthrow of capitalistic government, because "private industry is protected at the cost of human life." In the course of the evening, he received support from Brigadier-General Charles Smart, the MLA for Westmount, who said,

"There is no bank in the country that is not violating the criminal laws.... Bankers today are no more than racketeers and pirates.... Let a poor man take a loaf of bread and he gets two years in jail. Another man takes $10,000,000 and he is a captain of finance."

The Social Science Research Project, funded by the Rockefeller Foundation and sponsored by McGill, turned out a steady stream of reports on social and economic conditions in Montreal written by professors and graduate students under the direction of Leonard Marsh of the economics department. They were regarded by the governors of McGill as highly critical of the system, although they simply confirmed many of Herbert Ames's earlier findings. Perhaps the facts seemed more uncomfortable in the 1930s because of the temper of the times.

There were other incidents at McGill. *The Alarm Clock*, a student magazine espousing socialist principles, was virulent in its criticism of the economic system's inability to deal with the Depression. The publication was banned from sale on the campus, but not before it had been noted publicly by the *Montreal Star*. King Gordon, as faculty advisor to the Student Christian Movement chapter on the campus, helped lead that group in a socialist direction. Parents and governors were upset: the students were being corrupted. In early 1936, Chancellor Beatty sent a copy of one of F.R. Scott's letters published in the *Canadian Unionist* to Principal Morgan as evidence that "our university socialists are not only preaching socialism constantly, but are more active in trying to induce others to accept their doctrine than any other class of propagandists in the country." Morgan's response was that he hoped such controversy would always exist.

Accusations and complaints began to be made outside McGill. In early April, 1937, Sir Henry Gray, a distinguished surgeon, made the assertion in a speech to the Montreal Health Club that "right in McGill there are Communists now." His speech was widely quoted in the press. Principal Morgan denied Gray's claim, saying that, if it was so, he would like to know the names. However, on April 28, Morgan resigned as Principal—apparently (to judge by his and Beatty's letters) at the request of the Board of Governors. Morgan's failure to curb the "pinks" in the university was believed to be the cause for his removal and the *Toronto Daily Star,* the *Clarion*, the *Winnipeg Tribune*, the *Windsor Star* described Morgan as the champion of liberalism. Beatty defended his position in a convocation address, declaring that "no repression by the governors has been or ever

254

will be imposed on the Principals of this university.'' In the circumstances this seemed to mean that McGill principals might have the right to think as they like but not to their jobs. The choice (also free) was theirs.

The next Principal, Lewis Douglas, worked out with Beatty a policy of limiting tenure and promotions in such a way as to minimize ''the influence on the student population of certain members of the University staff.'' As a result, Forsey and Marsh were eased out of McGill along with some lesser lights. King Gordon had left even earlier. Scott retained his position perhaps because of his national reputation, although nothing is said about him specifically after the Morgan resignation. Nonetheless, it was the policy of the *Montreal Star* to give Scott as little publicity as possible. Whether this policy was decreed by the paper's publisher, J.W. McConnell, a governor of McGill and its great benefactor, is uncertain, though plausible. An ex-reporter for the *Star* remembers that such a policy existed, but says that it ''may have been only an effort of the *Star* staff to please J.W., knowing that he disliked Scott. People did those things then.'' ◊ Given Scott's prominence during McConnell's lifetime, this sometimes left strange gaps in *Star* coverage of the news.

The Depression also galvanized the enemies of St. James Street outside of Montreal. Western attacks on chartered banks, particularly the Bank of Montreal, led in 1934 to the establishment of the Bank of Canada. The Depression brought financial disaster to public and private borrowers alike, but the plight of the Western farmers was the worst. They had always desperately needed affordable capital on terms that met their fluctuating needs, but interest rates were consistently higher in the West and loans hard to get from the banks. Pressure mounted for the government to provide such loans. Finally, a Royal Commission on Banking and Currency was established in 1933 to investigate the advisability of establishing a central bank which could control the volume of currency in circulation, interest rates, credit conditions and external stability of the currency. It was believed by many, but denied by the banks, that the chartered banks were incapable of the disinterestedness and the flexibility required to meet the monetary needs of the country. The banks denied this. They had enough money, they said, all the country needed; but there were not enough sound borrowers. The banks' claims provoked considerable anger among members of the general public who felt that if money was so plentiful, there was no reason that the rate of interest should be so high and borrowing so difficult.

On the other hand, the Commission itself commented that "The commercial banker has very properly in the past regarded his responsibility as mainly confined to safeguarding the interests of his depositors and shareholders and to making judicious loans and investments with the funds entrusted to him." Not a single bank failed in Canada as a result of the Depression whereas in the United States more than 5,000 banks had to suspend payments between 1929 and 1932. Nonetheless, partly in response to those who believed that much of the distress and misery of the Depression was caused by the credit policies of banks, the Commission recommended the establishment of a central bank.

The new Bank of Canada which thus came into being reduced considerably the importance of the Bank of Montreal. It not only took over the issuing and control of currency, it also was now the government banker and manager of its finances, a role often assumed previously by the Bank of Montreal. An officer of the Royal Bank, Graham Towers, was appointed the Bank of Canada's first governor. The Old Guard was on its way out. The Bank of Montreal continued to prosper and to pay dividends even during the Depression, but like the CPR, it lost its dominance. It ceased to be Canada's largest and most important bank and an arm of the Dominion government.

In the same year that the governors of McGill were getting socialism under control in the university, there was another blow to the business community. The report of the Royal Commission on Price Spreads, published in 1937, concerned itself with some of Montreal's principal industries, several of which were represented on the McGill board. With regard to the textile industry, for example, the Commission declared:

> We cannot, in frankness, refrain from stating that the labour and wage conditions in this branch of Canada's industrial activity are such as to merit the most emphatic condemnation. They should not be tolerated in any state that claims to call itself civilized.

The shoe industry fared no better in the Commission's judgement:

> It is no surprise, in the light of these facts, to learn that the Minimum Wage Law is flagrantly violated. Out of the eight factories, six classified an illegal proportion of their workers as "inexperienced," and five paid a large proportion of them (35 to 83 percent), even then, less than the minimum rate.

Imperial Tobacco and the Macdonald Tobacco Company which held a virtual monopoly in manufacture of tobacco products, were singled out by the commission as bearing the major share of the responsibility for "the combination of low wages and high profits," in that industry. The report went on to point out that while in 1933 wage-earners received an average of $10.67 for a 44.7 hour week (less than $600 per year) an average of 28 chief executives received more than $15,000 each in salary and bonuses at Imperial Tobacco. At Macdonald Tobacco,

> ... undivided profits at the end of 1933 stood at $594,432, notwithstanding the withdrawal of $260,000 annually by the president since 1930. In 1933, 1,355 male and female employees of this firm received an average weekly wage of $12.80, 8 percent less than the 1929 average.

Such findings, pinpointing specific companies and individuals in Montreal might have embarrassed and infuriated those identified, had they been taken seriously. The report's recommendations that minimum wage and hour laws be rigorously enforced, that employees have the right to collective bargaining and to the strike weapon went far beyond the position employers took at the time. In fact, the amount of government regulation of business which the report recommended was a long time in coming. Even the right to collective bargaining through recognized union representatives was not generally accepted in the thirties.

As to the charges themselves, although a Montreal labour leader of the time says that "the workers were much impressed by these findings. They felt vindicated in their struggle." ◇ A retired businessman recalls that people felt at the time that the Royal Commission investigations were merely political ploys: attempts by Liberal businessmen in Toronto to shift the blame for the Depression to Tory businessmen in Montreal. ◇

A retired president of a construction company probably expresses a common attitude of leading Montreal businessmen of the thirties when he says that he doesn't remember much talk about the Royal Commission. The findings "never seemed to bother Blair Gordon [president of Dominion Textiles] a bit, and I knew him well. As for what they said about William Macdonald, don't forget that he gave millions to McGill. Nothing happens as a result of royal commissions, you know." ◇

Nonetheless, the attacks continued and spread. The Montreal Conference of the United Church passed a resolution in 1933 demanding the repeal of Section 98 of the Criminal Code which made it illegal to belong to, or even attend a meeting of an association deemed to be revolutionary. Under this law, labour meetings and all protest meetings of any sort, had been broken up and leaders arrested. The Montreal *Gazette* responded to the United Church resolution by branding it as one "which might have emanated from an organization of political radicals."

The split in the Montreal Anglo-Protestant community grew wider, the defensiveness of the older established Montreal business group more evident. After all, the attack was coming from within. McGill, which had been established by, directed, and nursed to international prominence by the philanthropy and efforts of the Montreal businessmen was biting the hand that fed it. The religious teachings on which the Square Milers had all been reared were being used against them. Even their own children were attending seditious meetings and following strange pipers. In fact, some of them *were* the pipers. Frank Scott was of the establishment born and bred. Of an old Quebec and Montreal family, his father was Canon F.G. Scott of World War I fame, his older brother a lawyer who was to become a judge. King Gordon was also a minister's son, albeit an American. Most of the McGill group of rebels were from solid middle-class British and Protestant backgrounds, and their socialism was based on Christian values.

There were others, not at McGill, from the same background: Stanley Ryerson, son of the dean of the faculty of medicine at the University of Toronto and a graduate of Upper Canada College, was a professor at Sir George Williams University. For him, Marxist socialism fitted familiarly with his Christian upbringing. A young dentist named Cyril (Flin) Flanagan, whose father was an Anglican minister in Montreal's north end, had attended Lower Canada College. He was a private with the Canadian Expeditionary Forces in World War I. At Passchendaele, his belly was ripped open by a shell; miraculously, he survived. He returned to study dentistry at McGill, where he was a football and hockey star who "regularly had to be carried off the field because he wouldn't give up as long as he could stand." ◊ He was much admired by the Montreal elite because he was an Old Boy who lived by all the values of loyalty, determination, courage and hard work. But Flanagan, disillusioned by the war and the Depression, became a socialist. He says that his socialism was a logical outgrowth of Christianity learned from his father. During the Depression, "watching kids eat out of garbage pails," he was part of the Montreal LSR and in 1945 ran for Parliament on the CCF ticket. He constantly attacked the injustices practiced by big business and tried to convert his wealthy friends to socialism, privately, in print, and from the speaker's platform. He worked from within, and although he made few converts in the business community, even he doesn't know how many patients, rendered speechless by wads of cotton and a dentist's drill, had their consciences disturbed by his exhortation. These and others like them were articulate, well-educated Anglo-Protestants who in other times might have fitted into a conservative Montreal business or professional life. Most of their generation did. Their friends and neighbors of the Anglo-Protestant community had to come to terms with their defection. Some tried earnestly to understand. Walter Johnson attended for the first time a lecture by J.S. Woodsworth, the first president of the CCF, in 1935. He wrote afterwards to a friend, that he was expecting ''to hear something very compelling. I found that he was weak as water, that he was upset by criticism, and had no come back in sound logic. I cross-examined him and he only became irritated. But he is listened to almost as a god by a great many Canadians.''

Peace movements were strong immediately after World War I, activated by the hideous nature of that war and the expectation that only the ''merchants of death,'' the capitalists, had gained by it or would want it repeated. The hope lay in the League of Nations, a concept which, however ineffectual it proved, fired the imagination. In the 1930s there appeared a barrage of photographic and personal reminiscences of that war, intended to thoroughly disabuse anyone of the notion that it was glorious. Books like Vera Brittain's *Testament of Youth,* and Robert Graves's *Good-bye to All That* contributed to the new generation's repudiation of the war as Canada's (or any other nation's) ''moment of glory.'' At the same time that pacifism was gaining ground, an anti-British, anti-Empire sentiment was growing. This feeling was, of course, the logical accompaniment to a growing Canadian nationalism, also much stronger in the younger generation than among their parents. The same woman who, as a child had quaked with awe at seeing the King and Queen in London before the war, was by the 1930s a thorough anglophobe. ''I hated the English,'' she says. ''They came here with their superior airs and treated us like colonials.'' ◊ Traditions were indeed crumbling.

Meanwhile, events in Europe threatened to engulf the world in another world war. Most socialists were also pacifists after

World War I, and believed that all wars were imperialistic; but the outbreak of the Spanish Civil War in 1936 caused an about-face. The Left saw the attack on the legally elected Spanish government by General Franco's Falangists, supported by Hitler and Mussolini, as an attack on the very principle of democracy. For the leaders of the Montreal French population and some of the more conservative of the English, Franco represented the forces of order, tradition and Christianity. Corporatism was widely admired and was advocated by Lionel Groulx, Archbishop Ville-neuve, and Mayor Camillien Houde of Montreal, accompanied by a marked (if unofficial) anti-semitism in the streets. For the rest of the decade, the struggle between communism and fascism, getting its dress rehearsal on the Spanish stage, divided Montreal along ethnic as well as generational lines. The Spanish Civil War brought about an uneasy united front among all left-wing groups, instigated by the Communist Party International line that only a united front of all anti-Fascist groups in the world could insure the defeat of those reactionary forces. The Spanish War was the catalyst which activated two other well-known examples of Anglo-Protestant defection to the Left.

Norman Bethune was already well known both for his radical methods of treating tuberculosis at the Royal Victoria Hospital and for his determined rebellion against the authoritarian conservatism of that stronghold of privilege. He was of Scottish and English descent, and his family included physicians and university professors. His own father was a Presbyterian minister. Bethune's decision to go to Spain and to set up a mobile blood unit in aid of the Spanish government is a well-known story. What he saw there converted him to Communism and, according to Stanley Ryerson, he became a member of the CPC on his return. Bethune was a charismatic character, bold, opinionated, quixotic, and romantic. He was hated and loved in Montreal and made a strong impression on the young intellectual and artistic generation.

One of the people who came under his influence was Hazen Sise, a member of an old and prominent Montreal family of British origins. His father, Paul F. Sise, was president of the Northern Electric Company and a director of the Royal Bank, Bell Telephone, the Montreal Trust, the Lake of the Woods Milling Company, Dominion Engineering, Price Brothers, Shawinigan Water and Power, and Dominion Bridge. Hazen's uncle, Charles Sise, was Chairman of Bell Telephone and a director of the Bank of Montreal, Northern Electric, the Royal Trust, the Maritime Telegraph and Telephone, and others. No one who knew Hazen would describe him as typical, and there is much evidence that he was a person not able to fit comfortably into any niche or to achieve any clear sense of direction in the society around him. His letters illustrate the ideological conflicts, particularly between generations, at the time. Not many of the young elite were so afflicted, and most people of Hazen's generation said, ''We were all sorry for his parents.'' ◇ But they were aware of the issues in the thirties, and clearly uncomfortable about them.

Hazen was in London hoping to practice the architecture in which he had been trained at McGill, or alternatively to get some work as a photographer. In truth, he was enjoying a year abroad, as was customary for young men of his position, and since he was unusually charming, he spent a lot of time entertaining and being entertained. Nonetheless, his rudderless existence bothered him, as his letters to his friends and family show. Hazen met Norman Bethune in London and after hearing him discuss his plans said, impulsively, ''My God, I wish I were going with you.'' Bethune said that he would be glad to have him—he needed a driver—but Sise should think it over. He refused to try to persuade him, but would see him the next day for his answer. Late in the afternoon of the next day, a rainy Sunday, Bethune was at the door of Sise's London flat, stern, unsmiling, waiting. In a letter to his father explaining why he decided to go to Spain, Hazen wrote:

> I am not a communist, but have been driven very close to their way of thinking both by the logic of their beliefs and by the trend of events, which, every day, go more and more to justify their position.... I believe that our futures will be very largely determined by the result of the conflict in Spain, so I am going to do my little bit.... If I had been of age in 1915 you would not have wanted to stop me—and the issues now are much clearer than then.

In December 1937, Hazen returned to Montreal firmly convinced of the righteousness of the Republican cause and prepared to speak his mind publicly. The family distress can be imagined from a letter Hazen wrote to Moran Scott: ''Off the straits of Belle Isle, Dad telephoned me and asked that I shouldn't give any interviews until I had had a chat with him. I agreed.'' When finally they were able to talk privately,

Father pointed out that Uncle Charlie and himself, as heads of public-service corporations depended, for their smoothe [sic] running, on the good-will of the provincial governments of Ontario and Quebec. He did not approve of Hepburn and still less of Duplessis but was in no position to do anything about it. He claimed, and I think with justice, that if I were to make any scathing attack on the Duplessis set-up (particularly the church) or even a damning analysis of the Franco situation, it would make endless trouble for them.... He claimed that if I came out fours-quare as a militant opponent of capitalism, he (and probably Uncle Charlie) would be put into such an embarrassing position that they would have to resign their jobs.

In fact, Hazen did speak at fund-raising meetings of the League for Peace and Democracy and wrote letters to newspapers, but these were more devoted to pleading the Spanish Republican cause than attacking local businessmen and politicians. His father did not have to resign from his job.

Meanwhile, Section 98 of the Criminal Code was being applied with vigour in Montreal. Even the older generation began to be concerned about the threat to freedom of speech and assembly inherent in the suppression of all social protest by political authorities, both municipal and provincial. Unemployed workers' meetings were consistently broken up by the police, and their leaders arrested as communists. Anyone distributing a notice of a meeting deemed by the police to be questionable under Section 98 was arrested. According to one member, every meeting of the League for Social Reconstruction was attended by police or the RCMP, who simply sat at the back of the room and listened. It was reported that the Montreal police broke up seventeen meetings, of presumed communist groups, and arrested sixty-nine persons, in 1934 alone. Fifty-three others were arrested by plain-clothesmen. Special police agents were said to have attended 802 communist meetings. One wonders how the police had time for anything else.

Matters became worse with the election of Maurice Duplessis as premier of Quebec in 1936. Duplessis had "a curiously morbid horror of socialist principles" which was activated by other events of that year. Ernest Lapointe, as federal minister of justice under MacKenzie King, had succeeded in rescinding Section 98 of the Criminal Code in response to much pressure. Immediately, there was pressure on provincial governments to pass compensatory anti-communist legislation.

Meanwhile, in October 1936 three delegates of the Spanish government were invited to address a public meeting in Montreal. Students at the Université de Montréal marched to City Hall and threatened to riot if the delegates were allowed to speak in public. Director Dufresne, the chief of police, forbade the meeting without explanation. A Westmount hall was then booked, but when the students threatened to invade that, it was also refused, although the reason given was that the hall was not available. Finally, a small group met in a salon of the Mount Royal Hotel and had just begun to listen to one of the speakers, when the management of the hotel suddenly announced that the meeting was cancelled and turned out the lights. On their way out, the group was jostled by students shouting "A bas les communistes!" Some of the demonstrators decided to extend their protest. On the pretext that all Jews were communists, they threw stones and damaged Jewish shops along St. Catherine Street on the way east to St. Denis Street.

Two days later, Sunday, October 25, was the Feast of Christ the King. Special sermons throughout the province warned of the communist peril represented by the Spanish visitors. Some priests and bishops congratulated the City of Montreal for preventing the meeting. Premier Duplessis announced, "I want to say how proud I was when I learned that the students had prevented the communists from speaking in Montreal." He contended that the grand theories of liberty, equality and fraternity were worthless; what counted was faith, hope, and charity. The acting mayor of Montreal, Leo McKenna, backed the police action: "They got just what they deserved ... the crowd mixed up in this are all communists." The *McGill Daily*, on the other hand, editorialized: "We feel that the attitude of certain students of the University of Montreal is against academic freedom, against the democratic principles of the British Empire."

Shortly afterward, petitions were gathered across the province requesting the government to ban communistic activities as the province of Ontario had already done. This led within the year to the passage of the Padlock Law, one of the most repressive measures ever enacted in North America. Section 3 made it illegal for any person who owned or occupied a building or house within the province, to use it or allow any person to make use of it "to propagate communism or bolshevism by any means whatsoever." Section 12 outlawed the printing, publication or distribution of any newspaper, periodical, pamphlet, circular or document propagating or "tending to propagate" communism or bolshevism. The judge of whether any of this was happening was the Attorney General, who could order the "padlocking" of establishments without any court proceedings. Those accused were presumed guilty until proven innocent, and could not appeal to a Superior Court judge for a year. The penalty was imprisonment. This law was passed unanimously by the Quebec National Assembly. With this weapon Premier Duplessis, who himself assumed the title and portfolio of Attorney-General, was able to suppress all opposition to his point of view, whether from labour unions, political dissidents, or religious sects.

Although Anglo-Protestant businessmen may not have been willing to carry matters to such length, and may even have had some sympathy for the Spanish Loyalists, they shared Duplessis' antagonism to unions, communists, and Jews. Duplessis, for his part, shared the English businessman's paternalistic sentiments, with the same odd mixture of generosity and penuriousness that we have noted in the Old Guard of the Square Mile (according to Pierre Laporte, who as a correspondent for *Le Devoir* followed Duplessis' political activities for fifteen years). He tells us that Duplessis could be very generous if one knew how to approach him, but he "paid his employees the lowest salaries ... and was always hostile to salary increases.... Instead of giving people a reasonable wage, he gave them meager salaries and distributed gifts at Christmas or Easter. He played at the generous man."

Duplessis had another characteristic in common with the Montreal businessman, according to LaPorte: "Anything new worried him: a new candidate, a new Minister, the face of a journalist he did not know, a new piece of legislation ... Duplessis was horrified at the thought of change ... Born in the last quarter of the 19th century, he apparently lived through the tremendous industrial changes of the past fifty years without being influenced by them in any way."

Laporte's description evokes the dictum of a Montreal clergyman heard by his daughter when she was growing up, about the time of World War I. "The Montreal businessman lives in the same neighborhood, sends his children to the same schools, belongs to the same clubs, and goes to the same summer resorts as his friends and relatives. In that way, he never risks encountering a new face or a new idea." ◊

Duplessis generally got along well with the English magnates. The premier's close relationship with J.W. McConnell has been well-documented; and he had other friendships as well. A businessman long past retirement reports that he came across a letter from Maurice Duplessis in the dead files of his company to Mr. F. "Dear George," it began, "I have taken your advice and I will see that McGill is given a grant." The informant added, "So that was how 'George' influenced politics. He had told Maurice how to get control of the private utilities companies and that, of course, led to Quebec Hydro, and in exchange Duplessis would support McGill." ◊ Mrs. H. says of the community of which she was a part : "I think one of the great shames of the English community is that they didn't fight Duplessis. They didn't because he was good for business. He did everything that they wanted and so they just closed their eyes to the dreadful things he was doing. They knew these things were going on." ◊ A lawyer whose practice involved political figures called it "an error of judgement" on the part of English business to "have played ball" with Duplessis since he "was the first premier to define Ottawa as the prime opponent of Quebec interests. When it suited Duplessis's purpose, he dumped them, and by supporting him, the English assisted in their own demise. He led us down the garden path." ◊

Although the political movements and ideological conflict of the 1930s did not persuade the Anglo-Protestant business leaders to change their ways, they did have repercussions in the community. The ideological conflict split generations, provided a value basis for the rejection of the authority of business leaders, and shook their confidence. Walter S. Johnson, a Montreal lawyer, in a letter to C.H. Carlisle, dated March 5, 1935, reported an acquaintance's "fair criticism," upon contemplating the intellectual turmoil of the thirties, that (much as he disliked the thought) capitalism was on the wane and was bound to be swept away, because "the enemies of capitalism are vociferous, they get thousands of columns of free advertising in the press, they have a triumphant note in their declamations, and gradually, they are getting a lot of people convinced that they must be right, because Capitalism does not seem to be able to hit back and justify itself."

A third-generation descendant of a prominent family remarked: "My grandfather did what he wanted to do and was proud of it. My parents' generation was terribly concerned with manners and doing the right thing. By the time my generation came along, we were ashamed to be who we were." ◊ It is reasonable to suppose that the contemporary political and ideo-

265

logical attacks on the ruling group must have had some part in producing this sense of shame—if not in the generation then in power, at least in their children.

Throughout this social and economic upheaval, Anglo-Protestant business leaders offered little leadership. The Montreal Board of Trade, the official voice and organization for English business, had few suggestions for alleviating the situation. Their annual reports show that they relied on old solutions: increased trade, particularly within the Empire, and reduction of taxes, especially corporation taxes. They did suggest that business firms "immediately give out contracts for construction work, and orders for goods, which might ordinarily not be placed until later. The adoption of such a policy by the majority of business firms would not only alleviate the unemployment situation but also tend to restore public confidence..." The Board of Trade became increasingly concerned with sound public finance which it believed to be threatened by enormous relief payments, corruption and incompetence. It first proposed that the province take over the city's finances in 1934. In 1940 under Camillien Houde, the city defaulted on a $7,500,000 bond issue; whereupon the Quebec Municipal Commission, established to administer the finances of collapsing municipalities, took over Montreal's financial affairs until 1944.

Even if sound, these were only piecemeal solutions. There was no one with the vision of a Franklin Roosevelt, or the idea of a New Deal, either in politics or in the business world. A man who was president of the Board of Trade at the time remarked that "if anyone had any sweeping ideas about what to do about the Depression, I think I would have heard of it, and I didn't." ◊

In fact, that keeper of the entrepreneurial conscience, Sir Edward Beatty, castigated the Canadian business community as a whole for their lack of leadership. In a speech entitled "What of Business Leadership in National Affairs?" in Toronto in 1937, Beatty accused business of failing to provide leadership in the economic crisis and ideological conflict of the Depression:

> The employer who does not consider the rights of his workers to reasonable stability of employment and reward will perforce pay the taxes needed to relieve distress.... To no little extent the attacks on the economic system ... are based upon legitimate discontent with things as they are. That there exist in this country obvious cases of suffering and misery is a direct challenge to those who believe with me in the established system of society....

266

Failure to criticize and to improve the system of society in which we believe is failure of leadership on the part of businessmen.

If Beatty found this to be true of the Canadian businessman in general, how much more it applied to those men in St. James Street where, until then, the major business decisions were made for the nation.

The Depression seriously reduced the standard of living of all Montrealers and ruined some of them, financially. Conservative business policies were cast in doubt—the National Policy had failed. In fact, all the values on which the Anglo-Protestant culture had been built were in disarray in the 1930s. More important still, the elite members of this group were unable to provide any real leadership in the crisis. The solutions they wanted—tax reductions for business, lower relief payments, tariffs, and Empire trade preference—were too easily dismissed as self-serving. Isolated, surrounded by enemies, the Montreal business elite stood at bay. The Bank of Montreal had lost its pre-eminent position; so had the Canadian Pacific Railway. Unable to fulfill its role as financial leader of the nation, the Montreal business group began to be replaced by newcomers, especially in Toronto, to whom these changes represented opportunity.

CHAPTER 12

From Depression to War

The majority of English Montrealers were not involved in the ideological turmoil of the 1930s. If they thought about it at all, as Mavis Gallant suggests in her play, *What's To Be Done?* many were simply confused. In fact, a public discussion about the play held in Montreal at Centaur Theatre in the Fall of 1984 and attended by people who were in the city in the thirties and forties, demonstrated how varied were the views of the ideological battles that continued from the Depression through World War II and later. People's ideas were largely a product of where they lived, what they were doing, and who they knew at the time. There were many more than two solitudes in Montreal. For the group with which we have been concerned, life was simpler and perhaps less fun than it had been when they were younger. They were rearing young children in ''reduced circumstances''; parties were less frequent and less fabulous.

Some of them were absorbed in sports, as they had always been. McGill University was a focus for amateur sports, and students and townspeople followed hockey, football, rowing, track, skiing, swimming, tennis, baseball, rugby, basketball, and soccer matches. Wins were celebrated and losses drowned with the same fervour that are now accorded the wins and losses of professional teams. People still remembered that in 1929, McGill teams won twelve out of fifteen intercollegiate championships. The Canadiens and the Maroons (a so-called English team) were playing on artificial ice at the Forum, where in 1924 Senator Donat Raymond had invested $1,250,000 to build an indoor rink and stadium. The popularity of hockey soared. Joining friends in the box seats for hockey night was a regular and exciting entertainment for those who could afford it.

People who might have had little interest in the Spanish Civil War and fascism in Germany and Italy were fascinated by activities of the Royal Family in the thirties. Montrealers had known or seen Edward, the Prince of Wales, when he was a frequent visitor to Montreal for balls and the Montreal Hunt, where the elite had met him personally. They followed his coronation and his subsequent abdication and marriage to Mrs. Simpson with interest and anguish. Scrapbooks of the period bulged with clippings on the subject. Even more of a favourite, one often producing an entire scrapbook, was the visit of King George VI and Queen Elizabeth in 1939, the first time a reigning British monarch had visited the city. Montreal indulged in an orgy of pomp and ceremony. Lamp-posts on the procession route were painted gold; streetcars flew Union Jacks; triumphal arches were built along the route; columns were crowned with lions and unicorns; bunting and flags hung from all downtown buildings. Fortunately, it did not rain. Crowds had gathered even before daylight to position themselves along the route. The royal couple arrived via a blue and silver train at Jean Talon Station. Then, in an open limousine, accompanied by a ''glittering hussar escort,'' the King and Queen travelled the twenty-three miles of route accompanied by cheers of welcome; by ringing church bells, by blaring bands and by the tooting of ships' horns. At the end of the day, a thousand guests joined George and Elizabeth for dinner at the Windsor Hotel and outside 100,000 uninvited admirers jammed Dominion Square, singing and shouting. A lady kept in her scrapbook a letter from her child's nanny who wrote that upon seeing the King and Queen, ''I had a sort of heaving in my chest, tears in my eyes, but I didn't cry because I was glad, very glad ... and I expect that ... their hearts go out to us as surely as ours to them.'' ◊ A great many Montrealers, not only the elite, still felt that they were British.

Although the lives of young married women in the 1930s were certainly not as glamourous as the social whirl of their debutante days, there were compensations. The Depression, requiring as it did that the whole family pull together, had given many women somewhat more responsible roles. Some had had to take jobs; husbands and fathers had not always been able to carry the financial responsibility which was expected of the male head of the family. Even elite women report equal sharing of budget and income information and decisions with their husbands. It began to be obvious that women were quite capable of managing such things.

It also became obvious that women would need more practical education than they had received in the past. Mothers who had themselves gone only to finishing school after Miss Edgar's, now accepted the idea of their daughters' attending McGill; and the daughters enrolled in increasing numbers. By 1940, there were about 2,500 women at McGill—35 percent of the enrolment. In the same year Quebec women were enfranchised; a right won in other provinces by 1921. The Montreal Suffrage Association, which began the effort to obtain votes for women, was organized in 1912 by the Montreal Council of Women, with Lady Drummond as honorary president. The English suffragists eventually realized that they could make no headway without the assistance of French women. They were joined in 1921 by a group headed by Mme. Marie Gérin-Lajoie and in 1927 by L'Alliance canadienne pour le vote des femmes au Québec. These women were greeted both in the national assembly, the press, and the pulpit with scorn, ridicule, and indignation. It took thirteen more years of patient persistence to achieve their goal. Their techniques were very low-key and lady-like. Like the women trying to enter McGill's medical school, they "walked very warily." Collard quotes the Hon. Jacob Nicol's comments on the successful passage of the bill enfranchising women. Nicol's remarks illustrate the misgivings about such a drastic move which had delayed its acceptance so long: "We have today come to an end of an historic era in Quebec, as elsewhere, whether we like it or not."

Most married women , however, continued to stay at home and reared their children as in the past. Members of the generation whose experiences we have been following were now approaching forty years of age. Although they may have moved to Westmount, their extended families were still nearby with parents and grandparents available for visits and advice. Continuity was reinforced by a desire to keep things as they were. Thus the community was somewhat insulated from child-care prescriptions being propounded by psychiatrists and psychologists in the United States and other parts of Canada. It was, after all, the era of scientific child-rearing, of which Canada's Dionne quintuplets were the most famous examples. But in Montreal children were still taught to obey and respect people in authority. Their schools were expected to be strict about discipline and to lay on the homework.

Children in public and private schools wore uniforms and stood at attention when the teacher walked into the room. They did not interrupt and they gave up their seats to anyone older than themselves. Elite children were still taught that they were privileged and had a responsibility to the community. Their parents might not have altered the basic values and social patterns which they hoped to pass on to their children, but during and after the Depression, there was less formality in child-parent relationships, just as there was less formality between husbands and wives. And a new note of uncertainty can be felt in parents' attitudes. Most agree that they were less rigid about rules and did more listening to their children than their own parents had done. One parent recalls: "We were softer with our children, more friendly and closer, but we still demanded the same standards that had been asked of us." ◊ Another says, "I think the Depression shook up our confidence. It seemed to cast doubt on a lot of the things we had been taught. It was hard to know what to tell our children." ◊

Whatever doubts they may have had, they continued to send their children to Miss Edgar's, the Study, or Trafalgar, to Selwyn House, L.C.C, or Bishop's College School. Summers were still spent with their friends and relatives at Métis, Como, Ste. Agathe, and Brome Lake, with considerable supervision of the children's activities and social contacts all year round.

MacKenzie King's foreign policy during the inter-war years had been largely isolationist, intended to keep Canada out of European entanglements, much like that of the United States at the time. This was consistent with King's historic effort to make Canada independent of Britain's foreign policy. He was joined by the other Dominions when in 1931 the Statute of Westminster declared that all members of the Commonwealth were equal partners. In this drive for national independence, one of the small but significant practices which fell into disuse was the proposal by the prime minister of a list of outstanding Canadians to receive titles bestowed by the British sovereign. Ties with Britain were being weakened and it was increasingly thought ridiculous for Canadians to aspire to an aristocracy that was rootless and regarded as absurd at home. And so elitism itself was weakened. It was, after the Depression, a source of wry amusement. "Would you believe, we had lords and ladies here in those days'!'" ◊

Nonetheless, in late August 1939, when Britain declared war on Germany after Hitler's invasion of Poland, the one week which it took MacKenzie King and the Canadian Parliament to follow Britain seemed more a token than a real gesture of independence. Once again Montrealers, particularly those of British origin, volunteered, but without the excitement and patriotic fervour they exhibited at the start of the first World War. No one had any illusions about a short and glorious war. Nonetheless, women got down to the business of making bandages, scarves, and mitts, and joining in volunteer war work. The war economy this time was organized and efficient. By 1941, wage and price controls were in place. The 400,000 still unemployed in 1939 were soon absorbed into war industries, and a labour shortage developed. By 1943, over a million Canadians were engaged in war production. Many of them were women. Rationing of scarce necessities and consumer goods was balanced by higher taxation and savings in Victory Bonds to prevent inflation. To keep labour peace in spite of the wage freeze, Ottawa passed regulations recognizing labour's right to bargain collectively and to organize. The year 1939 was set as the index year below which wages should not fall. Although wages were frozen, the national income per family rose sharply when every adult member of a family was working. Between 1939 and 1945 the gross national product rose from $5.6 billion to $11.8 billion, and the number of union members doubled.

The second World War was probably the finest hour of the Canadian businessman. C.D. Howe, as Minister of Munitions and Supply, chose for his executive and immediate subordinates the most capable, energetic, and imaginative businessmen in each industry. He then gave them individual responsibility for putting that industry on a war footing—for finding the resources and producing what was needed. They organized a war effort that met requirements with exceptionally little profiteering or waste. When the war was over, Howe's extraordinary "cabinet" inevitably constituted an in-group with connections and a knowledge of government that put them at a competitive advantage. Although Gordon Scott was on the Executive, J.R. Donald was a chemical specialist, and other Montreal businessmen served in various capacities, this was a national, not a Montreal group, chosen for competence. Members came from British Columbia, Ontario, the Maritimes—from every section of Canada, wherever the needed skills were found. And it is to be noted that Montreal had no predominance in this regard. Howe's creation of a new industrial base in Canada helped to break the hold of the Montreal Old Guard on the national economy.

Women by the thousands went to work in war industries in the early 1940s.

Montreal became a large manufacturing centre for munitions and chemicals and was headquarters for the Atlantic plane ferry service. People poured into the city to take war jobs. In one month a call went out for 2,000 additional employees to make shells. These jobs were taken mostly by women. For the first time in Quebec's history, the number one employer of labour was the iron and steel industry, not textiles. The iron industry paid higher wages. In 1943 textile workers earned an average of $1,000 each per year, while iron workers earned $2,000. Between 1939 and 1943 the number of wage-earners in the manufacturing sector of Quebec's economy rose from 180,448 to 374,605. Clearly, the average Montreal worker's income level rose. All these factors resulted in a new militancy in the Catholic unions and a drive toward modernization in Quebec.

Women who had been employed in munitions factories and paid good wages were no longer willing to take the abysmal wages and long hours of domestic service. Illustrating the prob- lem in one household, a lady reported that her mother, who "was one of those women who literally couldn't boil an egg," had a terrible time getting anyone to stay with her as maid of all work after the war. Girls came and went in a matter of days. One girl asked for a week's wages in advance to do some shopping. She took the money and never came back. "My mother called me in desperation and asked what she was to do. I said, 'Well, times have changed, you'll have to offer more money and treat them more like equals.'" Soon the mother had a new girl who actually lasted three weeks, after which the mother fired her and explained, "To have to pay $150 per month plus room and board and to have to be nice all the time, too—that's too much!" The lady telling the story believed that her mother was not nasty to servants but was used to being the boss and she couldn't change. ◇

New men and new corporations made fortunes during the war. The old English and Scottish families were still in Montreal, but the new rich often came from other parts of Canada, from the States, or, like the Bronfmans, from different ethnic groups. "For the first time, money began really to count," says a member of an old family. "You couldn't keep up the old style of life without it. Servants were very hard to get and demanded high wages. The *nouveaux riches* didn't know or care about who had been important before they came to town." ◇ It is generally conceded by elite Anglo-Montrealers that the Depression began the change and World War II finished the old elegant style, which could not exist without a corps of servants.

CHAPTER 13

The End of an Era

An even more important change brought on by the conditions of war was the rise of a successful French-Canadian labour movement in Quebec. As we have seen, there were many strikes in Quebec and in Montreal throughout the first half of the twentieth century. Most of them were unsuccessful. In the conditions of war production, where labour was needed and profits were high, strikes began to be won. In addition, new legislation changed the status of labour unions and of workers in general, increasing their power vis-a-vis the employers.

In 1939 Parliament had modified the Criminal Code to remove union militants from its jurisdiction. Presumably they could no longer be arrested or fired for union activities. This did not have much effect in Quebec because of the Padlock Law. In 1944, however, the federal government proclaimed P.C. 1003, which forced employers to recognize the union representing the majority of their employees and to negotiate with it, a right obtained ten years earlier in the United States. This order-in-council provided for conciliation of disputes and accepted the right to strike, if conciliation failed.

The Depression and the concerted anti-labour policies of the Church, Duplessis, and the employers, (with a little help from propaganda of the Left) had defined the economic interests of workers as fundamentally opposed to the interests of their employers. Since the majority of employers were English-Canadian or American, it was relatively easy to reinforce resentment of the economic control of French Canada by "foreign" bosses. Three strikes demonstrate this definition, and show the growing labour militancy and increasing public support for organized labour which arose in Quebec during and after the war. The Montreal Tramways strike (1943), the Dominion Textile strike (1946) and the Asbestos strike (1949) were against large English-Canadian or American companies employing mostly French-Canadian workers. All three demonstrate the unwillingness or inability of the employers, the state, and the Church to respond to new conditions except in old ways which were no longer appropriate or practicable.

In Montreal, between 1939 and 1944, when Duplessis was temporarily replaced by Adelard Godbout as premier, there were signs that the local police, if not provincial ones, were inclined to be sympathetic to strikers. The Montreal Tramway strike, though in some respects a jurisdictional dispute between rival unions, was also a strike caused by the refusal of the Quebec Regional Committee of the National Wartime Labour Council to allow an excess profits bonus to be paid to workers, in spite of the fact that it was included in a contract signed in 1942.

According to *Le Devoir* of March 29, 1943, the tramways company tried to convince the police that the strike was illegal; but "the police declared that they were not officially informed that the strike ... was illegal." *Le Devoir* went on to say that police headquarters even suggested that "the strike is the direct consequence of the policy of the company." Alderman Jean-Marie Savignac (later to become Chairman of the Executive Committee of the Montreal City Council) declared: "By going on strike, the tramways employees are using to the fullest a right conferred on them by federal law.... The public owes it to itself to show its sympathy with these heads of families who are fighting for their existence. For no one knows all the employees have endured from the Company in the last two years." This support from police and municipal officials was a far cry from the attitudes of the early thirties when any union was "communist."

The next significant strike was that of the United Textile Workers of America (AFL) against the Dominion Textile plants in Valleyfield and Montreal. Dominion was the biggest textile conglomerate in Canada. Its president was Blair Gordon, the son of Sir Charles Gordon of Montreal. Kent Rowley and Madeleine Parent were co-organizers of the strike of 6,000 workers, demanding a 25-cent hourly increase in pay, a 40-hour week and union recognition. Gordon and Duplessis fought the union, claiming that the strike was illegal because arbitration had not occurred, and because it was a "communist" conspiracy. After about a month, an agreement was reached in Montreal; but the company would not apply this to Valleyfield and continued to try to break the strike there. Trefflé Leduc, the much-respected president of the UTWA local, who had worked 48 years for the company, was arrested. Three weeks later, on August 13, a few hundred strikebreakers were escorted into the mill by provincial and company police. As the day went on, thousands of strikers and townspeople gathered outside the plant. When the scabs began to come out at closing time, a riot ensued. The crowd tore up cement slabs from the sidewalk and smashed the escorting automobiles' windshields and windows. They broke all the factory windows at ground level. After that, the plant stayed closed. The mayor of Valleyfield expressed the indignation of the people of the town when he said, "The attitude and action of the company lead me to conclude that the interests of the union are the interests of the people of Valleyfield." The strike was eventually won. The reaction of the community shows the growing support for workers' rights in the postwar years. On the other hand, the lawyer-son of an important Montreal iron and steel industrialist drove a judge out to Valleyfield for various legal activities and reports that "The union had a bunch of goons employed and the fellows that went to work, I mean sincere fellows, would come home and find their door busted in and notices saying, 'You go to work tomorrow and your wife and kids will get hurt.' I was involved only because I happened to be a lawyer acting for the company, but it shakes me what unions get away with." ◇

The climax of Quebec labour militancy during this period was the Asbestos strike in 1949. This time an American company was struck by a French-Canadian union. The Johns-Manville Corporation refused the asbestos workers' demands for higher wages, and improved safety and sanitary conditions in the mines. On February 13, 1949 the workers, organized by the CCCL (Canadian Confederation of Catholic Labour) went on strike. On May 5, company automobiles brought in strikebreakers, but all were stopped by the picketers. Provincial police told the strikers that 500 additional provincial police were arriving from Sherbrooke and that the Riot Act would be read the next day. Wishing to avoid bloodshed, the strikers agreed to withdraw the pickets. The next day the Riot Act was read amid violent attacks by the police, who broke into people's homes, routed out union members sleeping in a church hall, beat some of them savagely, and arrested 125 strikers and townspeople.

*Food trucks arriving for families of the miners
during the Asbestos strike of 1949. Collections were
taken at some Roman Catholic churches for the
relief of the strikers.*

The viciousness of this attack on a Catholic union aroused public opinion and certain members of the clergy. Archbishop Joseph Charbonneau of Montreal preached a sermon on Sunday, May 2, 1949, which disclosed the split that was developing in the Church with regard to workers' rights and led to his own banishment. Charbonneau said, "The working class is the victim of a conspiracy which seeks its destruction and when there is a conspiracy to crush the working class it is the duty of the Church to intervene."

The Archbishop of Sherbrooke, Maurice Roy, soon after appealed for support of the strikers, stating that "with all my soul as a Bishop, I support the Asbestos workers in their just demands." A number of bishops placed collection boxes at their church doors on behalf of the strikers' children, and $167,558.24 was collected. One of the strike leaders was Jean Marchand, later to be a cabinet minister in the Trudeau government. Newsreels of the time show a man in bermuda shorts, descending from a white Jaguar convertible to walk with the picketers: Pierre Trudeau. Both were prestigious names in French Canada. The Trades and Labour Congress and the Canadian Congress of Labour, arch-rivals of the Catholic unions, made public statements of support. The strike was successful and signalled a new militancy in the Catholic unions and a growing independence from those bishops Duplessis described as "eating out of my hand."

Trudeau, then editor of *Cité Libre*, an opinion journal, observed that: "For many people, the drama in Asbestos proclaimed violently the arrival of a new era.... For them this strike marks a step in the religious, political, social, and economic history of the province of Quebec."

The Asbestos strike, which started in February 1949, was not reported in *The Gazette* until May 6, after the outbreak of violence. When finally editorial comment was made, it was to discredit the motives of the strikers without giving information about the cause of the strike. In fact, the editorial said that there was no clear declaration of the demands of the strikers. Gérard Pelletier commented that in reporting the strike, even then, *The Gazette*, expressed "a certain remoteness, a superior tone, and an elegantly expressed but affected ignorance of the facts, as though it were an event taking place in Africa." In so far as it took such a position, *The Gazette* did its readers a disservice. In failing to provide the facts and in giving the impression that this strike was of little importance to the Montreal population of British descent, it encouraged the head-in-the-sand defensiveness to which they were already prone. Worse, it misinformed them. Organized workers had challenged the traditional employer-government-church coalition and had won. Workers in Quebec were now in a position to take advantage of new powers already being accorded by the federal and some provincial governments. After the war, these governments established labour relations boards with the power to certify union bargaining units and to adjudicate appeal. Through this legislation, labour unions and their leaders were given great power, while the power of employers to dictate terms and conditions of work was correspondingly reduced. Profits could be expected to decline in the face of increased labour costs and the steady rise in income taxes, individual and corporate.

The reactions of the business elite were predictable. A retired official of one of Montreal's most important industries remarked with regard to the new labour legislation: "I regard trade unions as combinations in restraint of trade. We have legislation that prosecutes companies for engaging in combinations in restraint of trade, but when unions go on strike they say, 'We won't work and we won't let anybody else work.' If that isn't a combination in restraint of trade, I can't think of anything that would be." He believes that other businessmen might have been cautious about saying too much in the forties and fifties when labour unions got the power to strike, but "I'm sure that they thought that unions had far too much power, even then."

Meanwhile, other challengers to St. James Street's power were gaining strength. Donald Kerr, a geographer, has demonstrated that Toronto had begun to be "a somewhat more attractive trading centre than Montreal during and, in particular, after the Depression." Although the population of Montreal continued to be greater than that of Toronto until the 1970s, all economic indicators collected by Kerr show that by 1961 Toronto had surpassed Montreal and these figures can be extended in some cases back to 1941. In 1961, for example, service receipts and retail sales show Toronto slightly ($120 million) higher than Montreal. Value added in total manufacturing activity was about $200 million greater in Toronto. Cheques cashed at clearing houses originating in Montreal totalled $78,593,811,000 compared to $109,570,868,000 in Toronto. Income taxes paid in Montreal represented 12.7 percent of the Canadian total, whereas Torontonians paid 19 percent. Finally, although the assets of leading corporations and financial institutions having their head offices in either city were nearly equal, Toronto had a slight edge in financial institutions. The value of stock market transactions showed a wide margin in favour of Toronto, which accounted for 67.1 per cent of all Canadian transactions, compared to 26.3 percent on the Montreal Exchange. Insofar as comparable statistics are available for 1941, the beginning of this process emerges: cheques cashed against Montreal banks totalled $9,904,907,000 while cheques cashed against Toronto banks totalled $11,344,826,471. In 1946, the earliest year in which taxation statistics were compiled, Toronto accounted for 19.34 percent of the grand total of Canadian taxes collected, while Montreal accounted for 17.38 percent. Toronto also had more taxpayers, and these had a very slightly higher average income. It was particularly in the area of financial institutions that Toronto began to supersede Montreal, which had exercised dominance for so long. As early as 1941 the number of people employed in finance and insurance was 21,346 in Toronto and 19,661 in Montreal. The economist E.P. Neufeld found that by 1939 Toronto accounted for 56.3 percent of the total value of stock exchange trading in Canada, while the Montreal Stock Exchange accounted for only 41.5 percent; by 1948 even the volume of trading in industrial stocks on the Toronto Exchange exceeded that on the Montreal exchange.

Contributing to this outcome, according to an ex-officer of the Royal Trust, was the fact that in 1936 the Toronto Standard Exchange rescinded the arbitrage arrangement which had existed between the two exchanges, which had permitted traders to buy and sell at the best price any shares quoted on either exchange. As a result, traders in Toronto could still do this, but Montreal traders could not. It was immediately advantageous to buy and sell from the Toronto Standard Exchange. Montreal could have retaliated, but did not; and according to this informant "this had a tremendous negative impact on the Montreal exchange." He explains the failure to respond to this challenge as another example of the lack of initiative in Montreal. "Toronto was really competitive. The Montreal exchange was a club." ◇

A retired officer of a large insurance company once based in Montreal was already aware of the shift by the fifties. Not only did he observe the new trends in the stock market; he also began to notice that important bond and stock houses were moving their senior people to Toronto. "A big West Coast firm I knew about felt that they had to have an eastern office and decided that it should be in Toronto, rather than Montreal. That was thirty years ago. Gradually such decisions made a difference." ◇

Another event often mentioned as making a difference was the building of the St. Lawrence Seaway. The construction, with the United States in the l950s, of a channel which would permit ocean-going vessels to sail to the Great Lakes did reduce Montreal's importance. This was an old project opposed by many Montreal businessmen, for obvious reasons. With their city no longer the gateway to the continent, the gate-keepers in shipping and railways could no longer reap the same profits. "If you were starting a manufacturing business that wasn't tied to water power," said an industrialist, "Ontario was a better place to be, after the Seaway was built." ◇ The evidence presented here suggests that the Seaway accelerated a process already under way, rather than that it initiated the change in the fortunes of the Montreal business elite.

Other factors were at work in Toronto's favour during the same period. The U.S. branch-plant invasion took place primarily in Ontario. By 1968, 68 percent of all branch plants were located there. This trend had developed through the twentieth century, beginning, as we have seen, with the National Policy in the latter part of the 19th century and was in full swing by 1914. This meant, of course, an influx of capital, of technical knowledge, a rise in employment, and a forward thrust to the industrialization of Ontario which put "the province far ahead of Quebec, where the Americans faced the additional barrier of language and in general a society which was much less anxious to industrialize," according to Jacob Spelt's study of the rise of Toronto. Ontario had always had closer ties with the United States and had at various times tried to break the hold of the Montreal group on transportation by getting permission to trade through New York. With the development of the industrial mid-west of the United States, Toronto was not only in the best geographical position to take advantage of trade and cooperation with U.S. firms, but was much more eager to encourage new industrial development than was the ruling group in Montreal. This was noted as early as 1937 by the Royal Commission on Dominion Provincial Relations. Discussing the Depression, the Report observed:

> When a measure of recovery in Canada did occur it came largely from expansion in new industries and frontiers which cut across

the established national pattern and, although secondary Montreal industries benefited to some extent, the basic situation was scarcely alleviated.... Montreal steadily lost ground to the rival metropolitan centre of Toronto with its close relationship to the new and expanding industries.

Between 1900 and the end of the second World War, London had ceased to be Canada's major source of foreign capital. Whereas in 1900, 85 percent of Canada's external capital financing came from London and only 14 percent from the United States, by 1954, 80 percent of external capital was American and only 18 percent was British. Furthermore, the United States had replaced Britain as the most powerful nation, economically and militarily, on earth. Naturally, the younger generation in Canada and elsewhere was turning to American models—from Lana Turner to Coca-Cola—and admiring its way of life as previous generations had admired things British. Part of the *raison d'être* of the English-Canadian life style was gone. It must be weighed along with the ideological and political attacks directed against capitalism in general, and the Montreal group in particular, as factors undermining the Montrealers' position.

Finally, changes in the Companies Act, in regulations applying to standards, prices, mergers, labour unions, and the operations of stock exchanges, as well as increases in corporate and individual income taxes, began to make a difference in the way business could operate. Administration and enforcement of these began to reflect a new mood of concern for the worker and the consumer which had not previously been notable in Canadian public policy. As one businessman put it: "The rules changed, and activities that businessmen had once regarded as sound practices were no longer possible, or at least no longer simple to do." ◊ New companies that had never operated under the old *laissez-faire* principles found it easier to adapt to the new situation than did older ones.

By the 1950s the Montreal business community gave the impression either that it had lost its nerve, or become alarmingly complacent, or both. In 1956, *Fortune* published an article describing the CPR as "encrusted in tradition." The author, Herbert Solow, catalogued the differences between policies followed by "an extremely conservative board of directors" and earlier ones:

> In the old days C.P.R. had a good healthy appetite for profits, and to increase them was willing to take risks. C.P.R.'s attitude

today might be summed up by the board member who sees his duty simply as "not to detract from earnings."... It has rejected proposals that it get into wildcatting (on its 9,800,000 oil-rich acres). Says management: "We have as freight customers oil companies with whom we don't want to compete. Anyway, this is a long-term proposition. We do all right."... The C.P.R. shows no more aggressiveness in running its far-west timber operations.... it has sold 1,400,000 of its two million acres of timberland ... and holds the remaining acreage for twenty Vancouver Island mills, including ... Macmillan & Bloedel. There is no competitive bidding. "We don't try to hold the mills up.... We're not out for the last cent. We consider how long a mill has been doing business with us. In return, the mills do the best they can to give us freight—when water rates permit."... C.P.R. hotels always keep plenty of rooms empty to avoid all risk of turning away a guest who is important to the railroad.

To its credit, the CPR reacted to these criticisms by establishing Canadian Pacific Investments to develop its natural resources. However, it was always a company with national scope, and as an example of a moribund company, directed by Montreal businessmen at that particular point in history, it will do nicely—especially since the CPR was one of the cornerstones of the Montreal group's rise to power. When the *Fortune* article was being prepared, in 1955, fourteen of twenty-four members of the board of directors were Montrealers, all English or Scottish, except for one token French-Canadian. All the executive officers were Montrealers, except for R.F. Tremayne of London, England. In the operating, maintenance, finance, and all other departments, twenty out of twenty-six officers were from Montreal. It is worth noting that half of the fourteen CPR board members who were Montrealers were, around the same time, also on the board of the Bank of Montreal. It would appear that the old Scots who had made Montreal the commercial centre of Canada had been succeeded by a generation whose primary interest was in maintaining things as they were. At the very least, they seemed to have lost the entrepreneurial leadership qualities of their forbears.

An elite can maintain its position only so long as it serves a necessary function in a society. When it ceases to do so, its members can no longer count on the people's loyalty, gratitude, admiration, or fear—the true sources of their authority. However, the *forms* of the privileged life may survive for a considerable period after the elite group has lost its usefulness. The institutions of exclusivity and privilege by which elites protect their positions

284

continue to be powerful citadels to be assaulted (and revered) by those who regard them as avenues to wealth and power. Schools like Selwyn House, Miss Edgar's, the Study, and Trafalgar continued to be almost entirely Anglo-Protestant until the day came when they had to depend on provincial government funds. Now their enrolment is almost as culturally diverse as any public school. As a board member and Old Boy of Selwyn House remarked, "Now absolutely anybody can get into my school. I can't even pronounce most of their names." ◊ When anyone can get in, schools cease to symbolize and maintain privilege.

The same process occurred in other institutions for which the English community had previously taken responsibility. A woman who was instrumental in founding the Arts Society as a liaison between the Montreal Museum of Fine Arts and the public said that when the government took over, the volunteer program "was just pushed out to give jobs for paid people. The people, mostly English, who had been patrons deserted the museum and have never come back. Now they don't give either money or paintings." ◊

Difficult as it was for the Anglo-Protestant patrons to accept being pushed aside in the new era, what they cannot forgive is the failure of successors to recognize their contribution to Montreal institutions. "I was furious at a story in *The Gazette* not long ago about the anniversary ball for the Museum. Not a word about the fact that the Gibbs gave the house on Phillips Square which was the first home of the Art Association, or of people like the Van Hornes who gave major collections, or like Cleveland Morgan who gave their time and money to keep it going. Oh, people are so ignorant, it's pathetic." ◊

Eric McLean, Montreal music critic, remarked that the English-speaking community has made a far greater contribution to the Montreal Symphony Orchestra, both in funds and in volunteer work, than is recognized today.

The Depression had forced governments at all levels to take responsibility for welfare. Unemployment insurance and "baby bonuses" (child-support payments made directly to mothers) had been established by the federal government during the war and were the beginning of a Canadian system of social assistance which began to replace private philanthropy. Large numbers of state-employed professionals increasingly took over the social service work which had once been the activity of upper class women in the English Protestant community of Montreal.

Increasingly, the volunteers encountered hostility from the professionals, and began to feel that they were not wanted. Professionals, on the other hand, no longer needed the money or the help enough to endure the dilettantism and snobbery of the elite volunteer. In response to this situation and to new definitions of the roles of women, young ladies of the post-war generation of the Anglo-Protestant old families were less prepared to spend their lives in leisure activities laced with philanthropic pursuits. They wanted a university education and even careers, in some cases. The Junior League began to have trouble recruiting members and keeping them seriously at work.

In addition, the graduated income tax, raised considerably during the war and never to fall, made it harder to accumulate individual fortunes, and families were turning fortunes over to be administrated by foundations. Most family firms became incorporated as joint-stock companies. Now, if large sums were needed by a university, a hospital, or other service organization, it was the corporation or foundation to whom they must turn—not an individual or a family. Philanthropy had become anonymous and impersonal; and the links between the groups within the Protestant community suffered the same fate.

In the mid-1950s, MacGregor Street was constructed through the Square Mile. A major traffic artery carried the noise and fumes of the vast post-war increase in automobiles through the tranquil gardens of the huge mansions where children used to play. Yet there was hardly a complaint. The old families no longer occupied those mansions. Their houses had been sold, changing owners frequently, or were in the hands of institutions such as the Salvation Army, the United Church, or McGill University. The James Ross house had become the McGill Law Faculty building. Sir Montagu Allan had bequeathed his "Ravenscrag" to McGill for the Allan Memorial Institute, a psychiatric hospital. The Purvis home on Pine Avenue housed faculty offices and classrooms. Sir Edward Clouston's mansion had become a nurse's residence. Other homes were bought for consulates or by philanthropic foundations. Kildonan, Senator Robert MacKay's estate, and the Redpath mansion were razed to make way for the Church of St. Andrew and St. Paul. Some were demolished and replaced by apartment buildings, or terraces. McGill's records of its acquisition of those elegant houses in its immediate vicinity show that of twenty-eight purchased or acquired as gifts, twenty had come into its possession by the mid-1950s. As another clue to the date of the decline of the Square Mile and its way of life, the most active turnover was in the 1940s.

Twenty years before the nationalist Quiet Revolution in Quebec in 1960, the die was already cast. The decline of the economic power of the families of the Square Mile was well advanced. The loss of their dominant position inevitably meant a loss of their ability to protect the interests of their community. As we have seen, in the division of social responsibility between the Protestants and the Catholics of Quebec, the Roman Catholic Church financed and operated the hospitals, schools, and social services required by the French-Canadian population. These institutions were staffed by nuns and brothers in the various religious orders dedicated to such services. Traditionally, every family gave one son and one daughter (usually the brightest ones) to be educated for the church. These then provided the large pool of unpaid labour needed for all these services. As urbanization proceeded, the Church saw its rural congregations decline and found its urban ones harder to control. The urban middle class and workers were more sympathetic to liberal, modern, and even materialistic ideas than Church teaching had allowed. When urban families ceased to follow the tradition of dedicating children to the Church, staffing the schools, hospitals, and social agencies on the old basis became impossible. The power vacuum that developed in the province as a result of the weakening of the hold of the Montreal financial group and of the Roman Catholic Church made the Quiet Revolution of 1960 not only possible, but also necessary. The government had to take over the social functions and many of the economic ones previously performed by these two groups.

It is not assumed here that the Montreal businessmen were utterly eliminated, or ceased to wield power in Canada. Wallace Clements, John Porter, and others have demonstrated conclusively that the economic elites of Canada continued to be largely English Protestants. Clements, in fact, shows that the difficulty of gaining access to this group has increased—especially in Quebec and Ontario. Pierre Fournier has documented that English-speaking businessmen continued to influence Quebec governments. The argument here is only that the Scottish, English, and Irish Protestants who had enjoyed a virtual monopoly of power and great wealth in the late nineteenth century were no longer in a dominant position, and that the centres of control were moving from Montreal to Toronto well before the Quiet Revolution in

Quebec. With this transfer of the locus of power, and changing times and values, went a change in the lifestyle which had been admired and envied.

September 28, 1940 was a Sunday and there was a double-header baseball game in the Delorimier Stadium. Over the loud-speaker came an announcement: Sir Herbert Holt had died. The next day there were long tributes by famous men to his "broad vision," his abilities as shown in the long list of enterprises he controlled or of which he was a board member. He was described as the last of the great pioneers, a builder of the nation as well as of such local benefactions as Montreal Light, Heat, and Power. *The Gazette* said, "But the man in the street would resort to the use of such colloquial phrases as 'a giant of industry,' or 'a great leader of finance' ... to give full and unrestricted voice to his admiration for such a notable career now ended." In fact, the people in the stadium (whom we may reasonably consider representative of the man on the street) broke into applause when the announcement was made. According to several eyewitnesses, the applause was followed by a few moments silence as people realized what they had done. Then there was an explosion of laughter. It was indeed the end of an era.

There are still wealthy people in Montreal, but few of them belong to the families that originally built the Square Mile. Peter Newman's 1979 list of the approximately 175 wealthiest and most powerful men in Canada included less than forty Montrealers. If we look back to the names of the Square Milers at the turn of the century, we see that very few of the same names appear on Newman's list. The Molson, Dawes, and Timmins families appear; Thomas Galt, Brian Drummond, Conrad Harrington (a Sir William Dawson grandson) and David Culver are mentioned. The Mortimer Davis and Elwood Hosmer estates, the Macdonald-Stewart and McConnell Foundations control millions. Members of the Webster, Birks, Nesbitt, Thomson, Morgan, Hallward, McCall, Clarke, and McMaster families are on the list. But newcomers representing many different ethnic groups share the stage: Bronfman, Steinberg, Cummings, Nihon, Louis Levesque, Kruger, and Desruisseaux. What happened to the old founding families? Sir Montagu Allan's only son was killed in World War I; Lord Mount Stephen had no sons; the James Ross fortune was dissipated by J.K.L. Ross in the twenties; J.W. McConnell's three sons all died tragically. Isaac Killam had no children; Lord Strathcona had one daughter. Sir Herbert Holt's son Robert was

288

killed in World War II. Most members of the old families believe, however, that too many generations tried to live on the fortunes without adding anything to them. Newman quotes W.K. Vanderbilt to the effect that "Inherited wealth is ...as certain death to ambition as cocaine is to morality," and perhaps that explains it. In this connection, it is interesting to note the persistence of the Molson family business and its prosperity. One of the oldest family fortunes in Canada, it is still a going concern. A member of the family was asked whether there were family patterns that might explain this continued success. The answer given was that "all the boys are always expected to work, to take on serious responsibility in the business." ◊

These developments did not produce noticeable social changes in Montreal until the late 1950s. In a new return to normal, elite girls "came out" again, a practice which had been dropped for the duration of World War II, but began again in 1948. In 1949, Mrs. Robert Reford gave her granddaughter what is reportedly the last coming-out ball to take place in a private residence. After that, debutantes were presented only at balls in hotels. It was, by then, acceptable (but not necessarily expected) that girls of this group should attend university; but most of them did not foresee a career, though they might take jobs while waiting to marry. They were expected to live in the parental home until that time. A woman who suggested to her father in the early 1950s when she was twenty-five years old and holding a job, that she might like an apartment of her own reports that "he was so upset that I never raised the question again." ◊ Young women continued to join the Junior League and to find it gave purpose and excitement to their lives. The membership in the League began to drop only around 1958.

The generation born a few years after the war was reared without nannies—reared, in fact, with few servants of any kind. Even this change was not abrupt. Baby-nurses who stayed only a few months were the accepted thing, at first. "It was still not done to try to take care of a new-born by yourself," says a woman whose children were born in the late 1950s. ◊ As to servants, "we made do with DPs for awhile." ("displaced persons" found in German internment camps or otherwise left homeless by the war could work out their passage to Canada through a year's service as live-in domestics.) Later, people could not "get live-in help at all, so somebody coming in to do the cleaning everyday or once or twice a week became the rule." ◊

When the generation reared in these circumstances grew up, its members were no longer interested in the customary ways. They did not want to "come out." They expected to go to university and to have careers. McGill was no longer the preferred, the "in" place to go. Instead, they went to Queen's University, to the University of New Brunswick, or Carleton University. After graduation they took jobs outside Montreal. "None of my friends' children are here, either. It isn't that they don't like Montreal or don't feel comfortable here; it's that the opportunities aren't here." ◊

A man approaching eighty reviewed his family situation: "The family managed to keep control of all our different enterprises until the 1960s. That was part of the responsibility to the family we tried to carry on. Of course, as time goes by, more and more descendants have to be provided for. But neither of my sons has the least interest in the business and both refuse to take it on. Not like my father's day or even when I was young, when the family business came first and sons didn't dream of going against their father's wishes. We have had to go public and the company is managed by outsiders, although I am still Chairman of the Board. We've moved our head office to Toronto, partly because of political and language problems here, but mostly because that's where the big decisions are made now so that's where you have to be. All my children except one daughter have left Quebec." ◊

Many of those who leave feel to some extent like strangers in other parts of Canada. It is a process of self-discovery in which they find that they are "French" in many of their attitudes—or at least Quebecers as much as Canadians. One woman said, "In Vancouver, I realized that I was part French-Canadian—not racially, but mentally." ◊ A Montreal woman now living in Toronto says, "It is so dull here. I miss the cosmopolitan atmosphere the French add to Montreal." ◊ Another native of Montreal moved to Toronto. Shortly after he moved, there was a national election. At a dinner party on election night someone asked him if he had voted that day. He replied, facetiously but with a straight face, "Oh, yes, I always say, 'Vote early and vote often.'" The shocked silence with which the assembled Torontonians greeted this remark reminded him that it was a Montreal joke. Its existence in the English-Protestant Montrealers' repertoire was a result of rubbing shoulders with the cynical view of politics often expressed by French-Canadians.

290

People who were born around the turn of the century speak in resigned voices of the changes that have occurred in the last sixty years: "Deplorable, on the whole." ◊ They feel that an admirable way of life has been displaced by a crass, unprincipled, rude, and irresponsible one. Their feelings echo those of all conservatives, all lovers of what W.B. Yeats calls "ceremony," all connoisseurs of the beauty of things that have endured. At every new democratic turn of human affairs in Western societies, these complaints have been heard. Edmund Burke said of the French Revolution, "The age of chivalry has gone. That of sophisters, economists and calculators has succeeded; and the glory of Europe is extinguished forever."

Representatives of nearly all the old, wealthy and prominent families are still living in Montreal. The middle-aged leave, if at all, only because their companies move. Some of the elderly follow their children to Ottawa, Toronto or Vancouver. Others will stay in Montreal. It is their home; and has been home to their families for generations. Very few still live in anything remotely approaching the old style. Where the descendants of the original Anglo-Protestant families are still living in huge mansions in Westmount, often they do not have enough servants to manage such houses. An elderly man in a large house near the top of the mountain in Westmount, serves tea himself in earthenware mugs to his visitor. His wife is out; and there is not a servant to be seen.

They tailor their activities to their means, and carry on. A woman from a prominent family, one of six children whose father had four brothers is now, except for a nephew, the only member of this large clan still in Montreal. From the small room she occupies in a senior citizens' home she attends board meetings of the various organizations in which she has been active and is writing another book with an enthusiasm undiminished by the fact that she is past eighty years of age. Another woman works in her home in upper Westmount, making stuffed toys by hand. She has more orders than she can fill. A man in his nineties, once the head of a large firm and still able to live in his own small house with a daily housekeeper to care for it and him, dresses impeccably in a three-piece suit and goes down to the Mount Royal club for lunch with his cronies—those that are still alive and able to get there. A woman approaching sixty lives alone in a farmhouse which was once the summer home of her prominent family. She and her husband are divorced, her children

291

gone. She works very hard keeping the small farm going, doing all the work of caring for the animals herself, waiting for an inheritance which grows smaller with every passing year. Yet on a cold night in mid-winter, when the snow lies deep and smooth under a star-crowded sky, she invites her visitor to take an old-fashioned sleigh ride. Under the fur robes, listening to the bells jingling in the utter silence as the horse-drawn sleigh glides past the sombre spruces, she laughs for pure joy, remembering the young men who accompanied her on such rides when she was young.

An old woman meets the visitor at the entrance to the senior citizens' residence. The house was once an elegant family home, as the curved mahogany staircase and panelling in the entrance hall attest. They go up to her room along winding corridors, off which lead many doors—all closed. The halls are silent. Hers is a small bedroom, just large enough for a single bed, two armchairs and two chests of drawers. "We'll have more privacy here." Sitting by the window, looking out on a parking lot and a cigarette and candy store, they talk: about her childhood, her school, growing up, marriage, wars, Depression and death—the usual stuff of any life, always the same and always different. At parting she says, "If I don't sleep tonight it will be your fault for stirring up all these old ghosts." ◇

The ghosts will not go away, whether we talk about them or not. These founding families have left their ideas and dreams, their successes and failures, as a permanent legacy. As with children, so with nations: succeeding generations of Canadians may have followed the pattern laid down by the Square Milers, or they may have rebelled against it; all have had to come to terms with it. When new Canadian ventures have to seek capital south of the border, while Canadian banks invest in Brazil; when careful, even tight-fisted banking and financial policies are more admired than business expansion; when our best artists, writers, thinkers must go elsewhere for recognition; when we assume that anything Canadian must be second-rate, the ghosts are abroad. When Western Canadians are convinced that business and government are dominated by Eastern interests out to exploit them; when Eastern Canadians fear the radicalism of the West; when French Canadians fight (or accept) the old stereotypes of inferiority, the ghosts are around. When we exhibit certain attitudes: our reticence; our cynicism and suspicion of too-easy enthusiasm; our love of pomp and ceremony, and of quiet, conservative taste in all things; our belief in elitism and in parliamentary processes, in strict discipline and severe punishment for wrongdoing, in a fascination with British ways and the monarchy and a certain distaste for American ways, the ghosts are with us. So they must be also when Canadians try to free themselves from these views.

Across Canada, the ex-Montreal "Anglos" are appearing. In Toronto, there are so many of them that they are beginning to be noticeable. They are called, wryly, "the boat people." They bring with them the social memories, attitudes, and abilities we have observed here. Their effort to fit into new niches may be expected to have some impact on the places where they now seek to "carry on."

Conclusion

Nearly all the Anglo-Protestant magnates who built the mansions in the Square Mile and lived in them between 1870 and 1910 were dead before 1950. Their children or grandchildren (mostly the latter) who were born around 1900 to 1910, were between seventy and ninety years old when they contributed the personal experiences on which this study was based. My account was concerned primarily with their lives up to 1950, although a few of their children (great-grandchildren of the early barons) were included to see how things turned out in the 1950s. By that time the way of life, the power, and the money they had inherited were rapidly vanishing. They were living a different kind of life in Westmount or the west of Montreal Island than their Square Mile parents and grandparents had enjoyed. They had fewer servants, less leisure and more work. The so-called Golden Age of the Montreal English-Scots Protestants had lasted less than one hundred years; its peak, barely fifty.

What happened? We noted the military, economic, political, and geographical events which led to Montreal's commercial and financial decline. To these we have added social and cultural characteristics which rendered the Montreal English-Scottish elite unwilling or unable to adapt to those changes. They thought of themselves as aristocrats and reared their children accordingly. They lacked, however, a rootedness in the land and its traditions, and the acceptance by the majority of native inhabitants of their right to power and privilege. These are the supports on which an aristocracy depends. Elite Anglo-Protestant children of the early twentieth century were offered little encouragement, on the other hand, to develop the ingenuity and risk-taking which had propelled their grandfathers' rise to wealth and power. Furthermore, by isolating themselves socially—as students at McGill, in their clubs as adults, at all ages at their summer places and in their social contacts—they insulated themselves against fresh ideas or new ways of doing things at a time when they sorely needed both. Not only were they mis-educated for life outside the Square Mile, but living and growing up there seemed to make it difficult for them to change.

That articulate, doughty champion of capitalism, Sir Edward Beatty, in a speech in 1937, pointed out some of the pitfalls of being, as he claimed businessmen to be, "the aristocracy of modern society." Aristocracies fell in the past, he warned, "when they failed to give their countries the leadership which the times demanded," when, "they thought too much of their privileges and too little of their duties, or "imagined that power could be transmitted by inheritance, or held by force." And, finally, "they fell because they failed to gain the confidence of those whom they were called to lead." Beatty's warning was to the point, and the business aristocrats of Montreal, who were unwilling or unable to change, fell from their places as leaders of the system. Having lost that, they were replaced in their community functions and an era in Canadian history came to a close.

We should, however, leave the last word to the people whose experiences have been the basis for this study. They have thought seriously about the problem long before talking to me. They have provided most of my own ideas on the subject—though the possibility that the training they received contributed to the decline is my own conclusion, gleaned from their statements and from my observations and research. The two explanations which they cited most frequently were conservative, unimaginative policies of Montreal business leaders after World War I and that too many people tried to live on family fortunes without adding to them. To their credit, not one blamed others for their decline—not even their known political enemies and business competitors. They take their responsibilities.

Notes

Since this is a work of popular history, it did not seem appropriate to interrupt the general reader with note citations in the text. The following references will direct more scholarly readers to all my sources that are ordinarily available to researchers.

My most valuable source material for this book was provided by 191 personal interviews described in the Introduction, as well as access to letters, diaries, and memoirs in the possession of my informants. Most of the interviews were tape-recorded. I have not attempted to provide detailed references for this material, since the majority of my informants insisted on anonymity. I have of course retained all my notes and tapes. Quotations from anonymous sources are marked with a diamond (◊) in the text.

Introduction

Background information on the composition of the Square Mile is based on the *Atlas of the City of Montreal* (Montreal: Atlas Publishing Co., 1906), plates 19, 24; on the *Census of Canada, 1901*, Vol. 1, *Population* (Ottawa: Dominion Bureau of Statistics), p. 376; and on Sir Herbert Ames, *The City Below the Hill* (Toronto: University of Toronto Press, 1972).

Information on the wealth of Montreal may be found in G. Myers, *History of Canadian Wealth* (Toronto: James, Lewis and Samuel, 1972), p. xxxi; and in Tom Naylor, *History of Canadian Business*, 2 vols. (Toronto: James Lorimer and Company, 1975).

CHAPTER 1
Grandparents. Parents, and Community

My historical treatment of the Bank of Montreal is based on Merrill Denison, *Canada's First Bank: The History of the Bank of Montreal*, 2 vols. (Toronto and Montreal: McClelland and Stewart, 1967), and on the annual reports preserved in the Bank of Montreal archives in Montreal.

Facts and figures on Montreal business in this chapter are derived from Wallace Clement, *The Canadian Corporate Elite* (Toronto: McClelland and Stewart, 1975); D.C. Masters, *The Rise of Toronto, 1850-1890* (Toronto: University of Toronto Press, 1947); and on the books by Myers and Naylor cited above. For the business activities of individuals, see C.W. Parker, ed., *Who's Who and Why in Canada* (Toronto: International Press, 1910-15)

For political relations between the Montreal group and the Macdonald government, see T.W. Acheson, ''The Social Origins of Canadian Industrialism: A Study in the Structure of Entrepreneurship, 1880-1910'' (Ph.D. dissertation, University of Toronto, 1971).

The history of the Canadian Pacific Railway is based on W. Kaye Lamb, *History of the Canadian Pacific Railway* (New York: Macmillan, 1977); Lorne McDougall, *Canadian Pacific* (Montreal: McGill University Press, 1968); and Pierre Berton, *The Last Spike* (Toronto: McClelland and Stewart, 1983).

Information on architecture was drawn from Alan Gowans, *Building Canada: An Architectural History of Canadian Life* (Toronto: Oxford University Press, 1966). On Montreal architecture see The Montreal Society of Architecture, *Exploring Montreal* (Toronto: Greey de Pencier, 1974); and Aline Gubbay, *Montreal: The Mountain and the River* (Montreal: Trillium books, 1981). Julia Gersovitz, ''The Square Mile: Montreal, 1960-1914'' (M.A. thesis, Columbia University, 1980) contains valuable information on both the mansions and the social life in the Square Mile before World War I.

For information on furnishings in the Square Mile mansions, see Elizabeth Collard, ''The Decorative Arts'' in *The End of an Era: Montreal, 1880-1914* (Montreal: McCord Museum, McGill University, 1977), pp. 7-9.

Edgar Andrew Collard's weekly columns, ''All Our Yesterdays'' and ''Of Many Things'' (*The Gazette*, Montreal, 1941-67, 1968-81), contributed a sense of Montreal life in general throughout the period 1900-1950.

p. 31. ''The roads are frightful ...'' Evelyn Cartier Springett, *For My Children's Children* (Montreal: The Unity Press, 1937), p. 52.

p. 36. ''... dug themselves into ... supervision'' Lloyd Reynolds, ''The Occupational Adjustment of the British Immigrant in Montreal'' (M.A. thesis, McGill University, 1933), p. 85.

CHAPTER 2
Getting the Right Start

For utilitarian values in Canadian child-rearing, see Brian Taylor, ''Utilitarianism and the Child: Jeremy Bentham'' in P.T. Rooke and R.L. Schnell, *Studies in Childhood History: A Canadian Perspective* (Calgary: Detselig Enterprises Ltd., 1982), pp. 4-27.

p. 40. ''Henceforth it was recognized ...'' Philippe Aries, *Centuries of Childhood: A Social History of Family Life* (New York: Alfred A. Knopf, 1962), p. 412.

p. 40. ''... the formation of a good English character ...'' Geoffrey Gorer, *Exploring English Character* (London: Cresset Press, 1955), p. 163.

p. 40. Material on the Nanny is from J. Gathorne-Hardy, *The Rise and Fall of the British Nanny* (London: Hodder and Stoughton, 1972).

p. 51. Howard Marler, ''An English Childhood in French Quebec'', *Country Life* (December 13, 1979), pp. 2327-8.

298

p. 53. "reinforcing class distinctions" Gathorne-Hardy, p. 73.

p. 54. "... the ordinary life ... is ... rewarding" Gorer, p. 197.

p. 57. For Victorian manners, see E.B. Aresty, *The Best Behaviour* (New York: Simon and Schuster, 1970), pp. 162-86.

p. 60. "A real lady ..." Ruth Lamb, " In the Twilight Side by Side" in the *Girl's Own Paper*, vol. XXIV no. 1204 (Jan. 24, 1903), p. 263.

p. 60. "... this sceptr'd isle ..." W. Shakespeare, *King Richard II*, act 2, sc. 1.

p. 61. "... only a soldier will do ..." and the theme of parents who believe that children are better off at home than abroad are to be found in a serial by Mrs. de Horne Vaiszey, "More about Pixie" in the *Girl's Own Annual*, vol. XXIV no. 1188-1219 (Oct. 4, 1902 to May 9, 1903).

CHAPTER 3
Schooldays

Histories of Montreal schools used in this chapter include M. Fripp, A. Elbourne, and M. Waters, *Roslyn: The Story of a Canadian School* (Westmount, Quebec: privately printed, 1977); E.C. Moodey and R. A. Speirs, *Veritas: A History of Selwyn House School* (Westmount, Quebec: Selwyn House Association, 1978); J. Graham Patriquin, *BCS: From Little Forks to Moulton Hill* (Lennoxville, Quebec: Bishop's College School, 1978); Stephen Penton, *Non Nobis Solum* (Montreal: Corporation of Lower Canada College, 1972); and E.I. Rexford, I. Gammell, and A. R. McBain, *History of the High School of Montreal* (Montreal: The Old Boys' Association, n.d.). A short history of the Trafalgar School was published by the school magazine, *Trafalgar Echoes*, in June 1937.

Information on Protestant public schools is taken from the *Report of the Protestant Board of School Commissioners, 1906* (Montreal: Eaton Printing Co., 1906).

p. 63. "Those things they will use ..." *Selwyn House School Magazine*, vol. 20 (1947-48), p. 35.

p. 65. "The lack of a suitable preparatory school ..." Moodey and Speirs, p. 2.

p. 68. "The masters were all Englishmen ..." Hugh MacLennan, *Two Solitudes* (New York: Duell, Sloan and Pearce, 1945), p. 205.

p. 69. See Joseph Campbell, *The Masks of God: Creative Mythology* (New York: Penguin Books, 1978).

p. 72. "... if the school has ... football ..." Penton, p. 65.

p. 72. Walter Molson, "Playing the Game," text of a speech published in the *Selwyn House School Magazine,* vol. 18 (1946-47), p. 15.

p. 72. "... ladylike behaviour ..." is from Donald Ross's will, in which he founded the Trafalgar Institute. *Trafalgar Institute*, published by the direction of the Trustees (Montreal: Gazette Printing Co., n.d.), p. 7.

p. 74. "... co-opts the senior ... boys" Ian Weinberg, quoted in M.P. Maxwell and James Maxwell, "Private Schools: The Culture, Structure and Processes of Elite Socialization in English Canada," in K. Ishwaran, *Childhood and Adolescence in Canada* (Toronto: McGraw-Hill Ryerson, 1979), p. 220.

p. 76. The description of fagging appears in Patriquin, vol. 2, pp. 250-51.

p. 78, 79. "Now to my mind ..." A *School Magazine* editorial quoted in Adelaide Gillard, *Affectionately Yours: A Collection of Letters* (privately printed, n.p., n.d.). Miss Gillard's rules of etiquette, and her letter, "You are the privileged ..." appear in the same collection.

p. 81. "Nothing is more characteristic ..." Mary Cramp and Maude C. Edgar, *Eternal Youth: Addresses to Girls, 1913-1930* (Toronto: Macmillan of Canada, 1931), p. 44.

p. 82. "One boy caught making the switch ..." Penton, p. 52.

p. 82. For Miss Edgar's assembly talk, see *Eternal Youth*, p. 144; for her speech, "And of our traditions ..." see p. 45; for her statement, "We want self-control ..." see p. 44.

p. 84. "... no one can learn ..." Penton, p. 304.

p. 85. "... in taking of just punishment ..." Moodey and Speirs, pp. 105-106.

p. 85. "... energies of aspiration," etc. Campbell, p. 5.

p. 87. Information on Sabbath schools is from R. Douglas Fraser, ed., *Home Study Quarterly* and the *Teachers' Monthly* (Toronto: Sabbath School Publications, Presbyterian Church in Canada, 1906-1916), copies of which are preserved in the Archives of the Presbyterian Church in Canada, in Toronto. For Anglican Sunday schools of the period, see *The Sunday School: Its Purpose and Place* (Toronto: The Sunday School Commission of the Church of England in Canada, n.d.), as well as uncatalogued Lesson Schemes for various years, in the Archives of the Diocese of Montreal.

p. 87. "... well-prepared lessons ..." J. Edgar Hill, *Annual Report of St. Andrew's Church* (Montreal, 1906). Archives of the Presbyterian Church in Canada.

CHAPTER 4
Play and the Holidays

p. 93. Murray Ballantyne, "J'ai grandi au Canada français," in Recherches et débats du centre catholique des intellectuels français, *Le Canada français, aujourd'hui et demain* (Paris: Librairie Arthème Fayard, n.d.), pp. 54-55.

p. 94. "In Scotland we banished ..." Marion Lochhead, *The Scots Household in the Eighteenth Century* (Edinburgh: The Moray Press, 1948), p. 264.

p. 99. "Going to the village for supplies ..." Robert Jellett, *History of the Hermitage Club* (privately printed, 1961), p. 45. Jellett's book also presents the by-laws of the Hermitage Club.

p. 103. See *The Knowlton Golf Club* (privately printed, February 1923), p. 16.

p. 105. "... the building of sand castles ..." Jean McEachran, "Metis Days," a holograph manuscript which forms p. 9 of the unpublished family memoirs of *The Clan Ross, 1798-1977*. By special permission.

p. 109. "They love her in the early Spring ..." Alice Baldwin, *Metis, Wee Scotland of the Gaspé* (privately printed, 1960), p. 10.

p. 110. "The streets glistened ..." McEachran, p. 16.

CHAPTER 5
Years of Trial: World War I

p. 111. For figures on participation rates, see Jacques Michel, *La Participation des canadiens français à la Grande Guerre* (Montreal: Éditions de l'A.C.F., n.d.), pp. 15-18; Kathryn M. Bindon, *More Than Patriotism* (Toronto: Personal Library, 1979), p. 37; and Col. G.W.L. Nicholson, *The Official History of the Canadian Army in the First World War* (Ottawa: Queen's Printer, 1962), pp. 212-13.

p. 112. "At approximately 9:15 ..." R.C. Fetherstonhaugh, *The 13th Battalion, Royal Highlanders of Canada, 1914-1919* (Montreal: privately printed, 1925), p. 7-8.

p. 114. For information on the non-military war effort, see MacPhail, *The Medical Services*; John Swettenham, *Canada and the First World War* (Toronto: McGraw-Hill Ryerson, 1969); and Dudley Oliver, "Report on the Work Done by the Bank of Montreal in London in World War I." Public Archives of Canada, MG.30, E.238.

p. 115. Molson family statistics are in Merrill Denison, *The Barley and the Stream* (Toronto: McClelland and Stewart, 1955), p. 300.

p. 115. "Out of the 1913-14 ... team" *Selwyn House School Magazine* vol. 24 (1951-52), p. 14.

p. 116. See Lt. Col. C. Beresford Topp, *The 42nd Battalion, C.E.F., Royal Highlanders of Canada in the Great War* (Montreal: Gazette Publishing Co., 1931), pp. 39, 49, 95, 170.

p. 118. Sir Andrew MacPhail, *Official History of the Canadian Forces in the Great War: The Medical Services* (Ottawa: King's Printer, 1925), p. 344.

p. 118. The description of the gas attack appears in Nicholson, p. 72.

p. 119. "It is some comfort to know ..." Kenneth L. Duggan to Mrs. Duggan, 19 Nov. 1915. Public Archives of Canada, Herrick S. Duggan file.

p. 119. "I was with Major Duggan ..." Sgt. Brooks to Mrs. Duggan, 16 Feb. 1918. Public Archives of Canada, Duggan Family Correspondence, Kenneth L. Duggan file, MG.30, E.304.

p. 120. The Ernest Spiller letter is quoted in William D. Mathieson, *My Grandfather's War* (Toronto: F.D. Goodchild, 1922), pp. 241-42.

p. 121. Scott's story about "the lovely night" is in Canon F.G. Scott, *The Great War As I Saw It* (Toronto: F.D. Goodchild, 1922), p. 241.242.

p. 121. For Ballantyne's remarks on the conscription crisis, see "J'ai grandi," p. 55.

p. 122. For an account of the crisis in Quebec, as well as the quotes from conservative newspapers, see Elizabeth Armstrong, *The Crisis of Quebec, 1914-1918* (Toronto: McClelland and Stewart, 1974), pp. 167, 196-97.

p. 122. "The hockey match left me ..." Public Archives of Canada, Letters of Dorothy MacPhail, MG.30, D.150, vol. 1.

p. 123. "Truly violent feelings ..." Beatrice Wyatt Johnson, *Memories of an Anglophone Quebecoise*, unpublished manuscript, pp. 29-30.

p. 123. "We felt ... that nearer" Scott, p. 299.

p. 124. "Whenever the Germans found ..." Bindon, p. 162.

p. 124. "... when a soldier thinks ..." W.H.S. Machlan, in Mathieson, p. 269.

p. 124. The description of the false armistice is in Col. William Wood, ed., *The Storied Province of Quebec: Past and Present* (Toronto: Dominion Publishing Co., 1931), vol. 3, p. 761.

p. 125. For casualty figures, see Nicholson, p. 535; Topp, p. 377; Fetherstonhaugh, p. 344; and Col. P.P. Hutchinson, *Canada's Black Watch* (Montreal: The Black Watch of Canada, 1962), p. 142.

p. 126. Figures on population ratios are from the *Census of Canada, 1921*, Vol. 1, population Ottawa: Dominion Bureau of Statistics), pp. 277, 340-41.

CHAPTER 6
The Winds of Change

p. 133. On education of women at McGill, see Margaret Gillett, *We Walked Very Warily* (Montreal: Eden Press, 1981).

p. 136. For information on population changes discussed in this chapter, see *Census of Canada, 1901*, vol. 1, p. 376; and *Census of Canada, 1921*, vol. 1, p. 305. See also P.A. Linteau, R. Durocher, and J.C. Robert, *Quebec: A History, 1867-1929*, tr. Robert Chodos (Toronto: James Lorimer and Co., 1983), p. 48.

p. 137. On the history of religion in Canada, see S. D. Clark, *Church and Sect in Canada*, 2nd ed. (Toronto: University of Toronto Press, 1948); J.W. Grant, *The Church in the Canadian Era*, Vol. 3, *A History of the Christian Church in Canada* (Toronto: McGraw-Hill Ryerson, 1972); and H.H.Walsh, *The Christian Church in Canada* (Toronto: Ryerson Press, 1956).

p. 138. I am indebted to N. Mair for the use of his unpublished manuscript, "The Protestant Churches and Nationalism," as well as for his insights on the development of ethnic churches.

p. 140. "... the organization of a united Protestant Church ..." and the response of the Presbytery's Committee appear in a press release (n.d., probably 1924) in the Archives of the United Church of Canada, in Montreal.

p. 140. "... to meet this combined strength ..." G.T. Daly, in Walsh, p. 296.

p. 141. The church union controversy is covered in issues of the Montreal *Daily Witness and Canadian Homestead* between 1920 and 1925 (Montreal: Fraser Hickson Library, repository). Dates of articles and correspondence cited are indicated in the text. The periodical changed its name several times; as a matter of convenience, the short title *Witness* is cited throughout. For a summary of various views on the church union issue, see Dougall's editorial in the *Witness* on the date cited.

p. 141. "The scheme took its impetus ..." Murray Ballantyne, *All or Nothing* (New York: Sheed and Ward, 1956), p. 33.

p. 142. Scott was "elected moderator ... and entered the pulpit ..." Walsh, p. 303.

p. 142. For statistics on the outcome of church union decisions in Montreal, see William Munroe, "The Uniting Churches and the Church Union Bill," issued by the Church Union Committee of the Presbytery of Montreal, 24 February 1925, Archives of the United Church of Canada (uncatalogued).

p. 143. The 1920 Lambeth Conference reports appear in Conference of Bishops of the Anglican Communion, *Encyclical Letter from the Bishops with the Resolutions and Reports* (New York: Macmillan, 1922).

CHAPTER 7
The Return to Normal

p. 150. "Oh, the parties of the twenties! ..." Ballantyne, *All or Nothing*, pp. 49-50.

p. 151. For information on the Montreal Amateur Athletic Association, see Alan Metcalfe, "Organized Sport and Social Stratification in Montreal" in Richard Grunear and J. Albinson, *Canadian Sport: Sociological Perspectives* (Don Mills, Ontario: Addison-Wesley, 1976). For information on specific sports and men's clubs I am indebted to club histories: The Royal Montreal Curling Club, *One Hundred and Fifty Years of Curling* (Montreal: privately printed, 1957); John Irwin Cooper, *The History of the Montreal Hunt* (Montreal: Montreal Hunt, 1953); and *The Royal Montreal Golf Club, 1873-1973* (Montreal: privately printed, 1973).

p. 152. For W.W. Johnson's remark on the Stock Exchange, and the stir over the lady riding astride, see Cooper, *Montreal Hunt*, pp. 73, 98.

p. 155. "... from the very early days ..." *Royal Montreal Golf Club*, p. 3.

p. 155. G.D. Mitchell, *Heritage Valdurn* (Papineauville, Quebec: Imprimerie Papineauville, n.d.) has given us the history of cross-country skiing in Quebec.

p. 157. For information on the St. James Club, see Edgar Andrew Collard, *The Saint James Club* (Montreal: privately printed, 1957). For the Mount Royal club, see Collard, "Mount Royal's Earlier Years," *The Gazette*, July 1971.

p. 158. See Paul P. Hutchinson, *The Black Watch (RHR) of Canada* (Montreal: The Black Watch, 1962).

p. 158. See *Dau's Blue Book of Montreal and Ottawa* (Montreal: Dau Publishing Co., 1928).

p. 160. "It may be asked if no doubts ..." Ballantyne, *All or Nothing*, p. 52.

p. 165. Information on the Junior League was drawn from *The Junior League of Montreal* (Montreal: Atelier Pierre Guillaume, 1963);, from the Constitution and By-laws of the League; from the *Junior League News*; and from the Minute Books for the years 1919 to 1930.

p. 167. Material on the Montreal Local Council of Women is available in the Council's annual reports. See also W.H. Atherton, *Montreal Under British*

Rule, 1760-1914, vol. 2, pp. 499-505; and Rosa L. Shaw, *Proud Heritage: A History of the National Council of Women of Canada* (Toronto: The Ryerson Press, 1957).

p. 169. For accounts of life at McGill in the 1920s, see Stanley B. Frost, *McGill University: For the Advancement of Learning*, vol. 2 (Montreal and Kingston: McGill-Queen's University Press, 1984); Margaret Gillet, *We Walked Very Warily*; and Edgar Andrew Collard, *The McGill You Knew, 1920-1960* (Don Mills, Ontario: Longman Canada, 1973).

p. 169. "McGill ... believed as firmly ..." Frost, vol. 2, p. 114.

p. 170. For statistics on university attendance, see W.M. Illing and Z.E.Zsigmond, *Enrolment in Schools and Universities, 1951-1952 to 1975-76*, Economic Council of Canada Staff Study no. 20 (Ottawa: Queen's Printer, 1976). See also the annual reports of McGill University , 1900, 1920, 1930.

p. 171. "... whole classes of freshmen ..." R. John Pratt, "Spanish Inquisition Was a Tea Party" in Collard, *The McGill You Knew*, p. 8.

CHAPTER 8
Entering the Business World

Information on the history of Canadian stock markets, business mergers, and trusts is drawn largely from Tom Naylor, *History of Canadian Business* (Toronto: James Lorimer and Co., 1975), vol. 1, pp. 186-221 and vol. 2, pp. 162-94. For the history of the Montreal Stock Exchange, see S. Johnson, "History and Organization of the Montreal Stock Exchange" (M.A. Thesis, Mcgill University, 1934). For information on political offices held by Montrealers, see T.W. Acheson, "The Social Origins of the Canadian Industrial Elite, 1880-1885" in D.S. Macmillan, *Canadian Business History* (Toronto: McClelland and Stewart, 1972), p. 167.

John English, *The Decline of Politics* (Toronto: University of Toronto Press, 1977) and R. M. Dawson, *William Lyon MacKenzie King* (Toronto: University of Toronto Press, 1948) have been valuable sources for much of the political history surveyed in this chapter.

p. 178. "It was a standard technique ..." Naylor, vol. 1, p. 211. The quotation from the *Monetary Times* appears on p. 215.

p. 182. For Simpson's views on wages, see J. S. Galbraith, *The Little Emperor* (Toronto: Macmillan of Canada, 1976), p. 16.

p. 185. "It carried out a great constructive policy ..." John Willison, quoted in English, *The Decline of Politics*, p. 9.

p. 186. "A very strenuous day ..." Dawson, p. 369.

p. 186. "The difficulty has been ..." Walter S. Johnson, *Letters* (Montreal: unpublished typescript).

p. 188. For an explanation of the conservatism of the Bank of Montreal, see Merrill Denison, *Canada's First Bank*, vol. 2, p. 138.

p. 189. "Come back when you have more." See Richard Rohmer, *E.P. Taylor* (Toronto: McClelland and Stewart, 1978), p. 35.

p. 189. For statistics on the three largest banks, see Clement, p. 83.

p. 189. "... did an unheard of thing ..." C.E. Bourne, "Advertising a Bank with 900 Branches," *Royal Bank Magazine* no. 94 (Nov. 1928), p.8; "to make friends with him ..." Ibid. p. 12.

p. 191. See H.W. Harper, "Service," *Royal Bank Magazine* no. 7 (April 1928), p. 11.

p. 192. "... the bank is keenly interested ..." Report of the Annual General Meeting of the Bank of Montreal, 1926.

p. 192. For information on CPR earnings, see appendices to Lamb, *History of the Canadian Pacific Railway*.

p. 192. "... largely with the object of breaking ..." *Report of the Royal Commission to Inquire in to Railways and Transportation in Canada* (Ottawa: King's Printer, 1917), p. xlviii.

p. 193. See Peter C. Newman, *The Canadian Establishment*, vol. 1 (Toronto: Seal Books, McClelland and Stewart-Bantam Ltd., 1977), p. 224.

p. 194. Correspondence and inter-office memoranda on the Rouyn-Noranda railway proposals are in the CPR Archives (Montreal), f. 1730/1-5. "... would very adversely affect our joint interests" Wanklyn to Taschereau, 5 Sept. 1923. "This, of course, would ... influence ..." Wanklyn to Grant Hall, 27 Oct. 1924. "...not sufficiently developed at present ..." E.N. Todd to W.M.Neal, 30 Oct. 1924. "We had hoped that the Canadian Pacific ..." Extract from a conference of the Hon. J.E. Perreault, Minister of Colonization, Mines and Fisheries, before the Reform Club, 28 Feb. 1925. "The only basis on which we could ... consider ..." Wanklyn to E.J. Herbert, 23 March 1925. See also Leslie Roberts, *Noranda* (Toronto: Clarke, Irwin and Co., 1956).

p. 196. "The gates of Canada should be ..." Canadian Pacific Railway, *Annual Report* (1919).

p. 197. "... to reduce it to ... inferiority ..." Lamb, p. 317.

p. 197. "... the construction programme of new branch lines ..." *Report of the Royal Commission on Railways* (Ottawa: King's Printer, 1932), ch. V.

p. 198. For the story of Thornton's career, see D'Arcy Marsh, *The Tragedy of Henry Thornton* (Toronto: Macmillan of Canada, 1935).

p. 198. "Within fifteen years ..." MacDougall, p. 107.

p. 199. Causes of labour unrest stated in Stuart Jamieson, *Times of Trouble: Labour Unrest and Industrial Conflict in Canada, 1900-1966*, Task Force on Labour Relations Study No. 22 (Ottawa: Privy Council, 1968), p. 86.

p. 203. For the growth of Westmount, see J.I. Cooper, *Montreal: The Story of Three Hundred Years* (Montreal: privately printed, 1942), p. 110.

p. 204. "too destructive to be tolerated" Michael Bliss, "Dyspepsia of the Mind: The Canadian Businessman and His Enemies, 1880-1914" in D.S. Macmillan, *Canadian Business History* (Toronto: McClelland and Stewart, 1972), pp. 190-91.

p. 204. "Has not the growing attempt ..." Sir Edward Beatty, "Obligations of Businessmen," speech to the Canadian Chamber of Commerce, 5 Feb. 1936. CPR Archives, B.37, vol. 1, p. 10.

CHAPTER 9
Providing for the Community

Services

p. 209. See Frost, *McGill University*, vol. 2, for details of McGill's financing. "... almost single-handedly ..." Ibid. p. 14.

p. 210. "... self-perpetuating body ..." Cooper, *Montreal Hunt*, p. 86.

p. 211. "There were great discrepancies ..." W. MacLeod, L. Park, and S. Ryerson, *Bethune: The Montreal Years* (Toronto: James Lorimer and Co., 1978), p. 33.

p. 213. "... whole families living ..." Terry Copp, *The Anatomy of Poverty: The Conditions of the Working Class in Montreal, 1897-1929* (Toronto: McClelland and Stewart, 1974), p. 71. Chapters 6 and 7 include valuable information on public health and social assistance.

p. 213. "... chiefly because of ignorance ..." Dr. J.G. Fitzgerald, in Copp, p. 102.

p. 214. Montreal Anti-Tuberculosis and General Health League, "A Survey of Public Health Activities" (1928), p.17. McGill University Archives, RG.2, C.69, f. 01358.

p. 215. For McLean's reports, see Copp, pp. 108, 110.

p. 216. "... the plain fact is that ..." *Annual Report of the Montreal Charity Organization Society, 1920*, p. 12.

p. 217. Frances O'Neill, "Summary of the Survey of the Protestant and Non-sectarian Relief Giving Organizations of Montreal, 1924" (Montreal: Financial Relief Federation); Howard Falk, "Report of a Committee of the Montreal Council of Social Agencies" (Montreal: Family Welfare Association), B.4. Archives of the Ville Marie Social Service Centre (Montreal), uncatalogued.

p. 217. "... traditionally, a major share ..." *The Province of Ontario: Its Social Services* (Toronto: Ontario Welfare Council, 1974), pp. 2-3.

p. 218. "Thus, for nearly two centuries ..." *Report of the Commission on Public Assistance*, the "Boucher Report" (Quebec: Government of Quebec, June 1963), p. 31. report is a valuable source of information on the history of social assistance in Quebec.

p. 218. "... a record of economy ..." N. R. Crump, radio address, 24 October 1930, CPR Archives, B.289.

Cultural Activities

p. 220. For Brown's analysis see *On Canadian Poetry* (Toronto: The Tecumseh Press, McGraw-Hill Ryerson, 1944), pp. 1-27.

p. 221. For information on the St. James Literary Society and Canadian Club programmes, see Fred C. Newman, *the First Fifty Years: A Brief History of the St. James Literary Society* (Montreal: privately printed, 1948); and Peter L. Walker, comp., "Papers and Debates Presented before the St. James Literary Society, 1898-99 to 1954-55" (typescript), McGill University Archives,

MG.3009. For the Canadian Club, see also McGill University Archives, MG.1605.

p. 222. "If the Academy of France ..." Lorne Pierce, "The Bonne Entente in Canadian Literature," speech to the St. James Literary Society, 12 March 1929, McGill University Archives, MG.3009, p. 3.

p. 223. "We were called bohemians ..." Leon Edel, "When McGill Modernized Canadian Literature" in Collard, *The McGill You Knew*, p. 116.

p. 225. The quotation from the *Mirror* appears in Anton Wagner, *Canada's Lost Plays*, vol. 3 (Toronto: Canadian Theatre Review Publications, 1980), p. 7.

p. 227. "I still had to go to Europe ..." William Watson, *Retrospective: Recollections of a Montreal Art Dealer* (Toronto: University of Toronto Press, 1974), p. 10.

p. 227. Information on the Montreal museum is taken from the annual reports of the Montreal Art Association, 1900-1930 and from "Historical Notes" (anon. typescript, 1983), Archives of the Montreal Museum of Fine Arts.

p. 229. "Dr. Martin looked at it ..." and "The big exhibitions were ..." Marian Scott, telephone conversation with author, 8 March 1990.

p. 229. "It was ... a great disappointment ..." Maurice Gagnon to Dr. C.F. Martin, president of the Art Association of Montreal, 22 March 1943, Archives of the Montreal Museum of Fine Arts.

p. 229. For the history of the modernists' struggle, see Christopher Varley, *The Contemporary Arts Society* (Edmonton: Edmonton Art Gallery, 1980).

p. 229. "That was very nice for young painters ..." Philip Surrey, interview with author, 18 Oct. 1989.

p. 230. "... rising merchant class ..." H. Kallman, "Historical Background" in Donald Walter, ed., *Aspects of Music in Canada* (Toronto: University of Toronto Press, 1969), p. 37.

p. 231. "... did not succeed in identifying ..." H. Kallman, G. Potvin, and K. Winters, eds., *Encyclopedia of Music in Canada* (Toronto: University of Toronto Press, 1981), p. 638.

p. 232. For architectural references, see notes to Chapter 1.

p. 233. "... as an act of self-preservation ..." Pierce, p. 6.

CHAPTER 10
Economic Catastrophe

p. 239. The story of the stock market crash is drawn from accounts in *The Gazette*, the *Montreal Star*, *Financial Times*, and other newspapers of the period. For statistics on the fall in share values, see Carl Bergithon, *The Stock Exchange* (Montreal: Gazette Publishing Co., 1940). For the fall in world prices, see J.L. Granatstein et al., *Twentieth Century Canada* (Toronto: McGraw-Hill Ryerson, 1983), p. 212.

p. 241. Statistics on suicides are taken from *Annuaire du Québec* (Quebec: Bureau de la statistique) 1930, p. 171; 1934, p. 170; and 1935, p. 189. The account of Kenneth Molson's death appears in Shirley E. Woods, Jr., *The Molson Saga, 1763-1983* (Toronto: Doubleday Canada, 1983), p. 257.

p. 241. For bankruptcies and proposals for coping with the Depression, see Montreal Board of Trade, *Annual Reports* for the years 1930-1937.

p. 242. For analyses of the causes and effects of the Depression, see chapters 6 and 7 of the *Report of the Royal Commission on Dominion-Provincial Relations*, the "Rowell-Sirois Report" (Ottawa: King's Printer, 1940), book 1, pp. 150-200; and Donald Creighton, *Canada's First Century* (Toronto: Macmillan of Canada, 1970), p. 205.

p. 243. "When a realization ..." Rowell-Sirois Report, book 1, p. 144.

p. 244. For information on relief payments and government financing, see Montreal Board of Trade, "Dominion, Provincial and Municipal Finance and Taxation," submission to the the Rowell-Sirois commission, 1940; and *Canada Year Book, 1934-35*, pp. 830-35.

p. 244. "... unemployment in Montreal ..." Rowell-Sirois Report, book 1, p. 191.

p. 245. See monthly reports of the Verdun Unemployment Relief Commission, Family Welfare Association, Verdun district, 1915-1935, Archives of the Ville Marie Social Services Centre, B.5, f. 8023.

p. 245. For the estimate on single men, see Creighton, p. 260.

p. 249. "The unemployed used to flow ..." Hugh MacLennan, *The Watch That Ends the Night* (Toronto: Macmillan of Canada, 1959), p. 119.

p. 249. The report on the Vitré Street refuge meals appeared in *The Alarm Clock* (Montreal: McGill University Labour Club), March 1933, p. 8. McGill University Archives, RG.2, c.51, Student Activities, 1924-1933.

p. 249. "In the moonlight ..." Libbie Park, "Bethune as I Knew Him" in *Bethune: The Montreal Years*, p. 89.

CHAPTER 11
Ideological Conflict

Information on the Left in the 1930s is drawn from A.L. Olssen, *The Canadian Left in Quebec During the Great Depression* (Ph.D. Thesis, Duke University, 1972); Merrily Weisbord, *The Strangest Dream* (Toronto: Lester and Orpen Dennys, 1983); the McGill University Archives, which contain a rich fund of information, including the university records of Sir Edward Beatty, the microfilm scrapbooks of F.R. Scott, and contemporary Montreal news clippings.

p. 250. "We had every reason to know ..." Sir Edward Beatty, "What of Business Leadership in National Affairs?" speech to the Rotary Club, Toronto, 22 Jan. 1937, CPR Archives, Speeches and Papers of Sir Edward Beatty, B.27, vol. 1, p. 6.

p. 253. "... private industry is protected ..." and "There is no bank ..." *Montreal Star*, 16 Dec. 1932, p. 6.

p. 254. "... our university socialists ..." Beatty to Morgan, 28 Dec. 1936; "[hoping the problem] will always be with us ..." Morgan to Beatty, 30 Dec.

1936; McGill University Archives, Correspondence of Chancellor Sir Edward Beatty, RG.2, c. 43, f. 301.

p. 254. "Right in McGill there are communists ..." *Montreal Star*, 9 April 1937, McGill University Archives, McGill University Scrapbooks, vol. 9, p. 67.

p. 254. For Morgan's letter of resignation and Beatty's letter of acceptance, see McGill University Archives, Correspondence of Chancellor Sir Edward Beatty, RG.2, c. 54, f. 729.

p. 254. Convocation address by Sir Edward Beatty published in the *Montreal Star*, 27 May 1937, McGill University Archives, McGill University Scrapbooks, vol. 9, p. 120.

p. 255. "... the influence on the student population ..." L. Douglas to Beatty, 23 November 1939, McGill University Archives. Correspondence of Chancellor Sir Edward Beatty, RG.2, c. 54, f. 730.

p. 255. For information on the establishment of the Bank of Canada, see R. Craig McIvor, *Canadian Monetary, Banking and Fiscal Development* (Toronto: Macmillan, 1958).

p. 256. "The commercial banker has very properly ..." *Report of the Royal Commission on Banking and Currency* (1933), McIvor, p. 148.

p. 256. For wages and prices in Montreal industries, see the *Royal Commission on Price Spreads Report* (Ottawa:King's Printer, 1935), pp. 111, 113, 115-116.

p. 258. "... which might have emanated from an organization of political radicals ..." Editorial, *The Gazette*, 10 June 1933, p. 10.

p. 258. "... watching kids eat out of garbage pails ..." C. Flanagan, interview with author, 4 May 1983.

p. 259. "... to hear something ... compelling ..." Walter S. Johnson to C.H. Carlisle, 5 March 1933, in Johnson, *Letters*.

p. 260. For Stanley Ryerson's statement, see *Bethune: The Montreal Years*, p. 145.

p. 261. "I am not a communist ..." Hazen Sise to Paul Sise. 4 December 1936, Public Archives of Canada. MG.30, D.187, vol. 6, f. 10.

p. 261. "Off the Straits of Belle Isle ..." Hazen Sise to Moran Scott, 1 Dec. 1937, Public Archives of Canada, MG.30, D.187, vol. 6, f. 3.

p. 262. "... curiously morbid horror ..." Creighton, p. 230.

p. 263. Duplessis' and McKenna's statements appeared in *La Presse*, 26 Oct. 1936. The *McGill Daily* remarks appeared on the same day. F.R. Scott Scrapbooks (microfilm), McGill University Archives, MG.2004, vols. 28-29/reel 34.

p. 264. "...paid his employees ..." Pierre, Laporte, *The True Face of Maurice Duplessis* (Montreal: Harvest House, 1970), p. 43. "Anything new worried him ..." Ibid., pp. 117, 119.

p. 265. "... the enemies of capitalism ..." Johnson, *Letters*.

p. 266. "... immediately give out contracts ..." Montreal Board of Trade, 88th Annual Report (1930), p. 55.

p. 266. For an account of Montreal's default, see Leslie Roberts, *Montreal: From Mission Colony to World City* (Toronto: Macmillan of Canada, 1969), p. 325.

p. 266. "The employer who does not consider ..." Beatty, "What of Business Leadership ...?" p. 10.

CHAPTER 12
From Depression to War

For the general history of Montreal from 1939 to 1945, see Kathleen Jenkins, *Montreal: Island City of the St. Lawrence* (New York: Doubleday, 1966); J.I. Cooper, *Montreal: A Brief History* (Montreal and London: McGill-Queen's University Press, 1969); and J.I. Cooper, *Montreal: The Story of Three Hundred Years* (Montreal: privately printed, 1942).

p. 270. "We have today come ..." Edgar Andrew Collard, "How Quebec Women Got the Vote," *The Gazette*, 20 Nov. 1976, p. 6.

p. 272. For statistics on the war effort, see Granatstein, p.275. See also Leslie Roberts, *The Life and Times of Clarence Decatur Howe* (Toronto: Clarke, Irwin & Co., 1957).

CHAPTER 13
The End of an Era

p. 276. See Evelyn Dumas, *The Bitter Thirties in Quebec* (Montreal: Black Rose Books, 1975), chapter 6, for an account of the Tramway strike.

p. 276. "... the police declared ..." Dumas, p. 86.

p. 276. "By going on strike ..." Dumas, pp. 87-88.

p. 276. See Charles Lipton, *The Trade Union Movement of Canada, 1827-1959*, 4th ed. (Toronto: NC Press, 1978), pp.272-74, for an account of the UTWA strike.

p. 277. "The attitude and action of the company ..." Lipton, p. 273.

p. 277. Pierre Trudeau, *La Grève de L'Amiante* (Montreal: Éditions Cité Libre, 1956) is the classic account of the Asbestos strike. See also Jack Williams, *The Story of Unions in Canada* (Toronto: J.M.Dent and Sons, 1975), and Lipton, *The Trade Union Movement of Canada*.

p. 279. "The working class is the victim ..." and "... with all my soul as a bishop ..." Lipton, p. 324.

p. 279. "For many people ..." Trudeau, p. 379.

p. 279. "... a certain remoteness ..." Gérard Pelletier, "La Grève et la presse" in Trudeau, p. 294.

p. 280. See Donald Kerr, "Metropolitan Dominance in Canada" in J. Warkentin, *Canada: A Geographical Interpretation* (Toronto: Methuen Publications, 1968), pp. 531-55, for statistics showing the rise of Toronto. Comparative figures for 1941 are taken from *Canada Year Book, 1942*, p. 81; *Taxa-*

310

tion Statistics (Ottawa: Department of National Revenue, 1948), p. 10; and *Census of Canada, 1941*, vol. 7, p. 846.

p. 281. See E.P. Neufeld, *The Financial System of Canada* (Toronto: Macmillan of Canada, 1972), p. 498, for stock exchange figures.

p. 282. "... the province far ahead of Quebec ..." Jacob Spelt, "Southern Ontario" in Warkentin, p. 358.

p. 282. "When a measure of recovery did occur ..." Rowell-Sirois Report, book 1, p. 191.

p. 283. "... encrusted in tradition ..." Herbert Solow, "The Canadian Pacific: Overdue," *Fortune*, August 1956, p. 86. "In the old days ..." Ibid., pp. 90, 91, 200.

p. 284. See CPR Annual Report for 1955, for board members.

p. 285. Eric McLean, telephone interview with author, 7 March 1990.

p. 287. See Clement, *The Canadian Corporate Elite*, pp. 225-27; John Porter, *The Vertical Mosaic* (Toronto: University of Toronto Press, 1965); and P. Fournier, *The Quebec Establishment* (Montreal: Black Rose Books, 1976).

p. 288. "... the man in the street would resort ..." Editorial, *The Gazette*, 29 Sept. 1940, McGill University Archives, McGill University Scrapbooks, vol. 10, p. 181.

p. 288. For Newman's list, see *The Canadian Establishment*, chapter 4 and Appendix D.

p. 289. "Inherited wealth is ... as certain death ..." Newman, *The Canadian Establishment*, p. 307.

p. 291. "The age of chivalry has gone ..." Edmund Burke, *Reflections on the Revolution in France* (1790) in the *Oxford Dictionary of Quotations*, 3rd ed. (Oxford University Press, 1980), p. 111.

Conclusion

p. 295. Beatty, "What of Business Leadership ...?" p. 16.

311

Printed in Canada